ROYAL CITY™

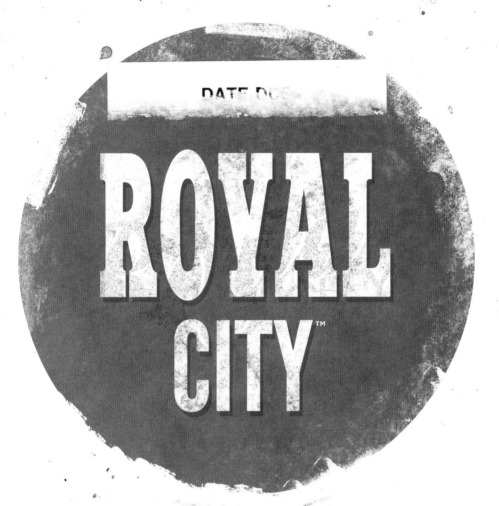

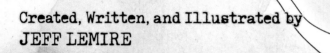

Created, Written, and Illustrated by
JEFF LEMIRE

Lettered by STEVE WANDS

Special Thanks to
RYAN BREWER,
WILL DENNIS

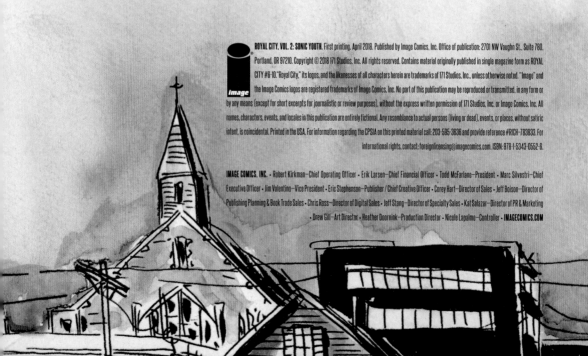

ROYAL CITY, VOL. 2: SONIC YOUTH. First printing. April 2018. Published by Image Comics, Inc. Office of publication: 2701 NW Vaughn St., Suite 780, Portland, OR 97210. Copyright © 2018 171 Studios, Inc. All rights reserved. Contains material originally published in single magazine form as ROYAL CITY #6-10. "Royal City," its logos, and the likenesses of all characters herein are trademarks of 171 Studios, Inc., unless otherwise noted. "Image" and the Image Comics logos are registered trademarks of Image Comics, Inc. No part of this publication may be reproduced or transmitted, in any form or by any means (except for short excerpts for journalistic or review purposes), without the express written permission of 171 Studios, Inc. or Image Comics, Inc. All names, characters, events, and locales in this publication are entirely fictional. Any resemblance to actual persons (living or dead), events, or places, without satiric intent, is coincidental. Printed in the USA. For information regarding the CPSIA on this printed material call: 203-595-3636 and provide reference #RICH-783833. For international rights, contact: foreignlicensing@imagecomics.com. ISBN: 978-1-5343-0552-6.

IMAGE COMICS, INC. • Robert Kirkman—Chief Operating Officer • Erik Larsen—Chief Financial Officer • Todd McFarlane—President • Marc Silvestri—Chief Executive Officer • Jim Valentino—Vice President • Eric Stephenson—Publisher / Chief Creative Officer • Corey Hart—Director of Sales • Jeff Boison—Director of Publishing Planning & Book Trade Sales • Chris Ross—Director of Digital Sales • Jeff Stang—Director of Specialty Sales • Kat Salazar—Director of PR & Marketing • Drew Gill—Art Director • Heather Doornink—Production Director • Nicole Lapalme—Controller • **IMAGECOMICS.COM**

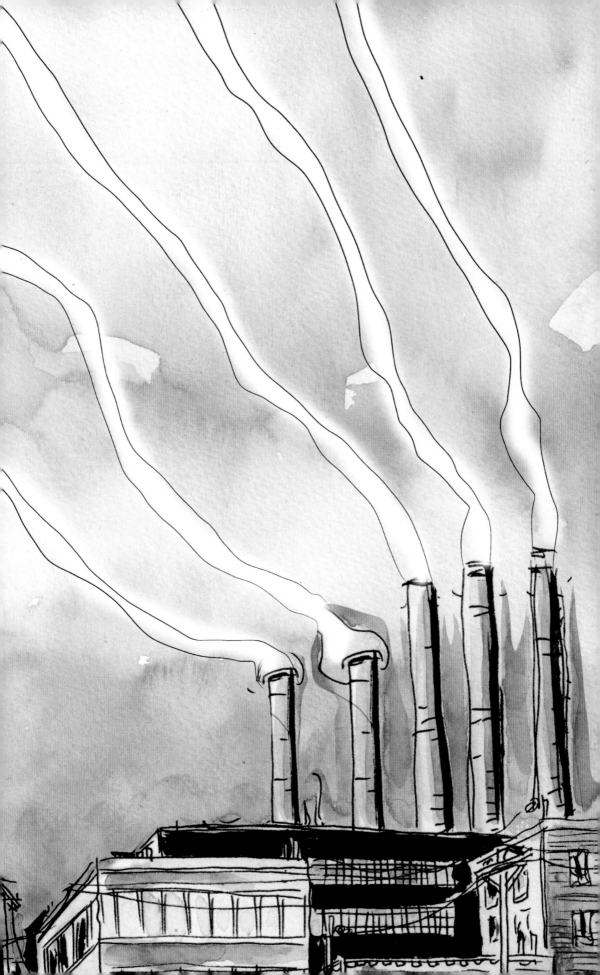

CHAPTER SIX

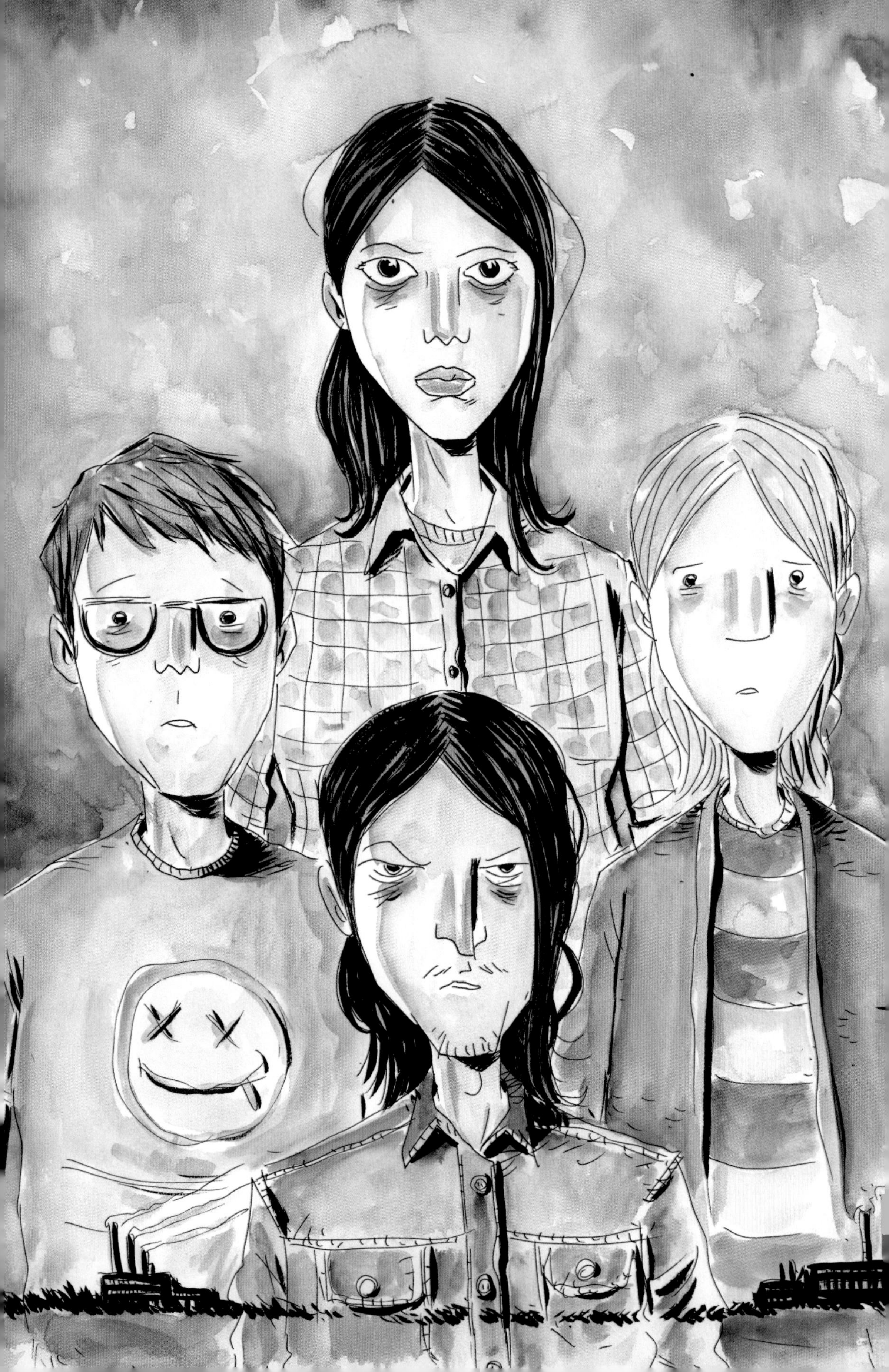

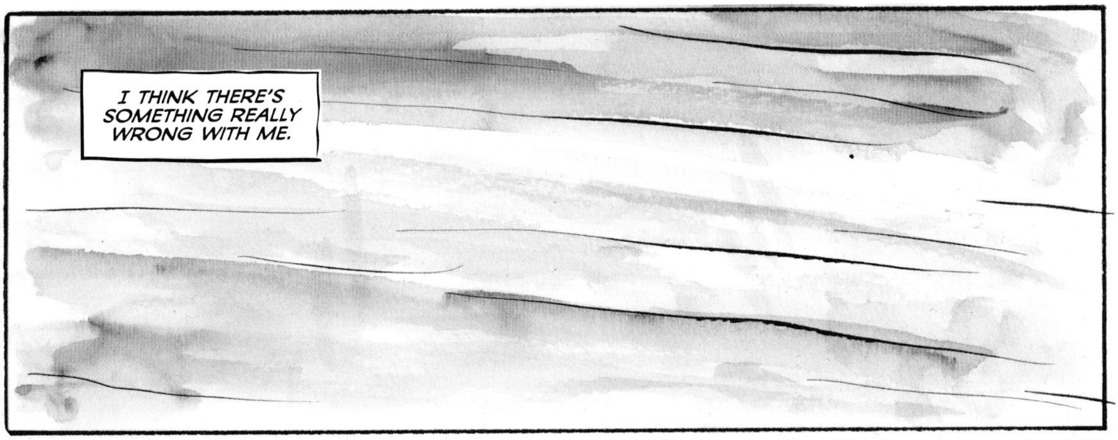
I THINK THERE'S SOMETHING REALLY WRONG WITH ME.

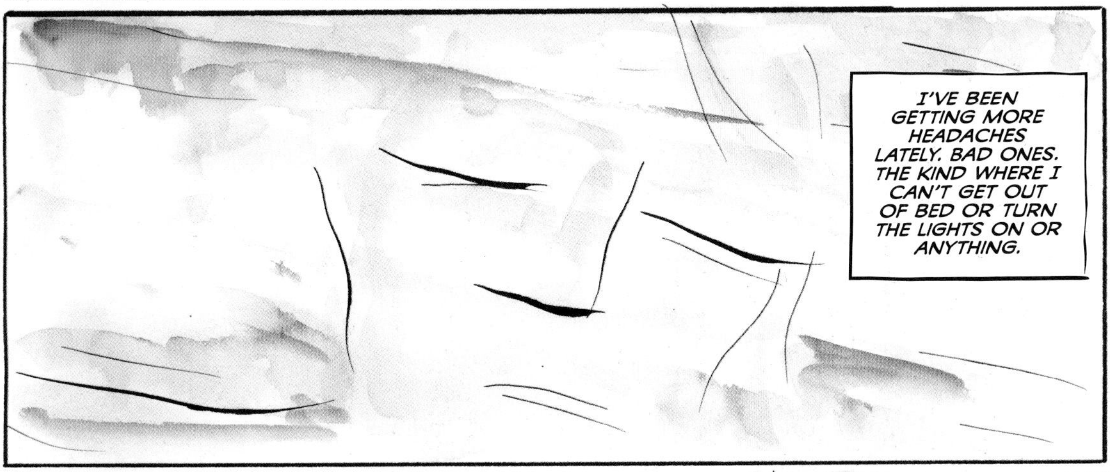
I'VE BEEN GETTING MORE HEADACHES LATELY. BAD ONES. THE KIND WHERE I CAN'T GET OUT OF BED OR TURN THE LIGHTS ON OR ANYTHING.

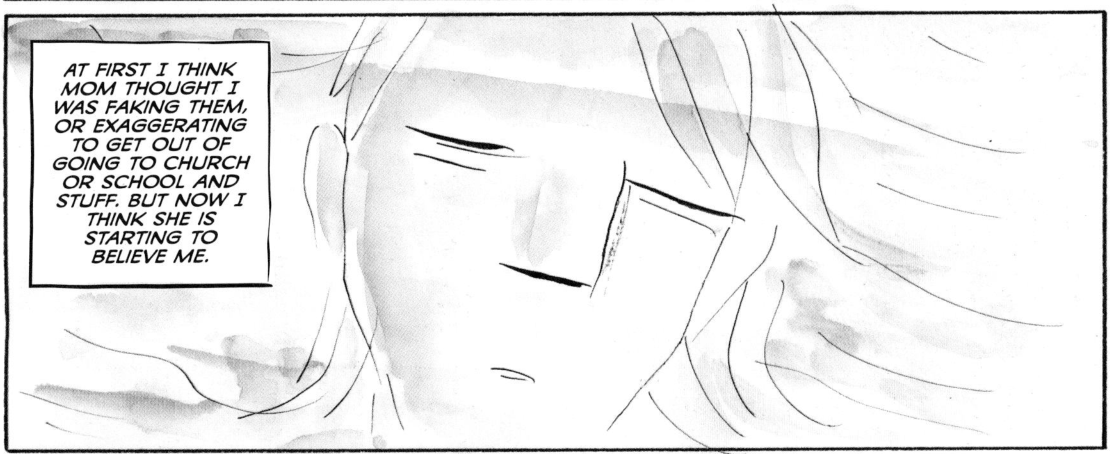
AT FIRST I THINK MOM THOUGHT I WAS FAKING THEM, OR EXAGGERATING TO GET OUT OF GOING TO CHURCH OR SCHOOL AND STUFF. BUT NOW I THINK SHE IS STARTING TO BELIEVE ME.

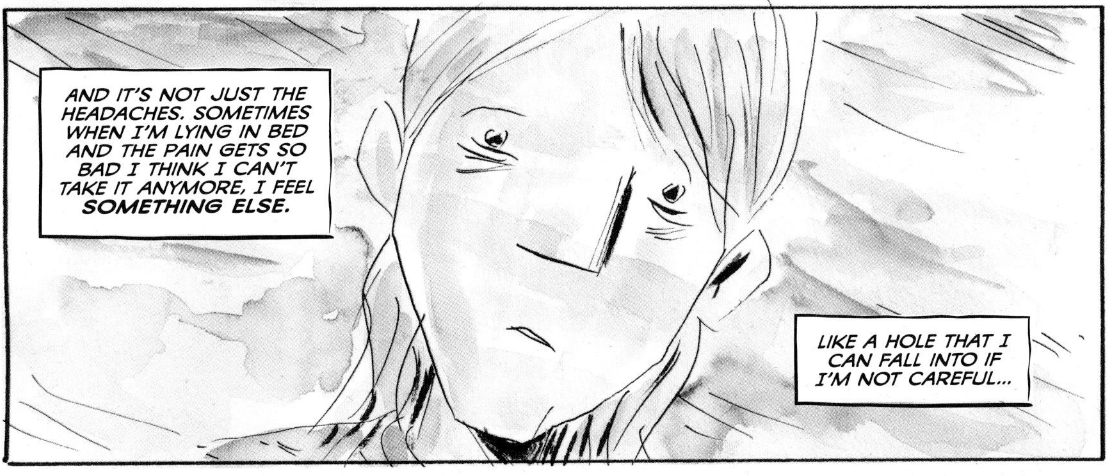
AND IT'S NOT JUST THE HEADACHES. SOMETIMES WHEN I'M LYING IN BED AND THE PAIN GETS SO BAD I THINK I CAN'T TAKE IT ANYMORE, I FEEL **SOMETHING ELSE.**
LIKE A HOLE THAT I CAN FALL INTO IF I'M NOT CAREFUL...

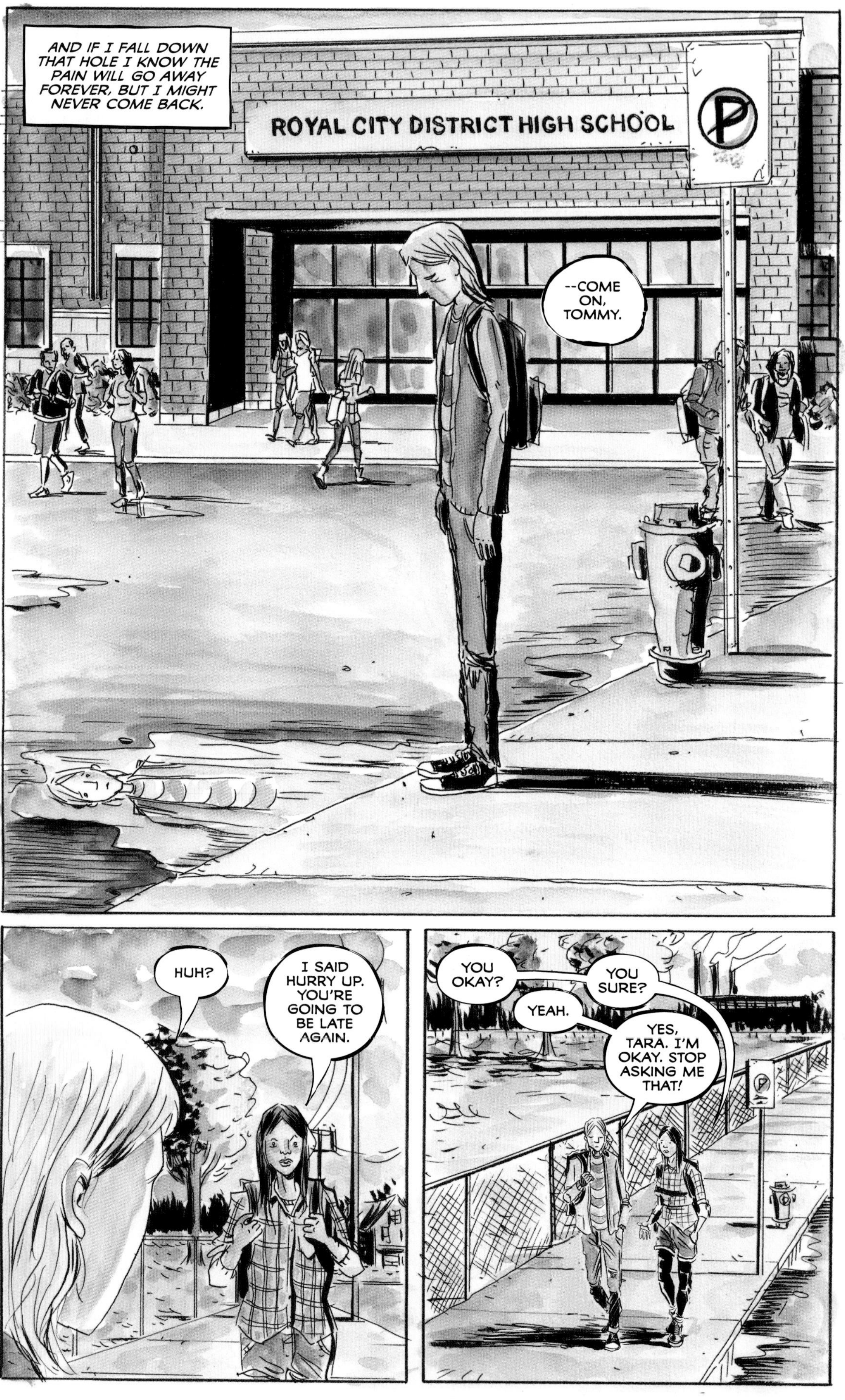
AND IF I FALL DOWN THAT HOLE I KNOW THE PAIN WILL GO AWAY FOREVER, BUT I MIGHT NEVER COME BACK.
ROYAL CITY DISTRICT HIGH SCHOOL
--COME ON, TOMMY.
HUH?
I SAID HURRY UP. YOU'RE GOING TO BE LATE AGAIN.
YOU OKAY?
YEAH.
YOU SURE?
YES, TARA. I'M OKAY. STOP ASKING ME THAT!

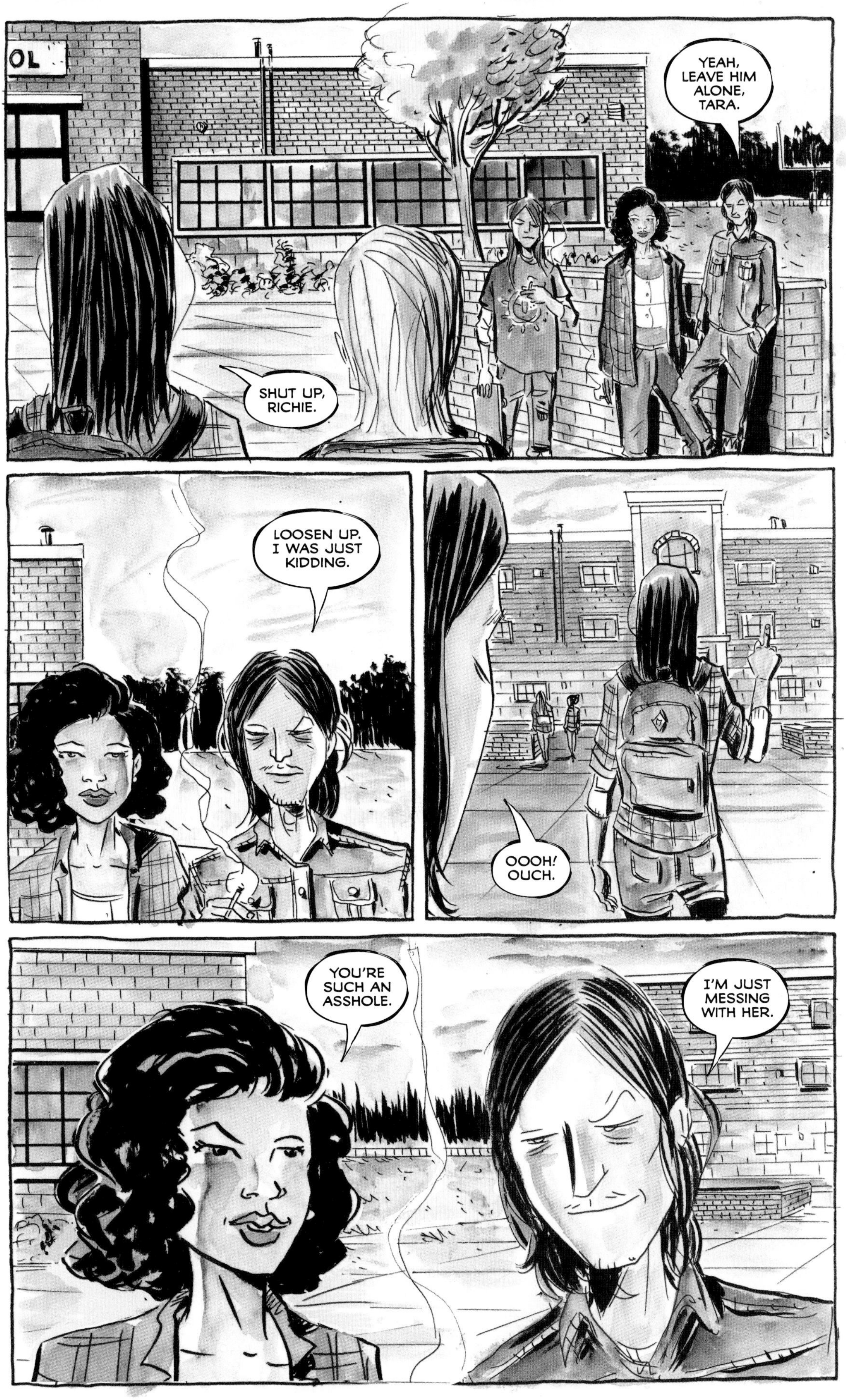
YEAH, LEAVE HIM ALONE, TARA.
SHUT UP, RICHIE.
LOOSEN UP. I WAS JUST KIDDING.
OOOH! OUCH.
YOU'RE SUCH AN ASSHOLE.
I'M JUST MESSING WITH HER.

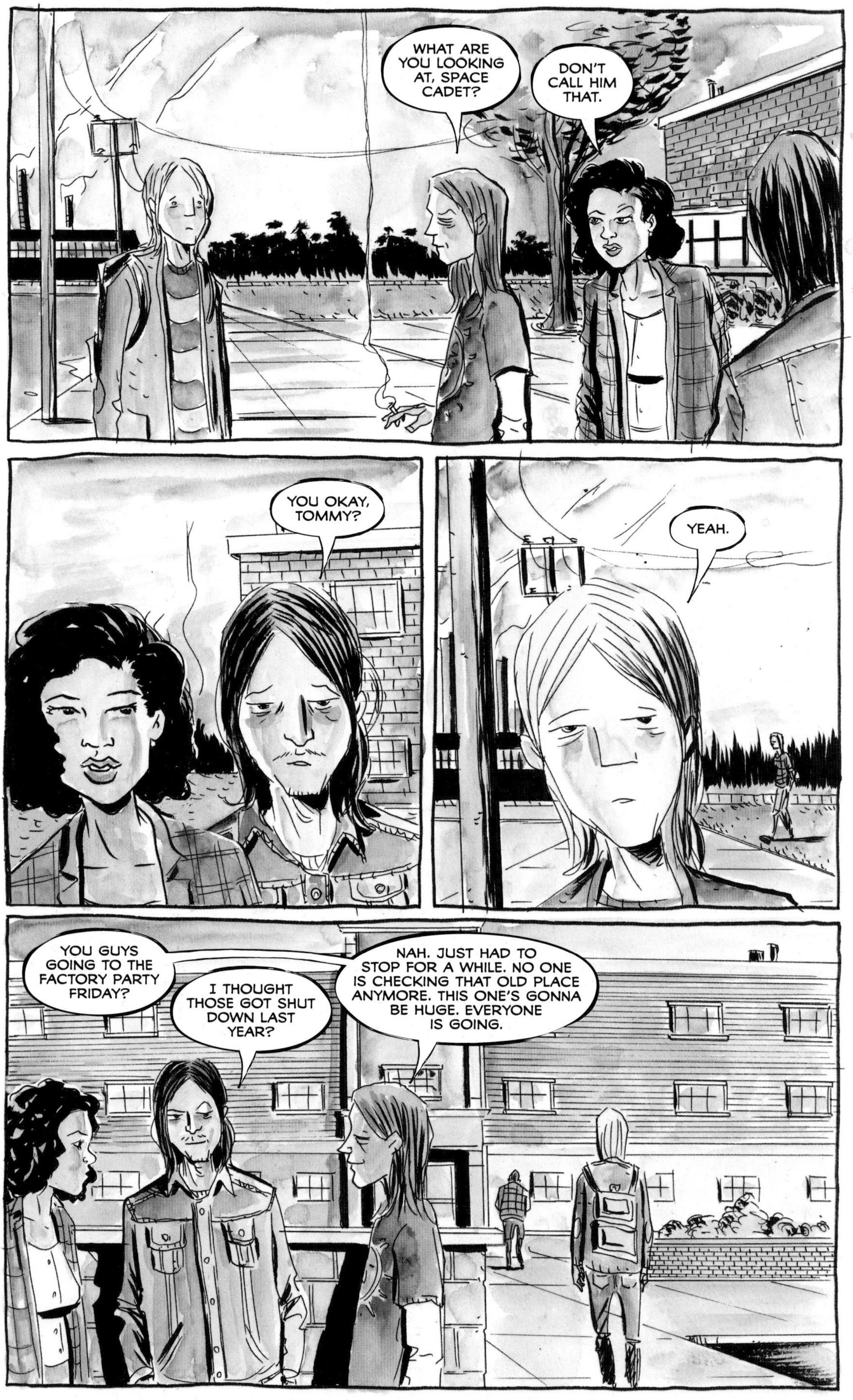
WHAT ARE YOU LOOKING AT, SPACE CADET?
DON'T CALL HIM THAT.
YOU OKAY, TOMMY?
YEAH.
YOU GUYS GOING TO THE FACTORY PARTY FRIDAY?
I THOUGHT THOSE GOT SHUT DOWN LAST YEAR?
NAH. JUST HAD TO STOP FOR A WHILE. NO ONE IS CHECKING THAT OLD PLACE ANYMORE. THIS ONE'S GONNA BE HUGE. EVERYONE IS GOING.

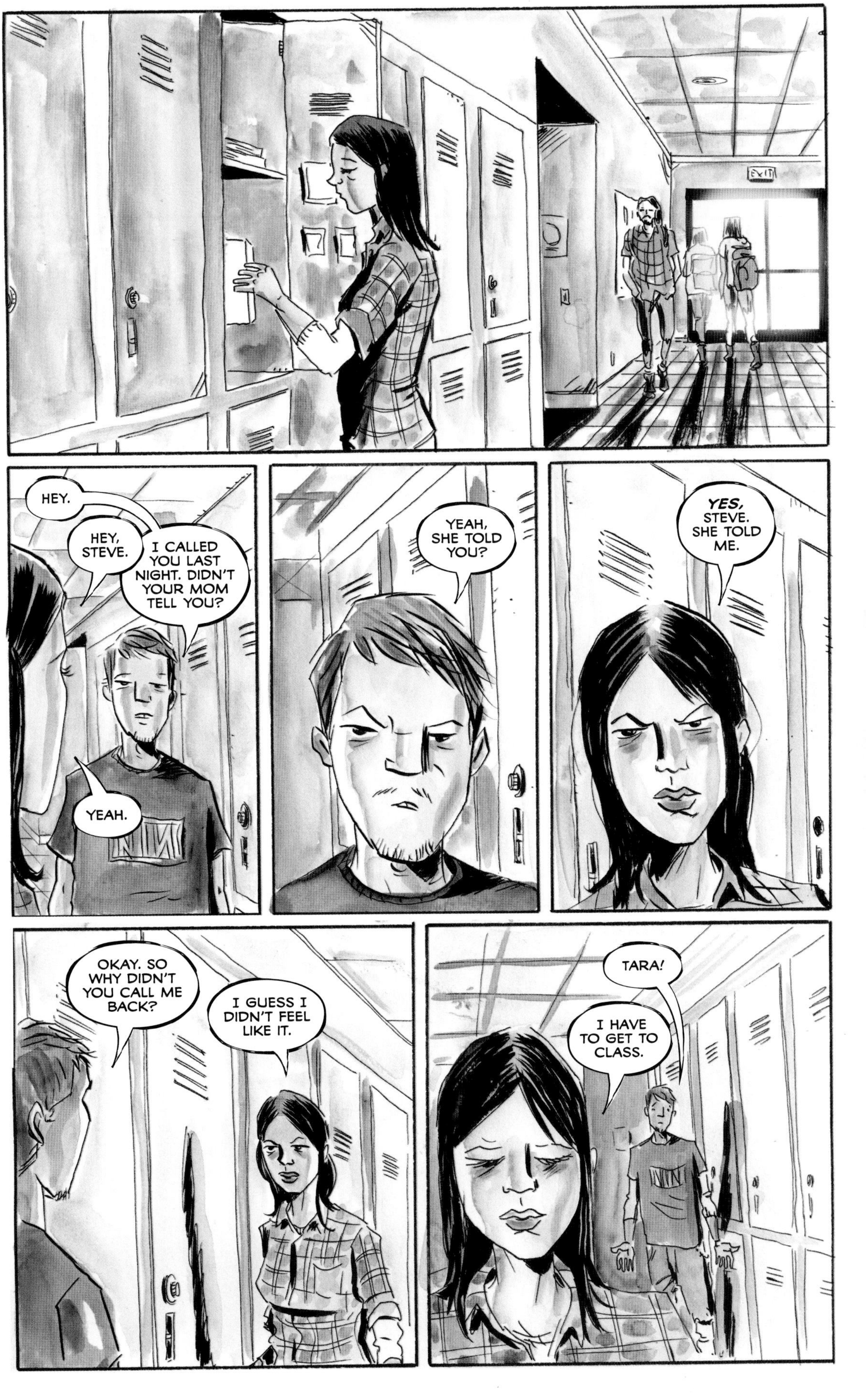
HEY.
HEY, STEVE.
I CALLED YOU LAST NIGHT. DIDN'T YOUR MOM TELL YOU?
YEAH.
YEAH, SHE TOLD YOU?
YES, STEVE. SHE TOLD ME.
OKAY. SO WHY DIDN'T YOU CALL ME BACK?
I GUESS I DIDN'T FEEL LIKE IT.
TARA!
I HAVE TO GET TO CLASS.

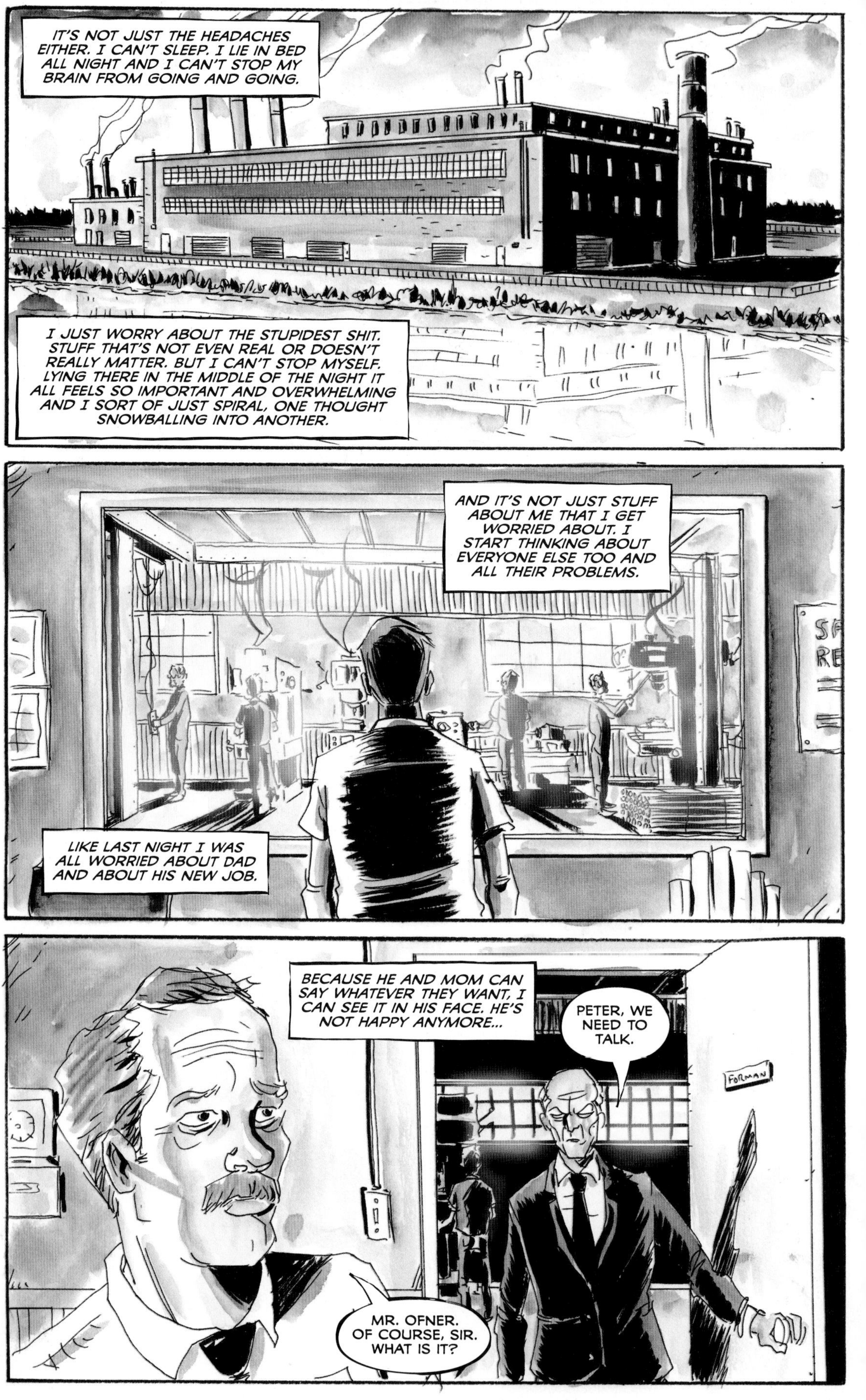
IT'S NOT JUST THE HEADACHES EITHER. I CAN'T SLEEP. I LIE IN BED ALL NIGHT AND I CAN'T STOP MY BRAIN FROM GOING AND GOING.
I JUST WORRY ABOUT THE STUPIDEST SHIT. STUFF THAT'S NOT EVEN REAL OR DOESN'T REALLY MATTER. BUT I CAN'T STOP MYSELF. LYING THERE IN THE MIDDLE OF THE NIGHT IT ALL FEELS SO IMPORTANT AND OVERWHELMING AND I SORT OF JUST SPIRAL, ONE THOUGHT SNOWBALLING INTO ANOTHER.
AND IT'S NOT JUST STUFF ABOUT ME THAT I GET WORRIED ABOUT. I START THINKING ABOUT EVERYONE ELSE TOO AND ALL THEIR PROBLEMS.
LIKE LAST NIGHT I WAS ALL WORRIED ABOUT DAD AND ABOUT HIS NEW JOB.
BECAUSE HE AND MOM CAN SAY WHATEVER THEY WANT, I CAN SEE IT IN HIS FACE. HE'S NOT HAPPY ANYMORE...
PETER, WE NEED TO TALK.
FORMAN
MR. OFNER. OF COURSE, SIR. WHAT IS IT?

SOME OF THESE TIME CARDS DO NOT MATCH THE HOURS YOU HAVE BEEN INVOICING FOR THE DAY SHIFT.

WHAT? I'M PRETTY SURE I DID THEM CORRECTLY, SIR. I CAN DOUBLE-CHECK THOUGH. I MAY HAVE ADDED THEM UP WRONG.

YOU ADDED THEM UP WRONG, ALL RIGHT. EMPLOYEES COME IN FIVE OR TEN MINUTES LATE AND YOU STILL LET THEM COUNT THE FULL HOUR!

OH, WELL, IT'S ONLY A FEW MINUTES OFF. SOME OF THE GUYS ARE COMING IN ALL THE WAY FROM THE COUNTY SO I THOUGHT--

PETER, YOU ARE LETTING THEM WALK ALL OVER YOU!

ORDERS
200 PIECES   OCT 17
350 PIECES   OCT 31
1500 PIECES   DEC 17
800 PIECES   JAN 5

I GAVE YOU THIS POSITION BECAUSE I THOUGHT YOU COULD HANDLE IT. BUT THAT MEANS YOU'RE *IN MANAGEMENT* NOW. YOU'RE NOT THEIR BEST FRIEND. THEY DON'T HAVE TO *LIKE YOU*, PETER.

YOU'RE-- YOU'RE RIGHT. I'M SORRY.

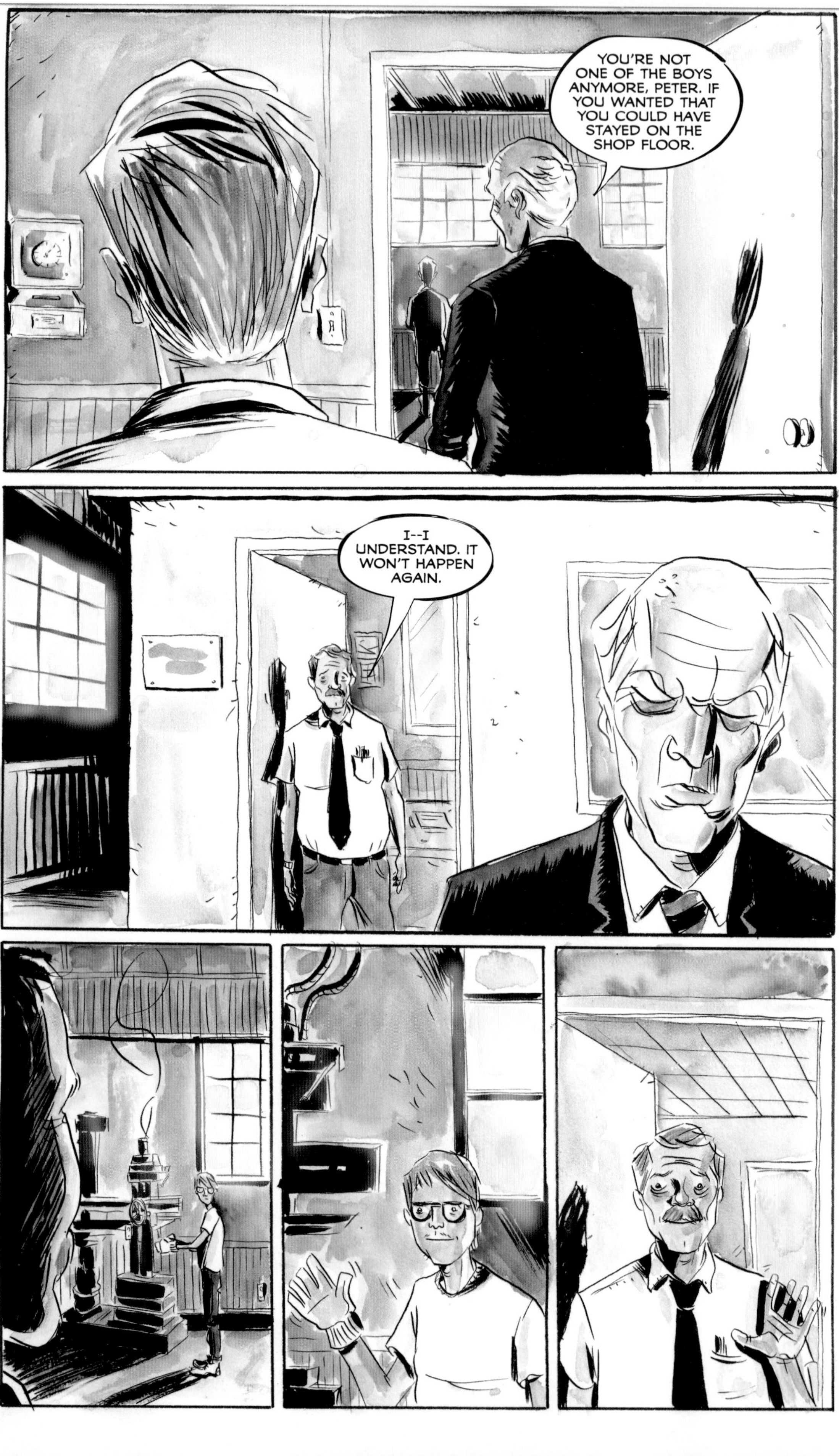
YOU'RE NOT ONE OF THE BOYS ANYMORE, PETER. IF YOU WANTED THAT YOU COULD HAVE STAYED ON THE SHOP FLOOR.
I--I UNDERSTAND. IT WON'T HAPPEN AGAIN.

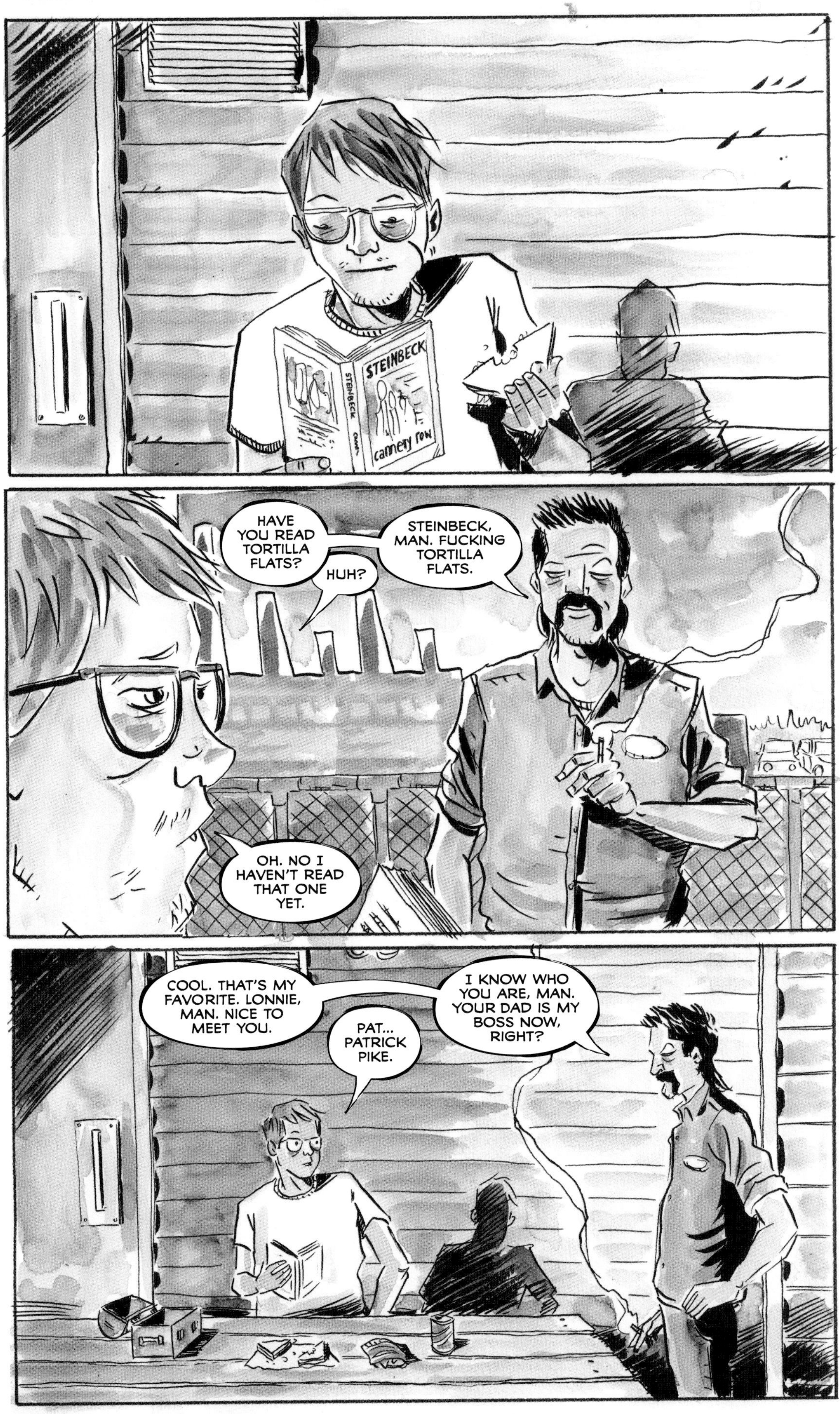
STEINBECK
STEINBECK
cannery row
HAVE YOU READ TORTILLA FLATS?
HUH?
STEINBECK, MAN. FUCKING TORTILLA FLATS.
OH. NO I HAVEN'T READ THAT ONE YET.
COOL. THAT'S MY FAVORITE. LONNIE, MAN. NICE TO MEET YOU.
PAT... PATRICK PIKE.
I KNOW WHO YOU ARE, MAN. YOUR DAD IS MY BOSS NOW, RIGHT?

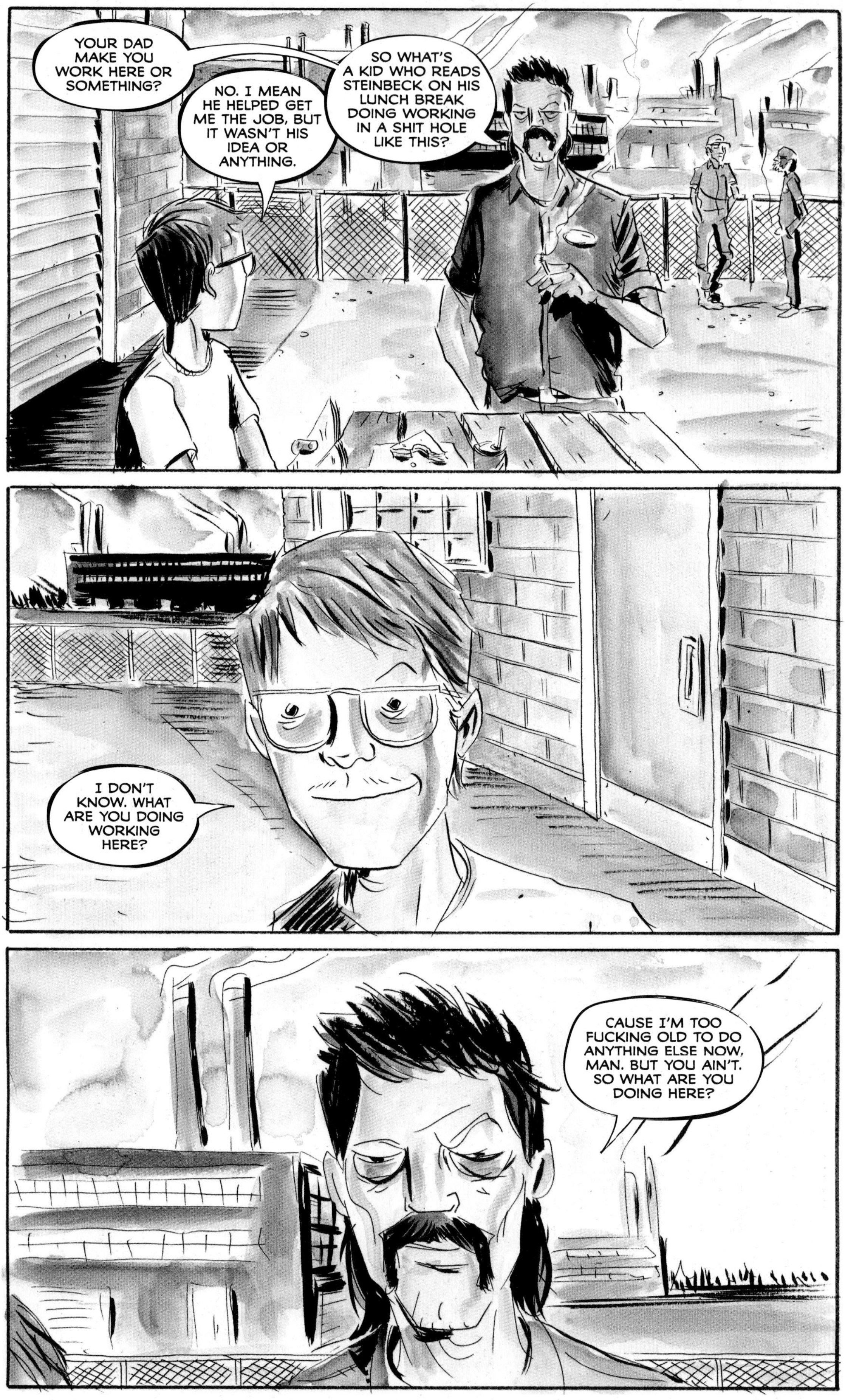
YOUR DAD MAKE YOU WORK HERE OR SOMETHING?
SO WHAT'S A KID WHO READS STEINBECK ON HIS LUNCH BREAK DOING WORKING IN A SHIT HOLE LIKE THIS?
NO. I MEAN HE HELPED GET ME THE JOB, BUT IT WASN'T HIS IDEA OR ANYTHING.
I DON'T KNOW. WHAT ARE YOU DOING WORKING HERE?
CAUSE I'M TOO FUCKING OLD TO DO ANYTHING ELSE NOW, MAN. BUT YOU AIN'T. SO WHAT ARE YOU DOING HERE?

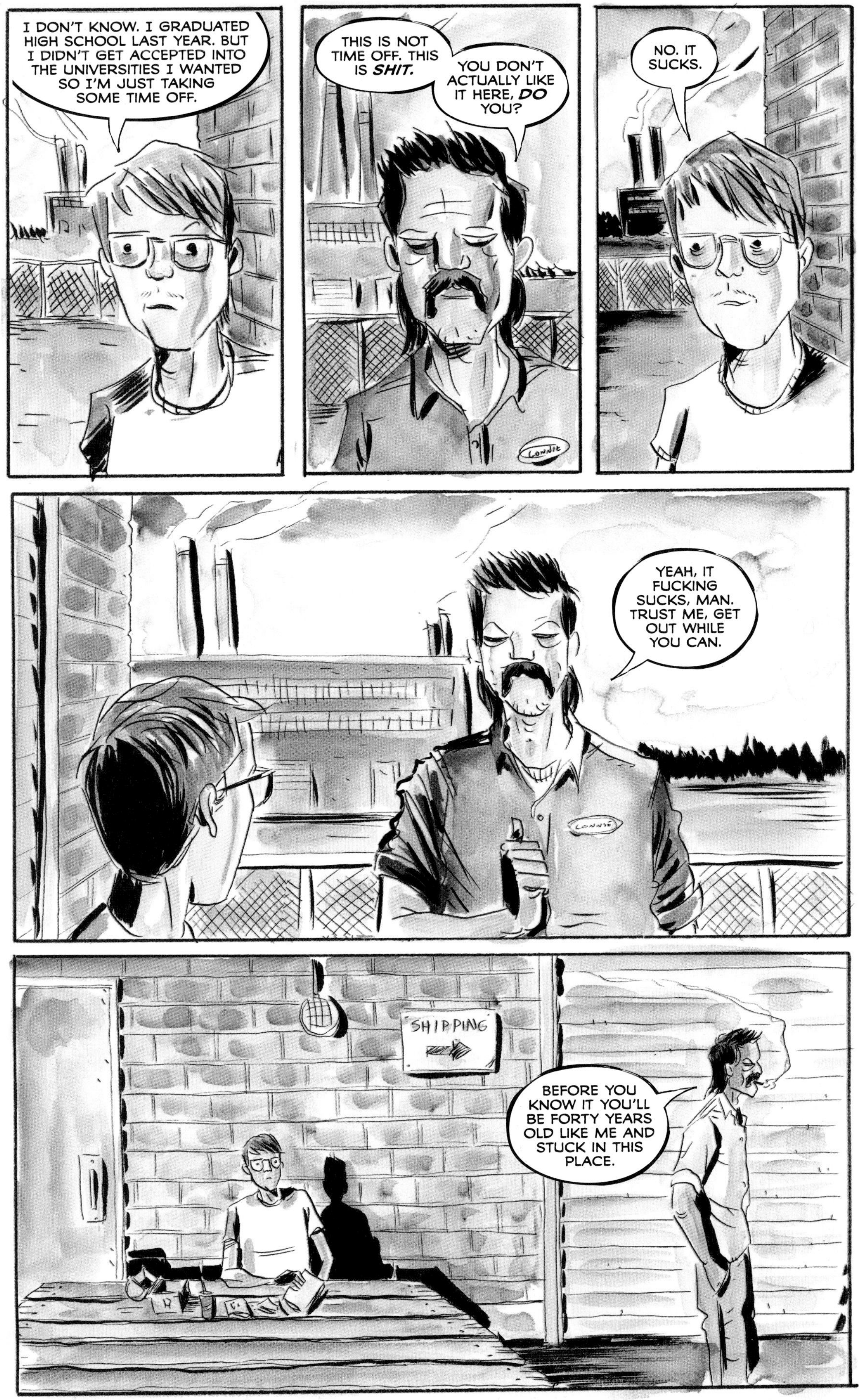
I DON'T KNOW. I GRADUATED HIGH SCHOOL LAST YEAR. BUT I DIDN'T GET ACCEPTED INTO THE UNIVERSITIES I WANTED SO I'M JUST TAKING SOME TIME OFF.
THIS IS NOT TIME OFF. THIS IS *SHIT.*
YOU DON'T ACTUALLY LIKE IT HERE, ***DO*** YOU?
NO. IT SUCKS.
YEAH, IT FUCKING SUCKS, MAN. TRUST ME, GET OUT WHILE YOU CAN.
SHIPPING
BEFORE YOU KNOW IT YOU'LL BE FORTY YEARS OLD LIKE ME AND STUCK IN THIS PLACE.

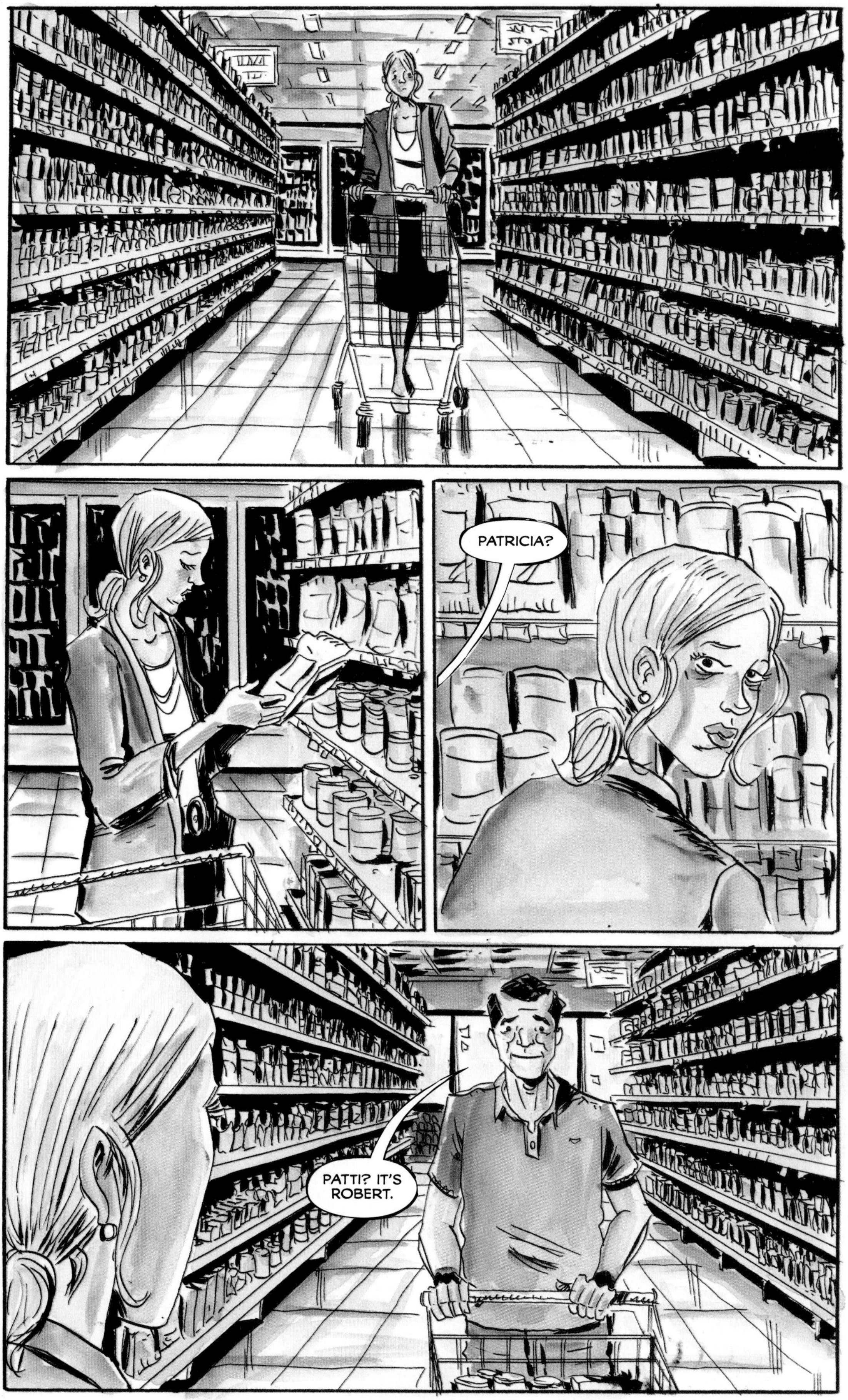
PATRICIA?
PATTI? IT'S ROBERT.

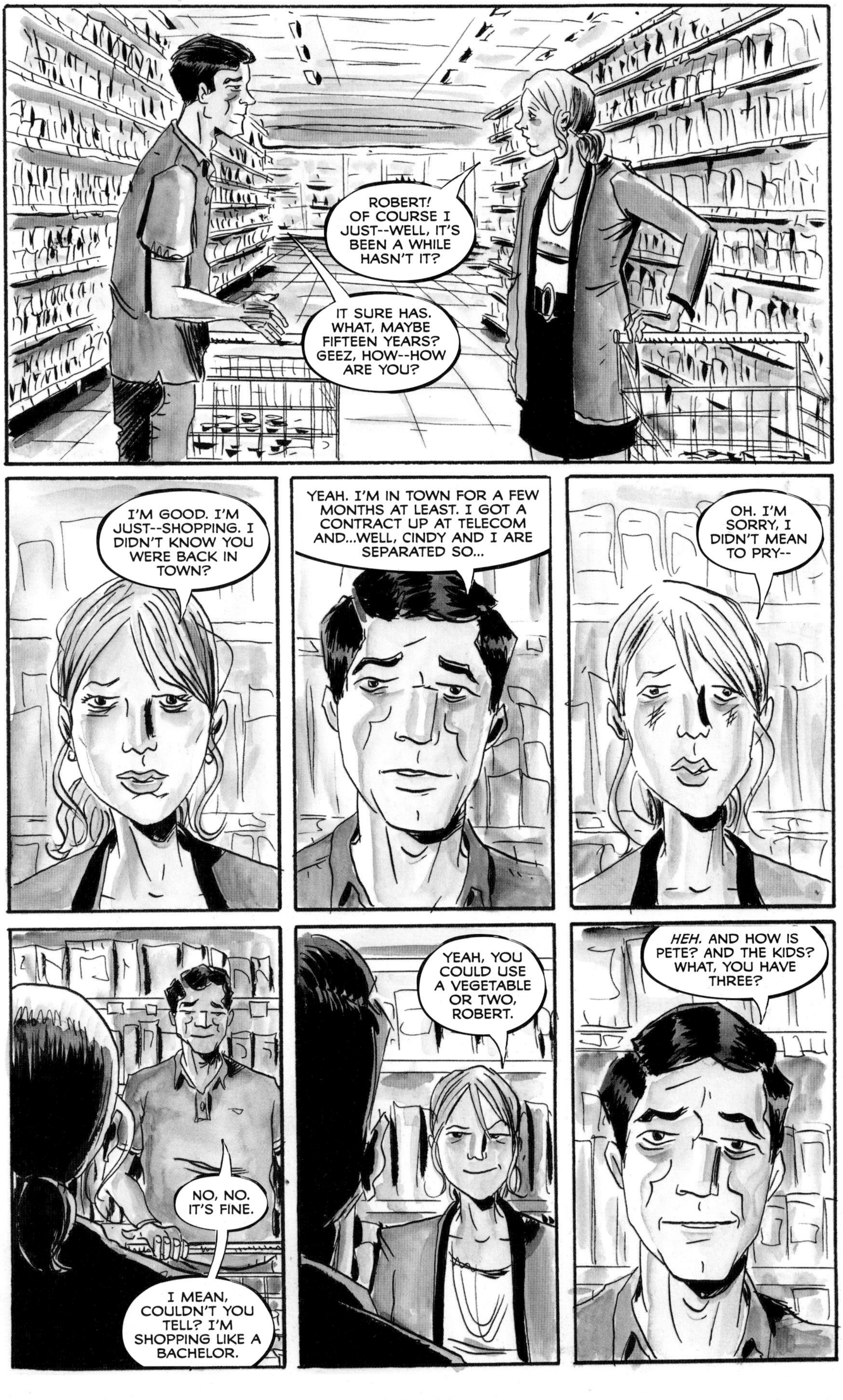
ROBERT! OF COURSE I JUST--WELL, IT'S BEEN A WHILE HASN'T IT?
IT SURE HAS. WHAT, MAYBE FIFTEEN YEARS? GEEZ, HOW--HOW ARE YOU?
I'M GOOD. I'M JUST--SHOPPING. I DIDN'T KNOW YOU WERE BACK IN TOWN?
YEAH. I'M IN TOWN FOR A FEW MONTHS AT LEAST. I GOT A CONTRACT UP AT TELECOM AND...WELL, CINDY AND I ARE SEPARATED SO...
OH. I'M SORRY, I DIDN'T MEAN TO PRY--
NO, NO. IT'S FINE.
I MEAN, COULDN'T YOU TELL? I'M SHOPPING LIKE A BACHELOR.
YEAH, YOU COULD USE A VEGETABLE OR TWO, ROBERT.
HEH. AND HOW IS PETE? AND THE KIDS? WHAT, YOU HAVE THREE?

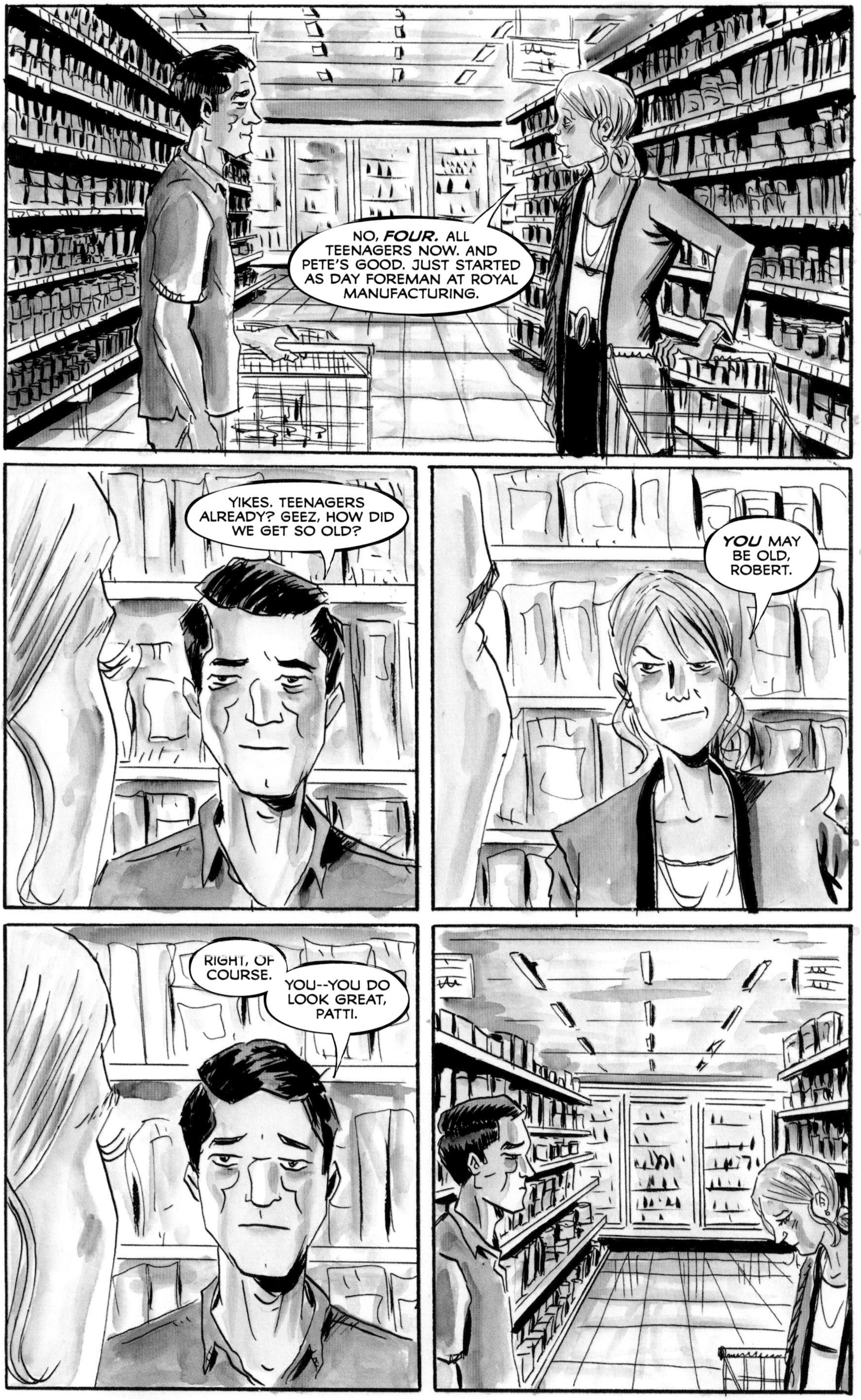
NO, *FOUR.* ALL TEENAGERS NOW. AND PETE'S GOOD. JUST STARTED AS DAY FOREMAN AT ROYAL MANUFACTURING.
YIKES. TEENAGERS ALREADY? GEEZ, HOW DID WE GET SO OLD?
YOU MAY BE OLD, ROBERT.
RIGHT, OF COURSE.
YOU--YOU DO LOOK GREAT, PATTI.

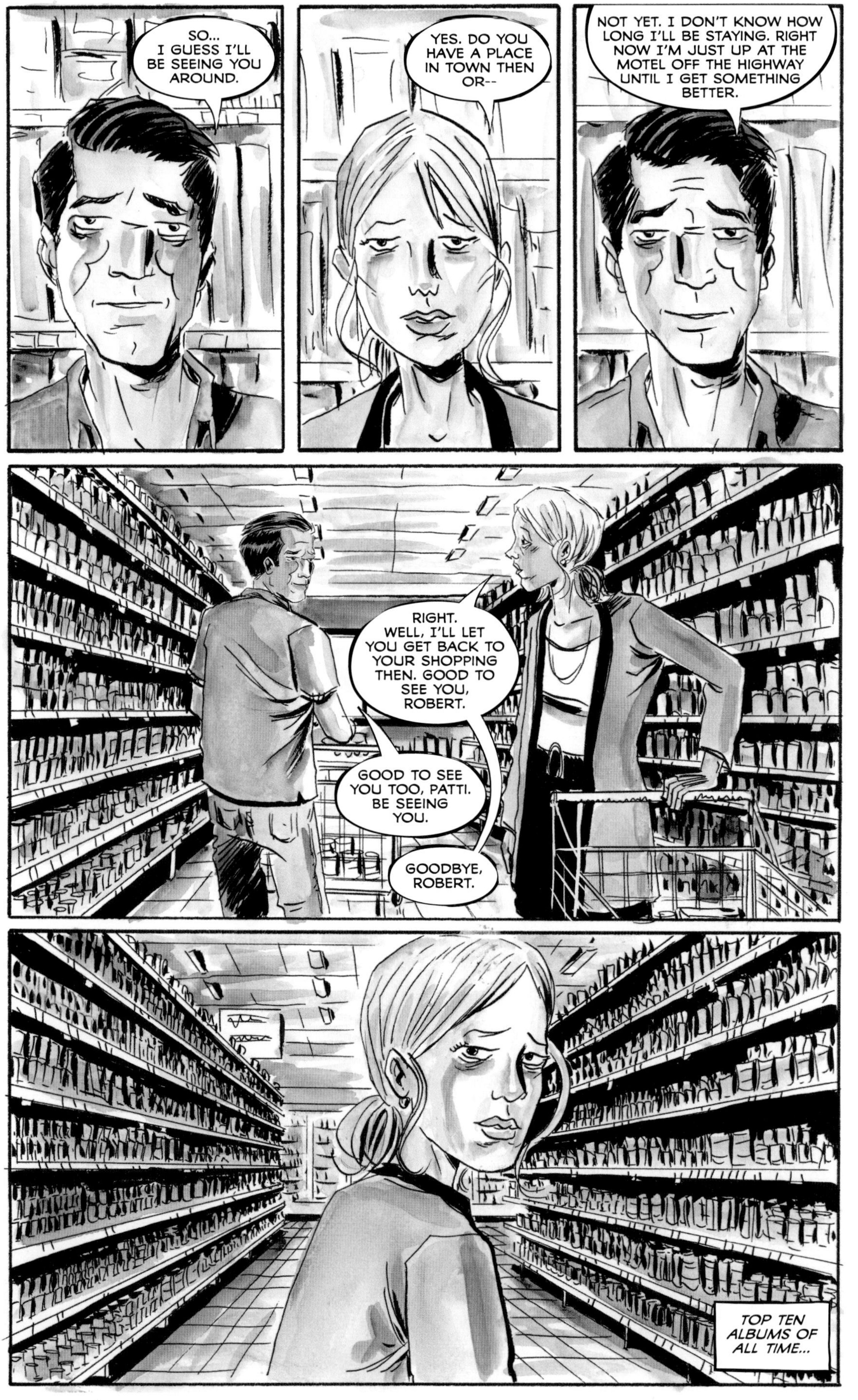
SO... I GUESS I'LL BE SEEING YOU AROUND.
YES. DO YOU HAVE A PLACE IN TOWN THEN OR--
NOT YET. I DON'T KNOW HOW LONG I'LL BE STAYING. RIGHT NOW I'M JUST UP AT THE MOTEL OFF THE HIGHWAY UNTIL I GET SOMETHING BETTER.
RIGHT. WELL, I'LL LET YOU GET BACK TO YOUR SHOPPING THEN. GOOD TO SEE YOU, ROBERT.
GOOD TO SEE YOU TOO, PATTI. BE SEEING YOU.
GOODBYE, ROBERT.
TOP TEN ALBUMS OF ALL TIME...

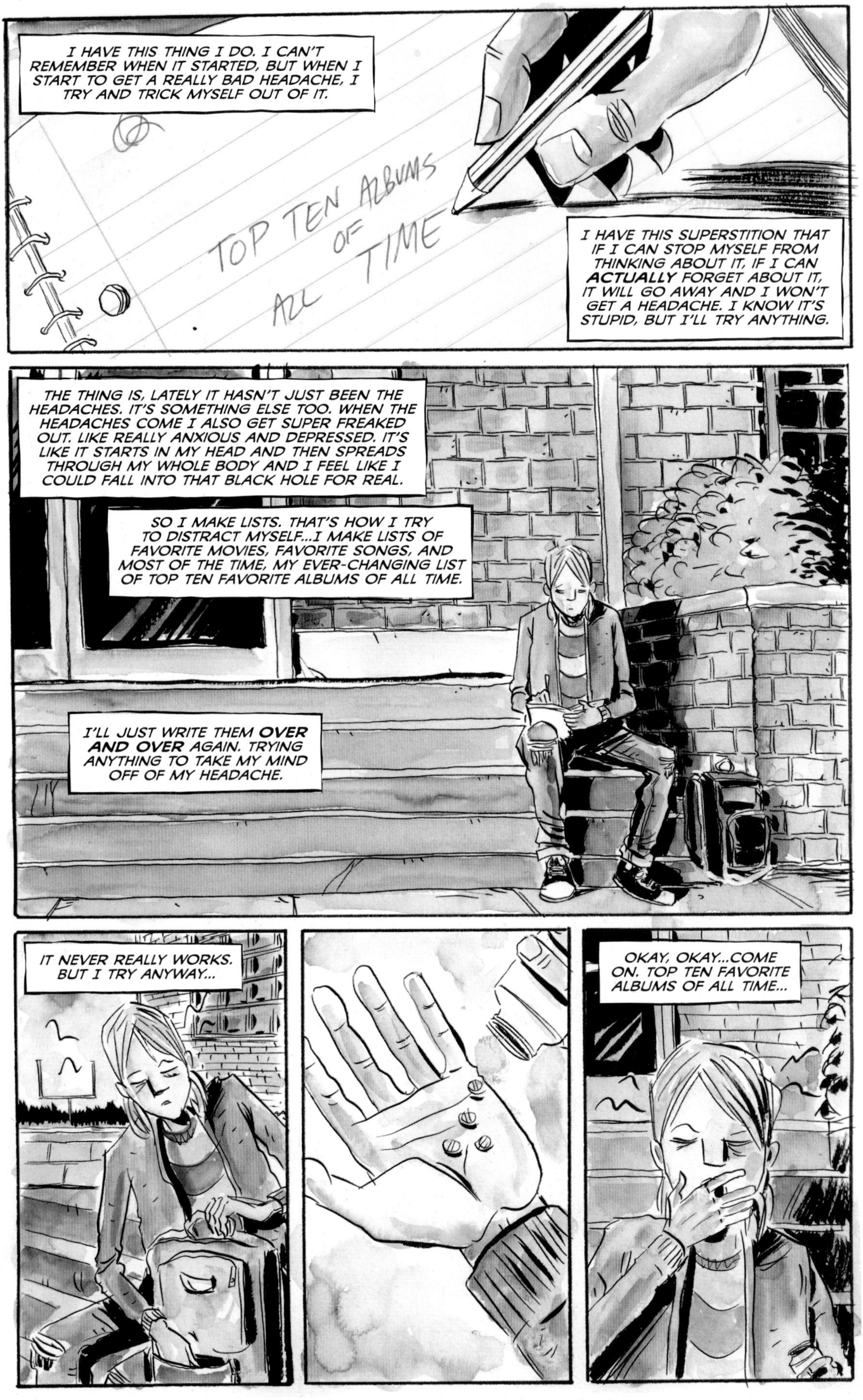
I HAVE THIS THING I DO. I CAN'T REMEMBER WHEN IT STARTED, BUT WHEN I START TO GET A REALLY BAD HEADACHE, I TRY AND TRICK MYSELF OUT OF IT.
TOP TEN ALBUMS OF ALL TIME
I HAVE THIS SUPERSTITION THAT IF I CAN STOP MYSELF FROM THINKING ABOUT IT, IF I CAN **ACTUALLY** FORGET ABOUT IT, IT WILL GO AWAY AND I WON'T GET A HEADACHE. I KNOW IT'S STUPID, BUT I'LL TRY ANYTHING.
THE THING IS, LATELY IT HASN'T JUST BEEN THE HEADACHES. IT'S SOMETHING ELSE TOO. WHEN THE HEADACHES COME I ALSO GET SUPER FREAKED OUT. LIKE REALLY ANXIOUS AND DEPRESSED. IT'S LIKE IT STARTS IN MY HEAD AND THEN SPREADS THROUGH MY WHOLE BODY AND I FEEL LIKE I COULD FALL INTO THAT BLACK HOLE FOR REAL.
SO I MAKE LISTS. THAT'S HOW I TRY TO DISTRACT MYSELF...I MAKE LISTS OF FAVORITE MOVIES, FAVORITE SONGS, AND MOST OF THE TIME, MY EVER-CHANGING LIST OF TOP TEN FAVORITE ALBUMS OF ALL TIME.
I'LL JUST WRITE THEM **OVER AND OVER** AGAIN. TRYING ANYTHING TO TAKE MY MIND OFF OF MY HEADACHE.
IT NEVER REALLY WORKS. BUT I TRY ANYWAY...
OKAY, OKAY...COME ON. TOP TEN FAVORITE ALBUMS OF ALL TIME...

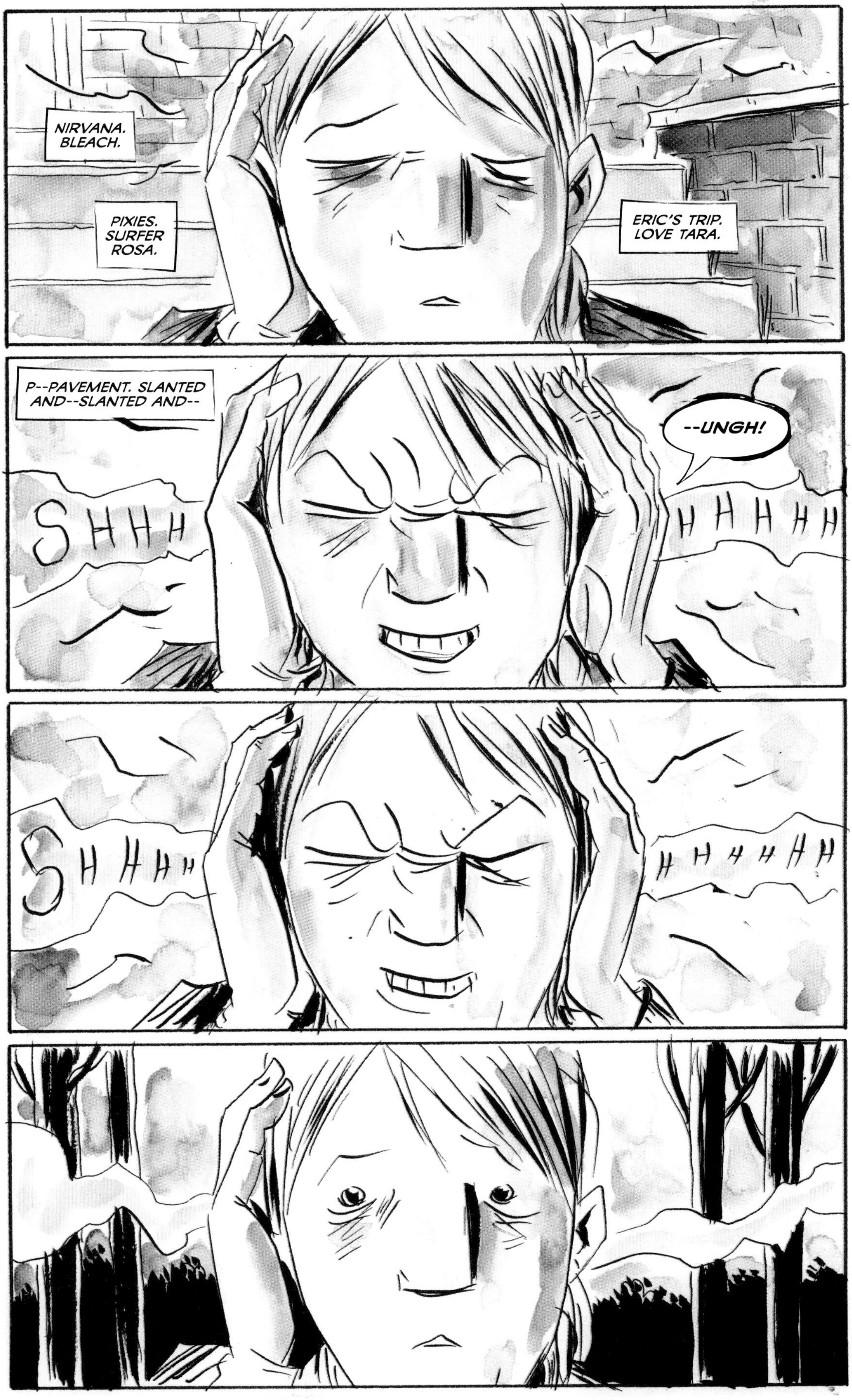
NIRVANA. BLEACH.
PIXIES. SURFER ROSA.
ERIC'S TRIP. LOVE TARA.
P--PAVEMENT. SLANTED AND--SLANTED AND--
--UNGH!
SHHH
HHHHH
SHHHH
HHHHHH

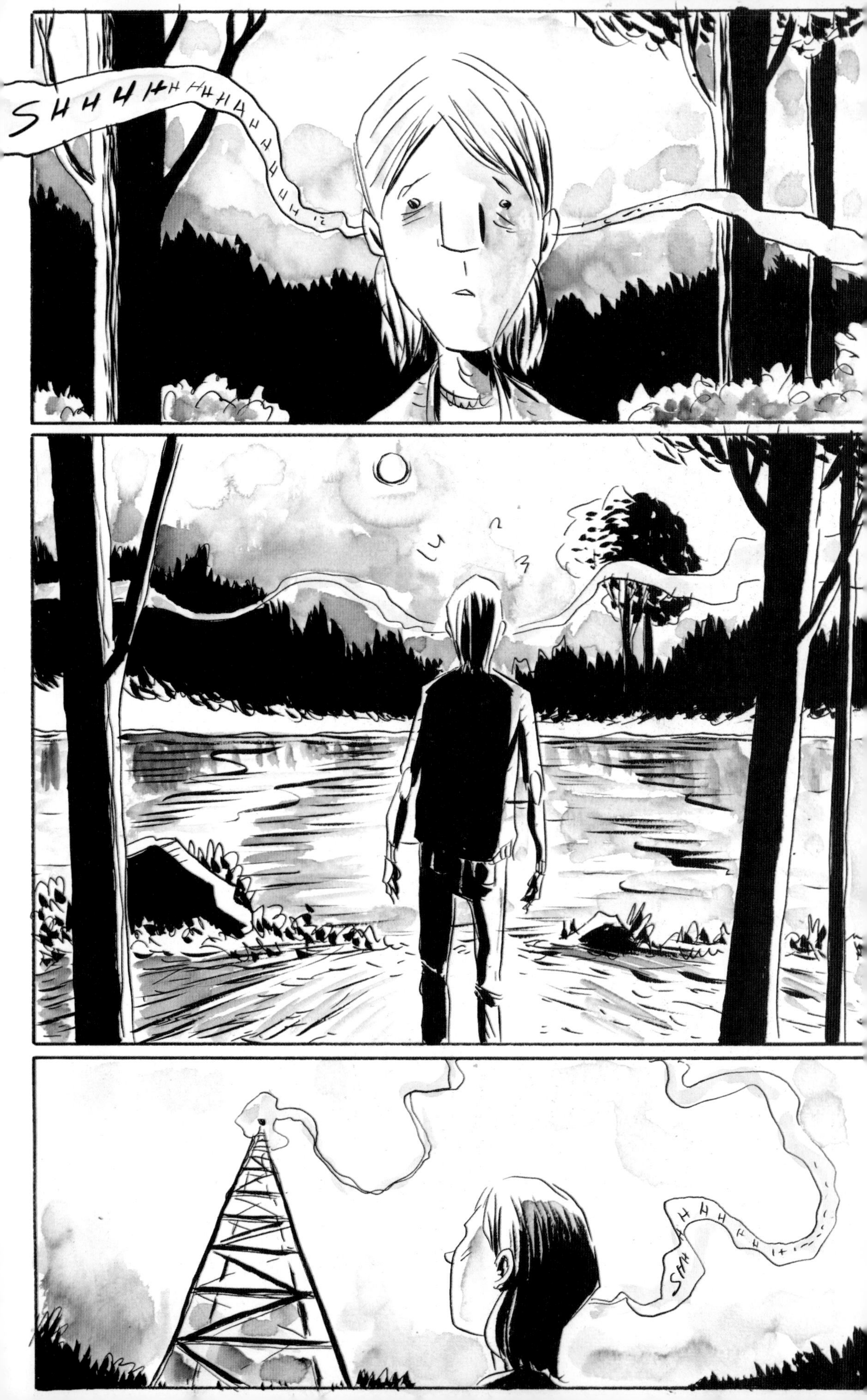
SHHHHHHHHHHHHHHHH
SHHHHHHHH

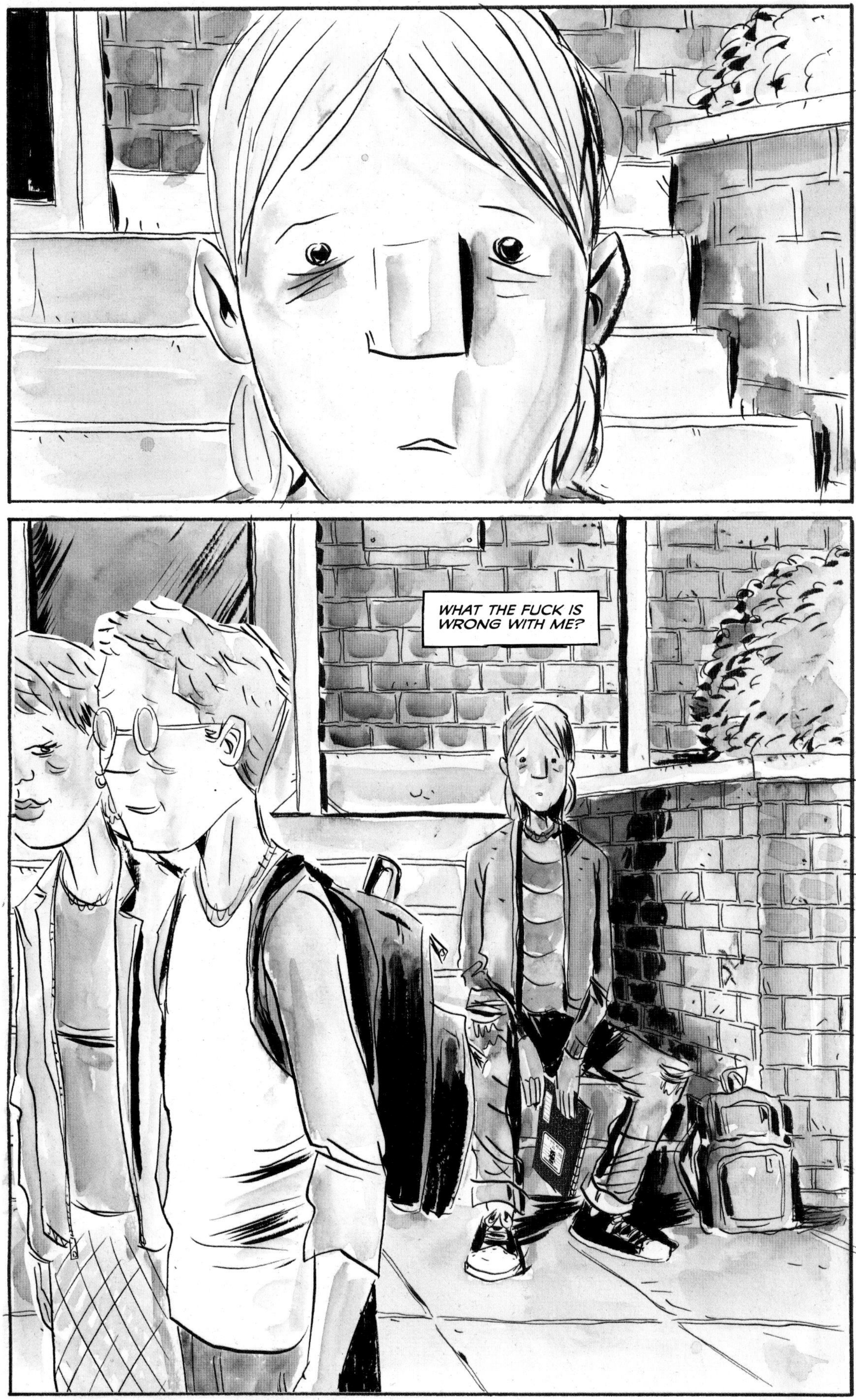
WHAT THE FUCK IS
WRONG WITH ME?

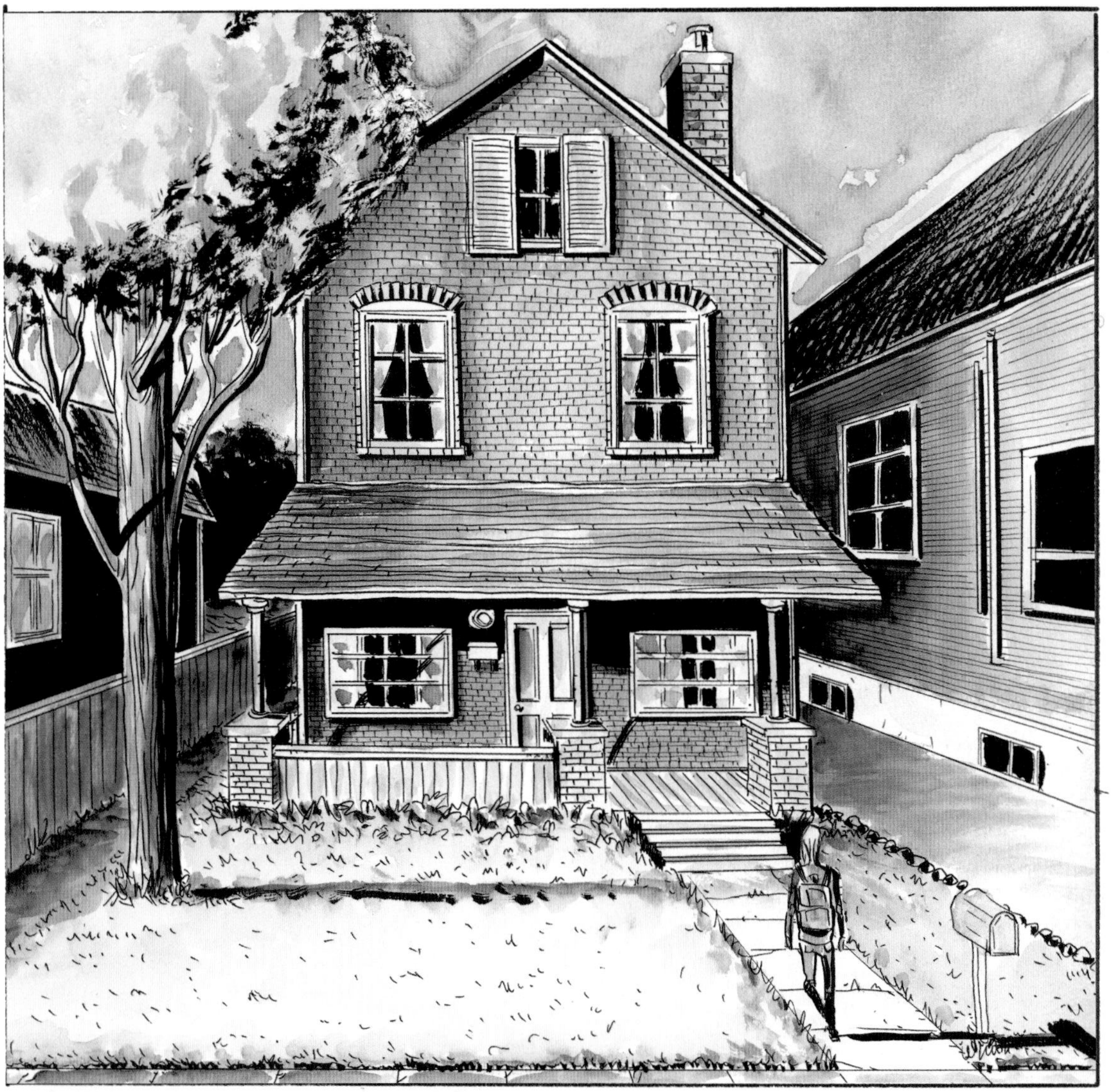

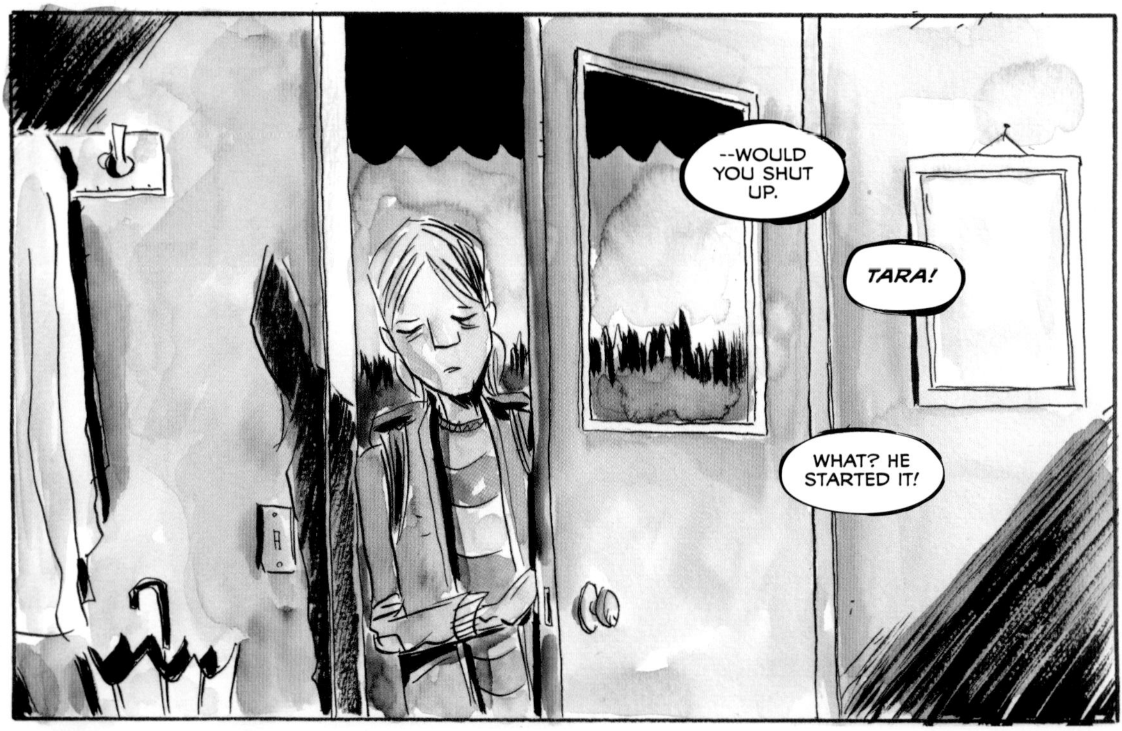
--WOULD YOU SHUT UP.
TARA!
WHAT? HE STARTED IT!

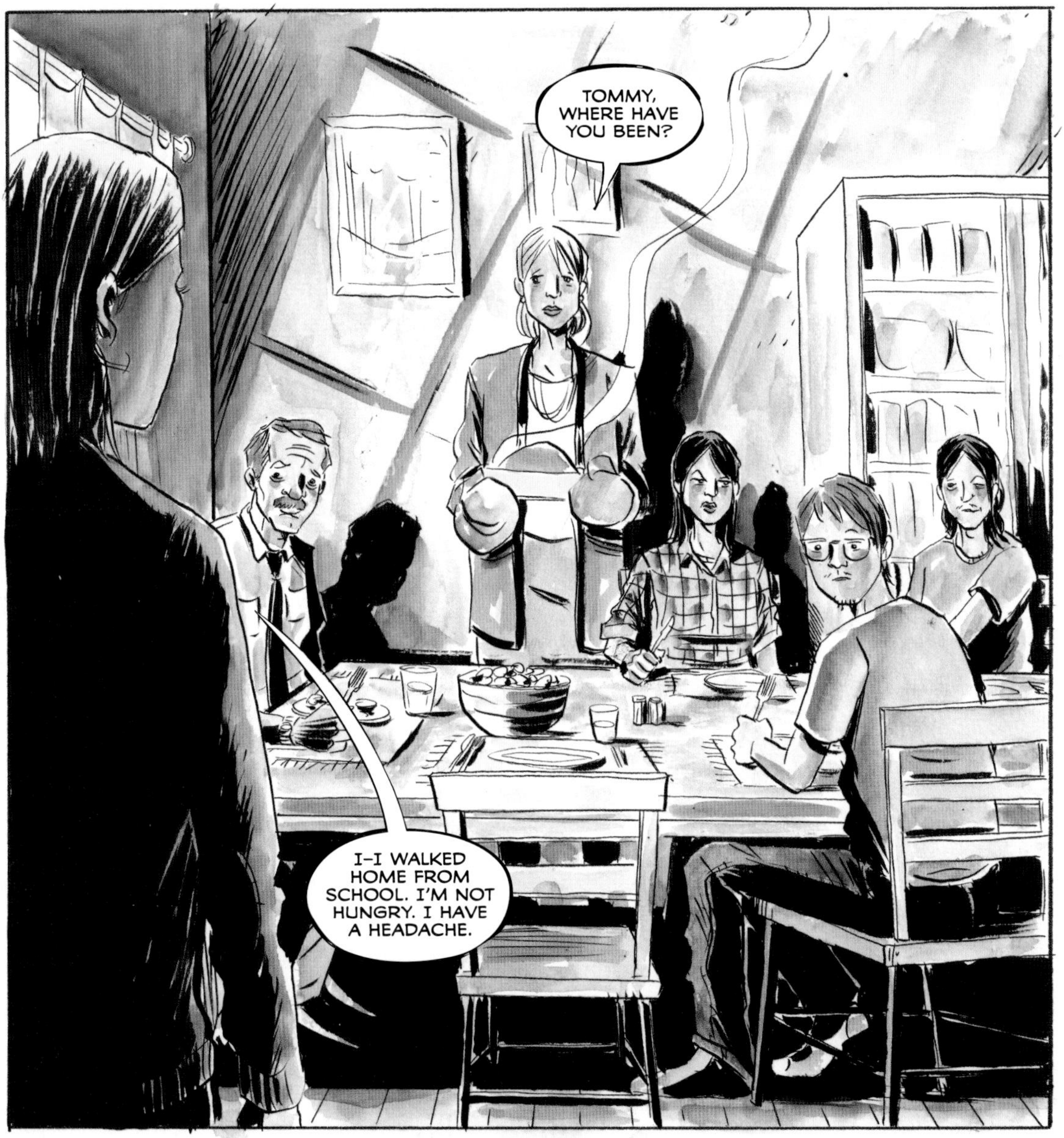
TOMMY, WHERE HAVE YOU BEEN?
I-I WALKED HOME FROM SCHOOL. I'M NOT HUNGRY. I HAVE A HEADACHE.

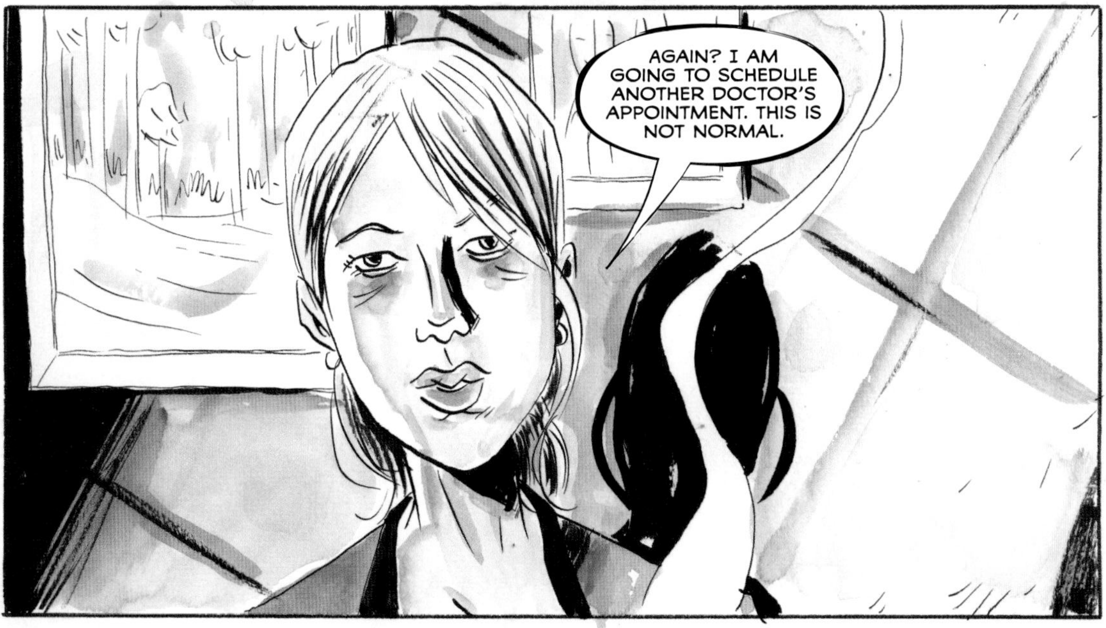
AGAIN? I AM GOING TO SCHEDULE ANOTHER DOCTOR'S APPOINTMENT. THIS IS NOT NORMAL.

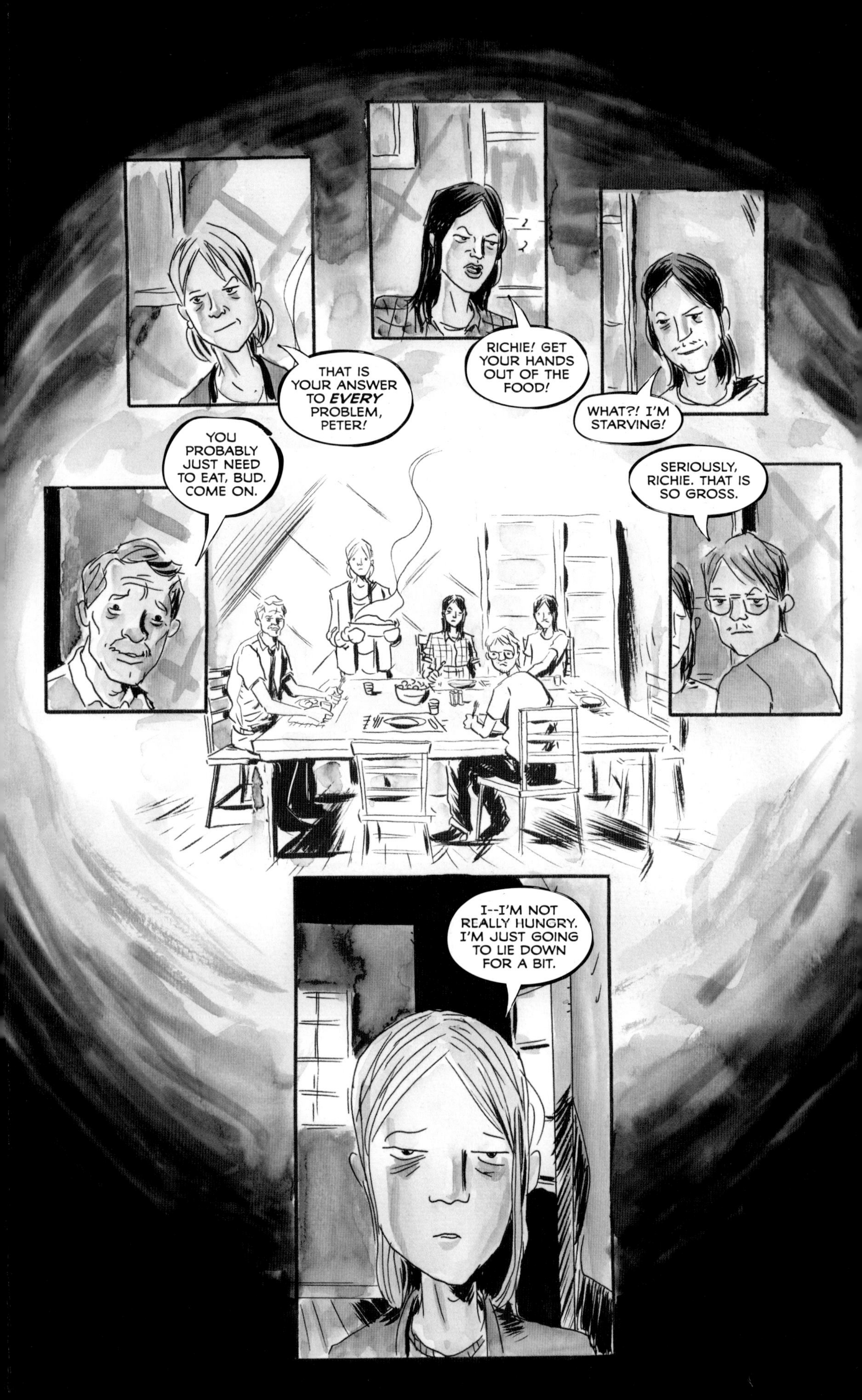
THAT IS YOUR ANSWER TO EVERY PROBLEM, PETER!
RICHIE! GET YOUR HANDS OUT OF THE FOOD!
WHAT?! I'M STARVING!
YOU PROBABLY JUST NEED TO EAT, BUD. COME ON.
SERIOUSLY, RICHIE. THAT IS SO GROSS.
I--I'M NOT REALLY HUNGRY. I'M JUST GOING TO LIE DOWN FOR A BIT.

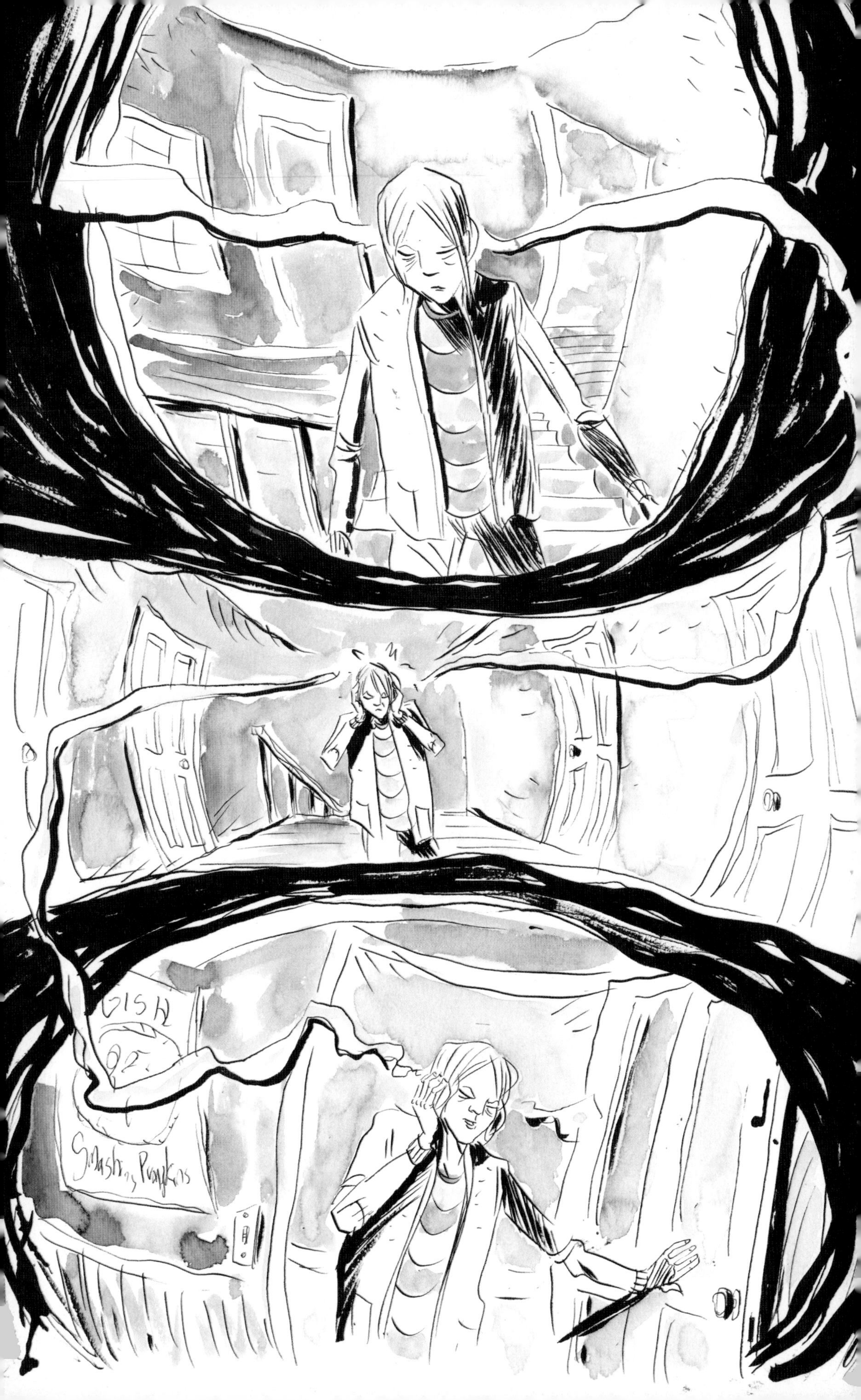

WISH
Smashing Pumpkins

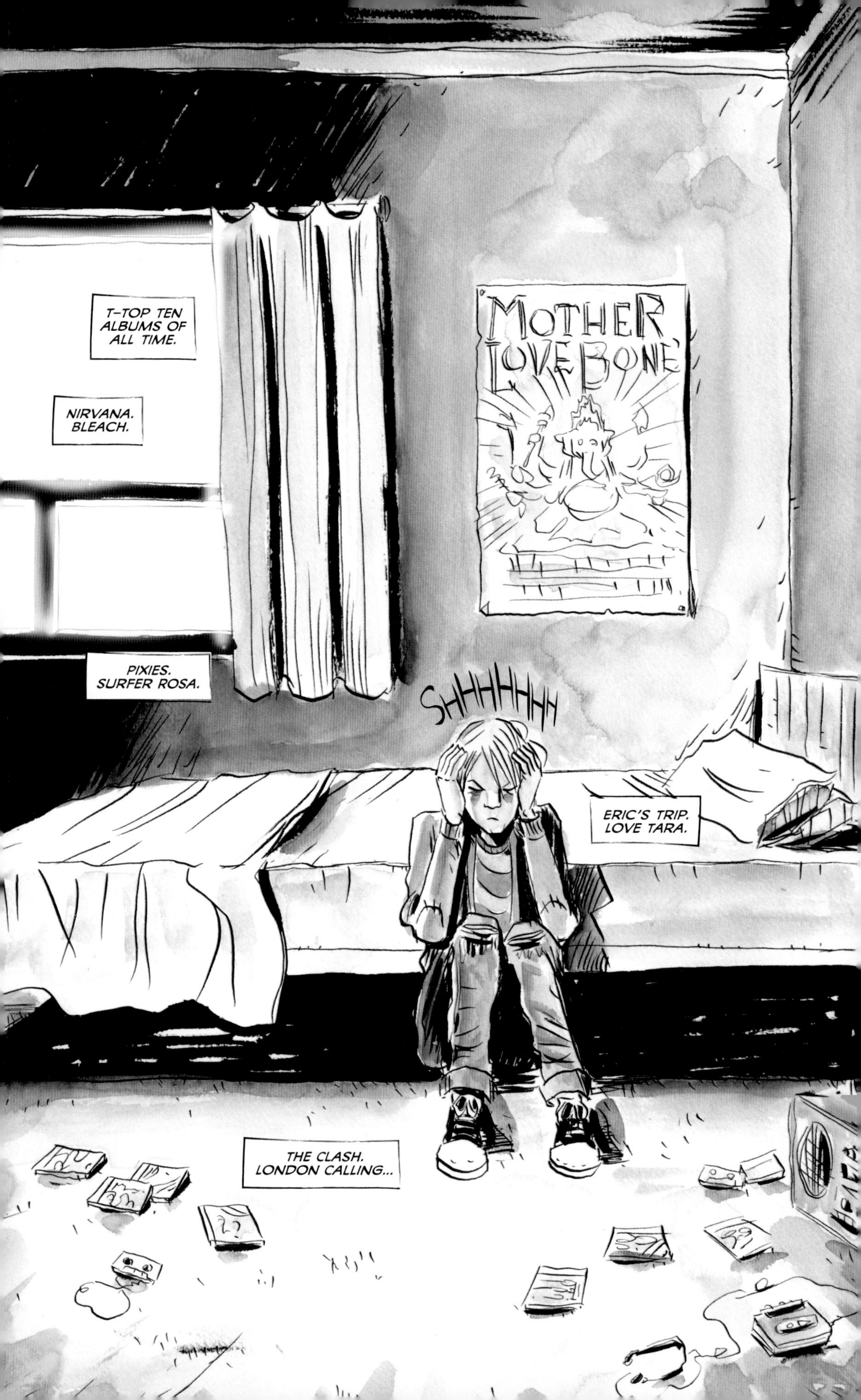
T-TOP TEN ALBUMS OF ALL TIME.
NIRVANA. BLEACH.
MOTHER LOVE BONE
PIXIES. SURFER ROSA.
SHHHHHHH
ERIC'S TRIP. LOVE TARA.
THE CLASH. LONDON CALLING...

CHAPTER SEVEN

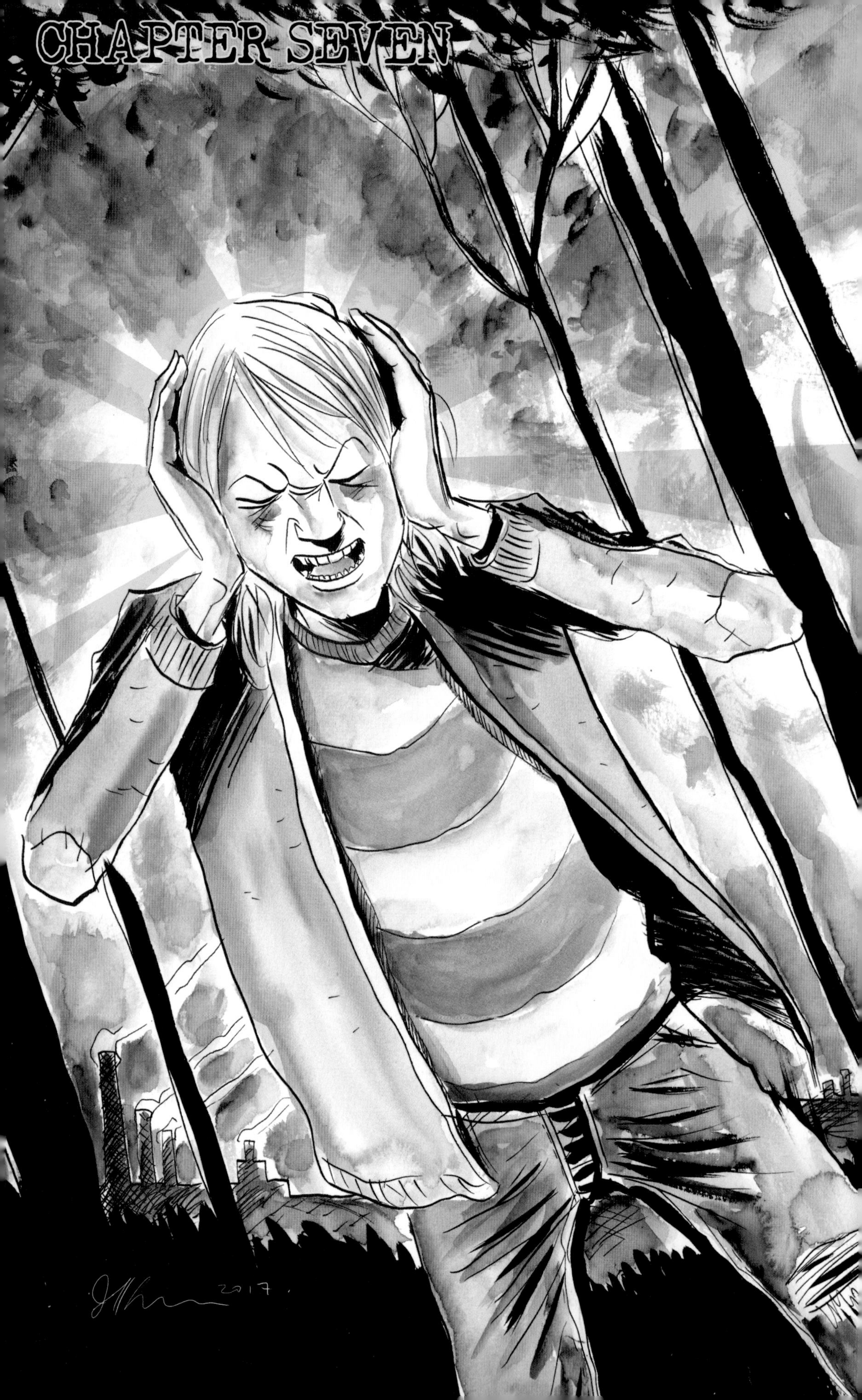

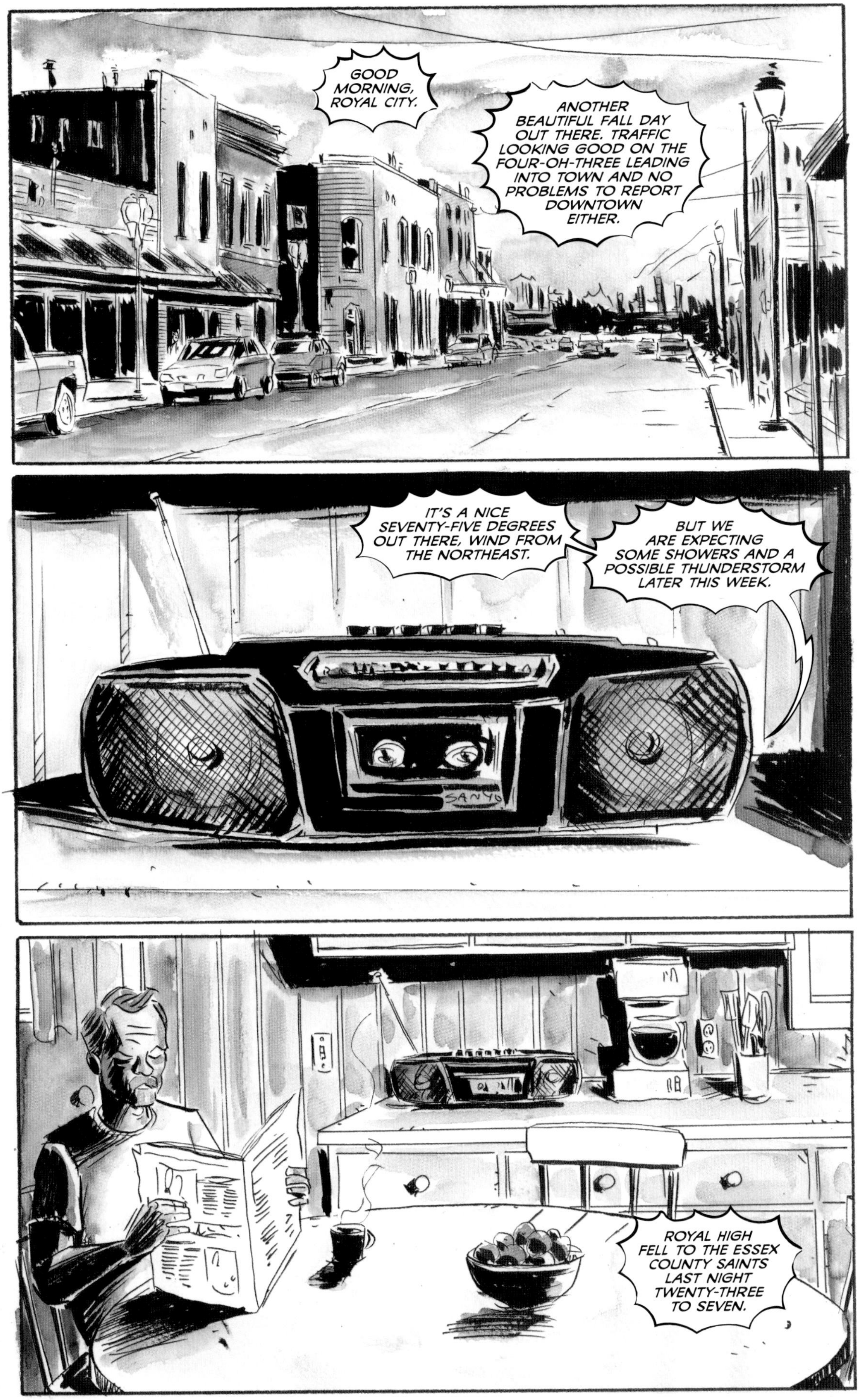
GOOD MORNING, ROYAL CITY.
ANOTHER BEAUTIFUL FALL DAY OUT THERE. TRAFFIC LOOKING GOOD ON THE FOUR-OH-THREE LEADING INTO TOWN AND NO PROBLEMS TO REPORT DOWNTOWN EITHER.
IT'S A NICE SEVENTY-FIVE DEGREES OUT THERE, WIND FROM THE NORTHEAST.
BUT WE ARE EXPECTING SOME SHOWERS AND A POSSIBLE THUNDERSTORM LATER THIS WEEK.
SANYO
ROYAL HIGH FELL TO THE ESSEX COUNTY SAINTS LAST NIGHT TWENTY-THREE TO SEVEN.

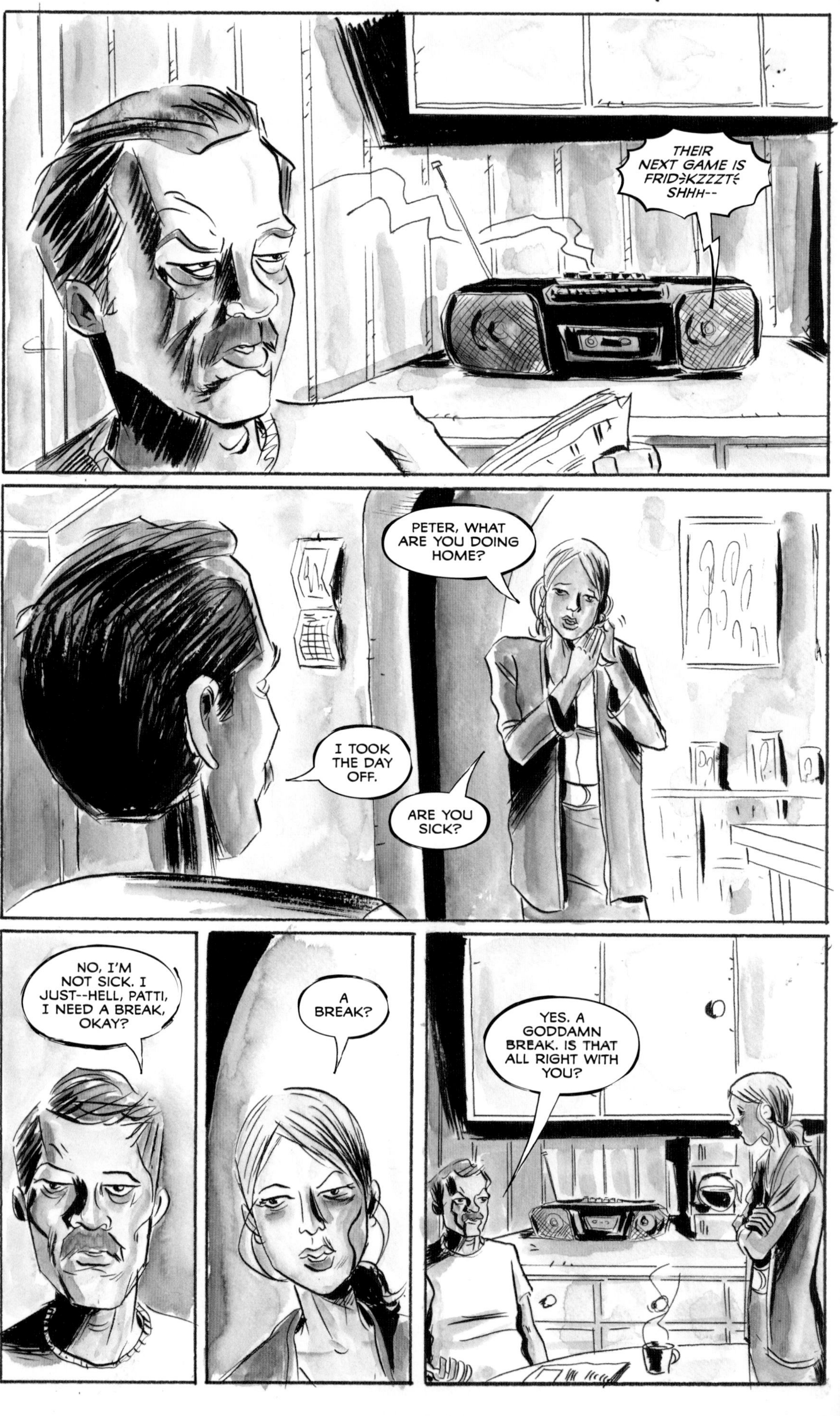
THEIR NEXT GAME IS FRID⚡KZZZT⚡ SHHH--
PETER, WHAT ARE YOU DOING HOME?
I TOOK THE DAY OFF.
ARE YOU SICK?
NO, I'M NOT SICK. I JUST--HELL, PATTI, I NEED A BREAK, OKAY?
A BREAK?
YES. A GODDAMN BREAK. IS THAT ALL RIGHT WITH YOU?

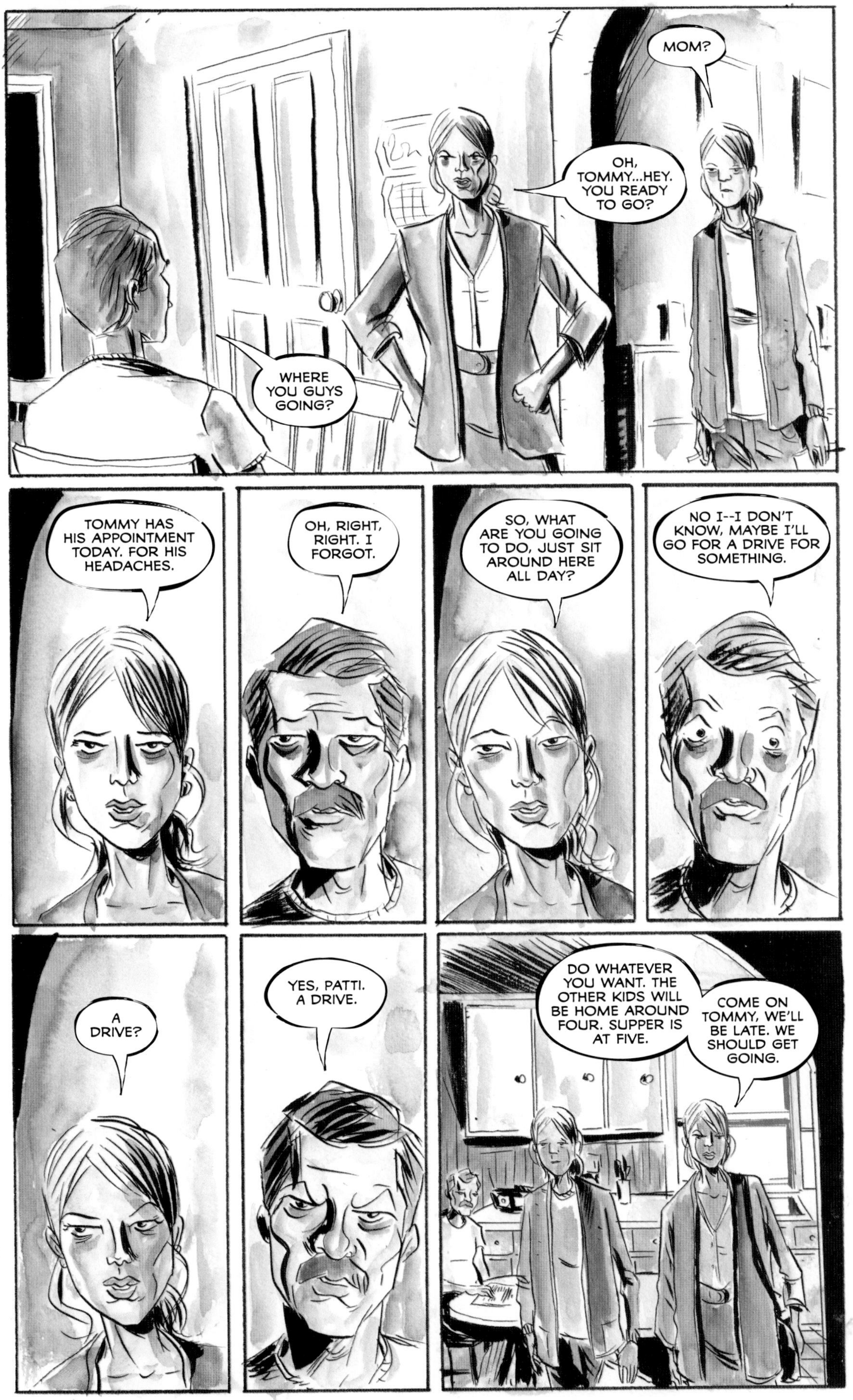
MOM?
OH, TOMMY...HEY. YOU READY TO GO?
WHERE YOU GUYS GOING?
TOMMY HAS HIS APPOINTMENT TODAY. FOR HIS HEADACHES.
OH, RIGHT, RIGHT. I FORGOT.
SO, WHAT ARE YOU GOING TO DO, JUST SIT AROUND HERE ALL DAY?
NO I--I DON'T KNOW, MAYBE I'LL GO FOR A DRIVE FOR SOMETHING.
A DRIVE?
YES, PATTI. A DRIVE.
DO WHATEVER YOU WANT. THE OTHER KIDS WILL BE HOME AROUND FOUR. SUPPER IS AT FIVE.
COME ON TOMMY, WE'LL BE LATE. WE SHOULD GET GOING.

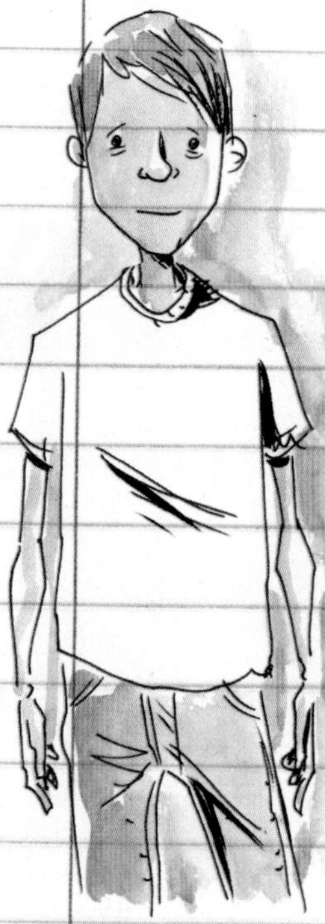

It's wierd how you suddenly realize your parents are REAL people too. I mean, of course I know that, I'm not stupid, but lately it's like I've been seeing them differently.

So, this is what I do know...
My mom + dad were both born here in Royal City. Neither of them had any brothers or sisters, and they actually grew up just a few streets away from one another. I wonder if they ever used to play together when they were little? It's sort of crazy to think about them ever even being kids.

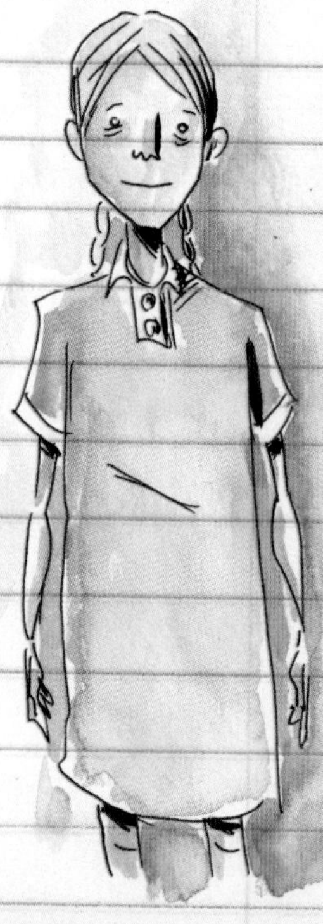

Anyways, they went to high school together too, but I don't think they were close until after the fire.

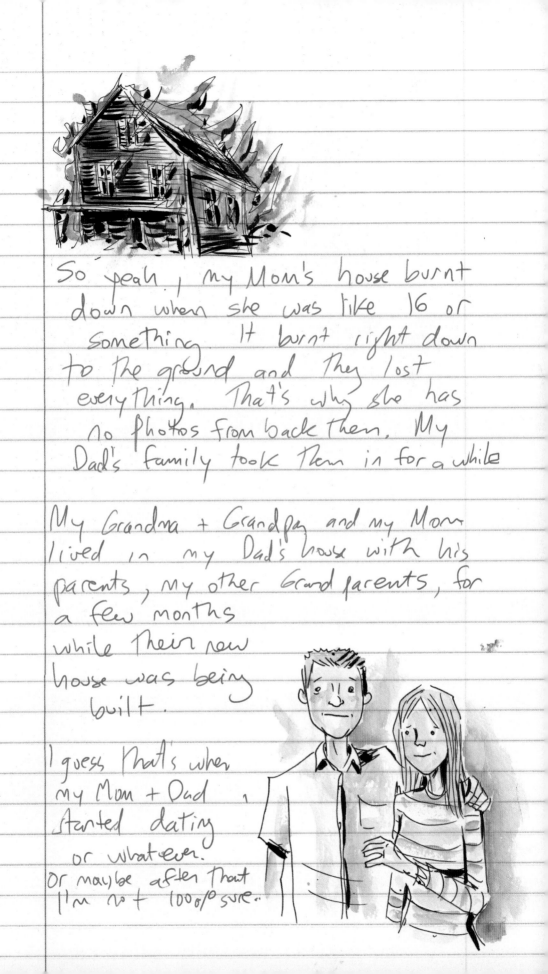

So yeah, my Mom's house burnt down when she was like 16 or something. It burnt right down to the ground and they lost everything. That's why she has no photos from back then. My Dad's family took them in for a while

My Grandma + Grandpa and my Mom lived in my Dad's house with his parents, my other Grandparents, for a few months while their new house was being built.

I guess that's when my Mom + Dad started dating or whatever. Or maybe after that I'm not 100% sure..

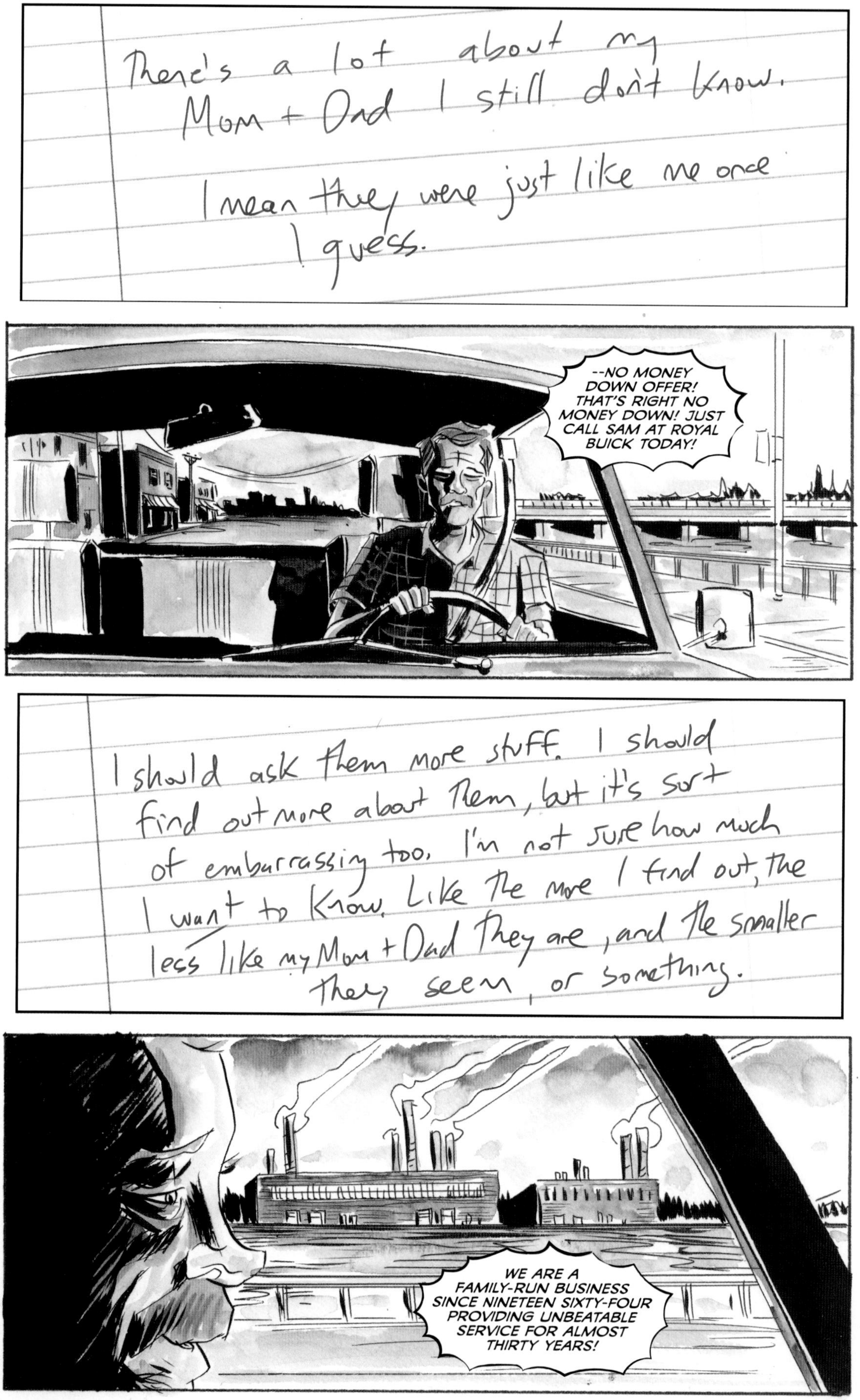
There's a lot about my
Mom + Dad I still don't know.
I mean they were just like me once
I guess.
--NO MONEY DOWN OFFER! THAT'S RIGHT NO MONEY DOWN! JUST CALL SAM AT ROYAL BUICK TODAY!
I should ask them more stuff. I should
find out more about them, but it's sort
of embarrassing too. I'm not sure how much
I want to know. Like the more I find out, the
less like my Mom + Dad they are, and the smaller
they seem, or something.
WE ARE A FAMILY-RUN BUSINESS SINCE NINETEEN SIXTY-FOUR PROVIDING UNBEATABLE SERVICE FOR ALMOST THIRTY YEARS!

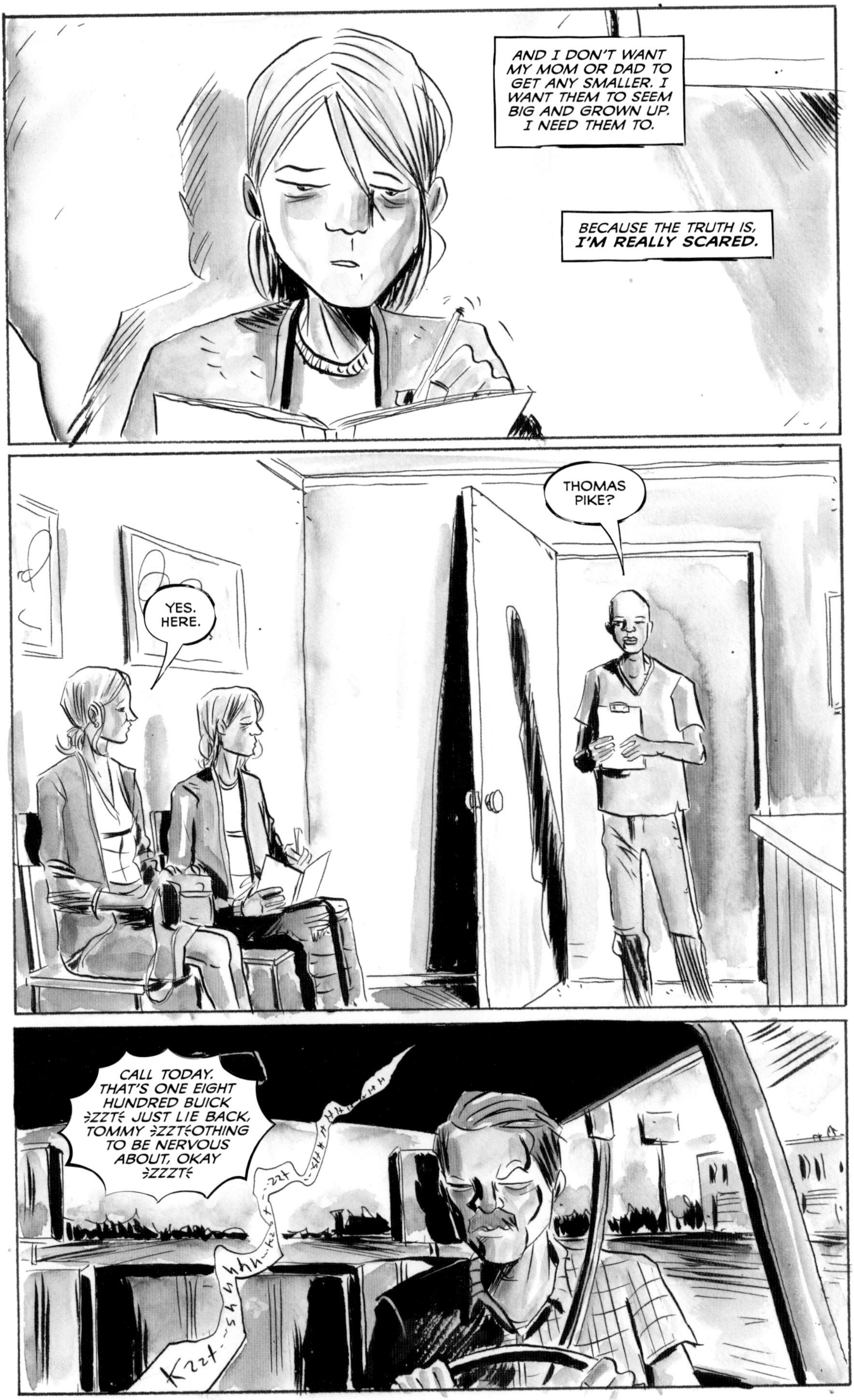
AND I DON'T WANT MY MOM OR DAD TO GET ANY SMALLER. I WANT THEM TO SEEM BIG AND GROWN UP. I NEED THEM TO.
BECAUSE THE TRUTH IS, I'M REALLY SCARED.
THOMAS PIKE?
YES. HERE.
CALL TODAY. THAT'S ONE EIGHT HUNDRED BUICK ≯ZZT≮ JUST LIE BACK, TOMMY ≯ZZT≮OTHING TO BE NERVOUS ABOUT, OKAY ≯ZZZT≮

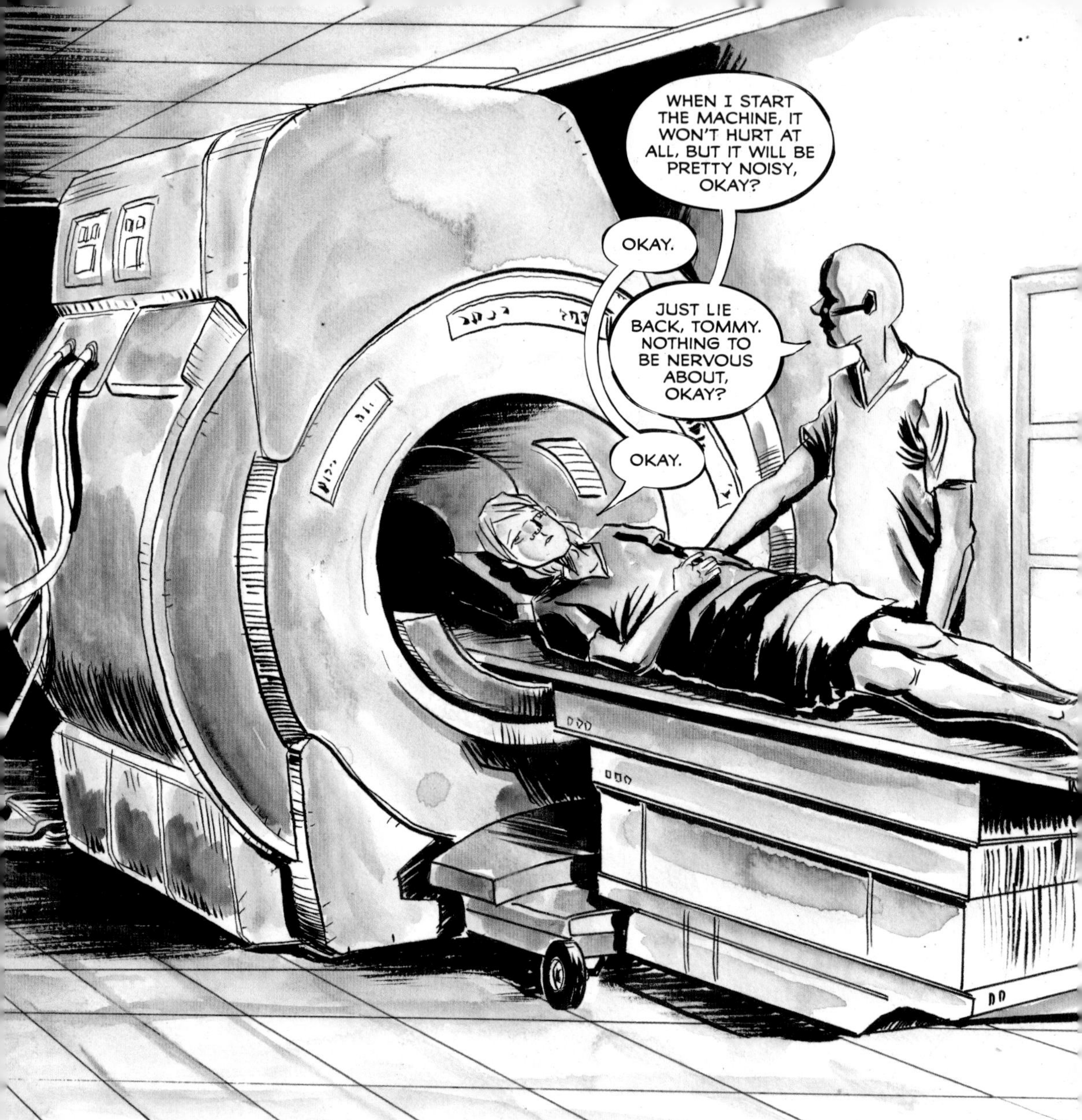
WHEN I START THE MACHINE, IT WON'T HURT AT ALL, BUT IT WILL BE PRETTY NOISY, OKAY?
OKAY.
JUST LIE BACK, TOMMY. NOTHING TO BE NERVOUS ABOUT, OKAY?
OKAY.

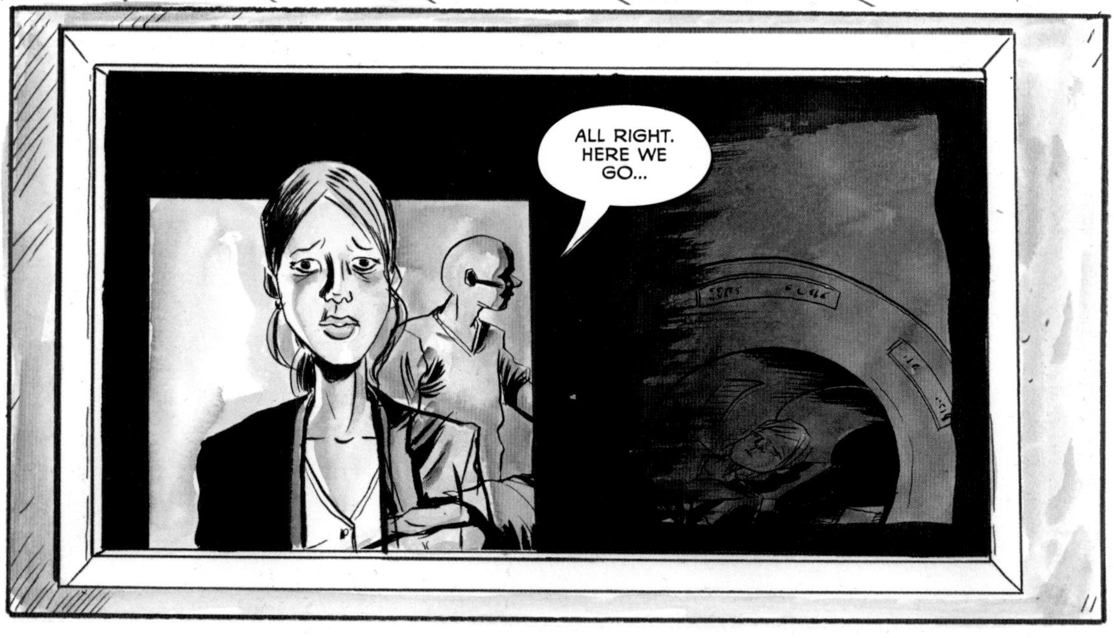
ALL RIGHT. HERE WE GO...

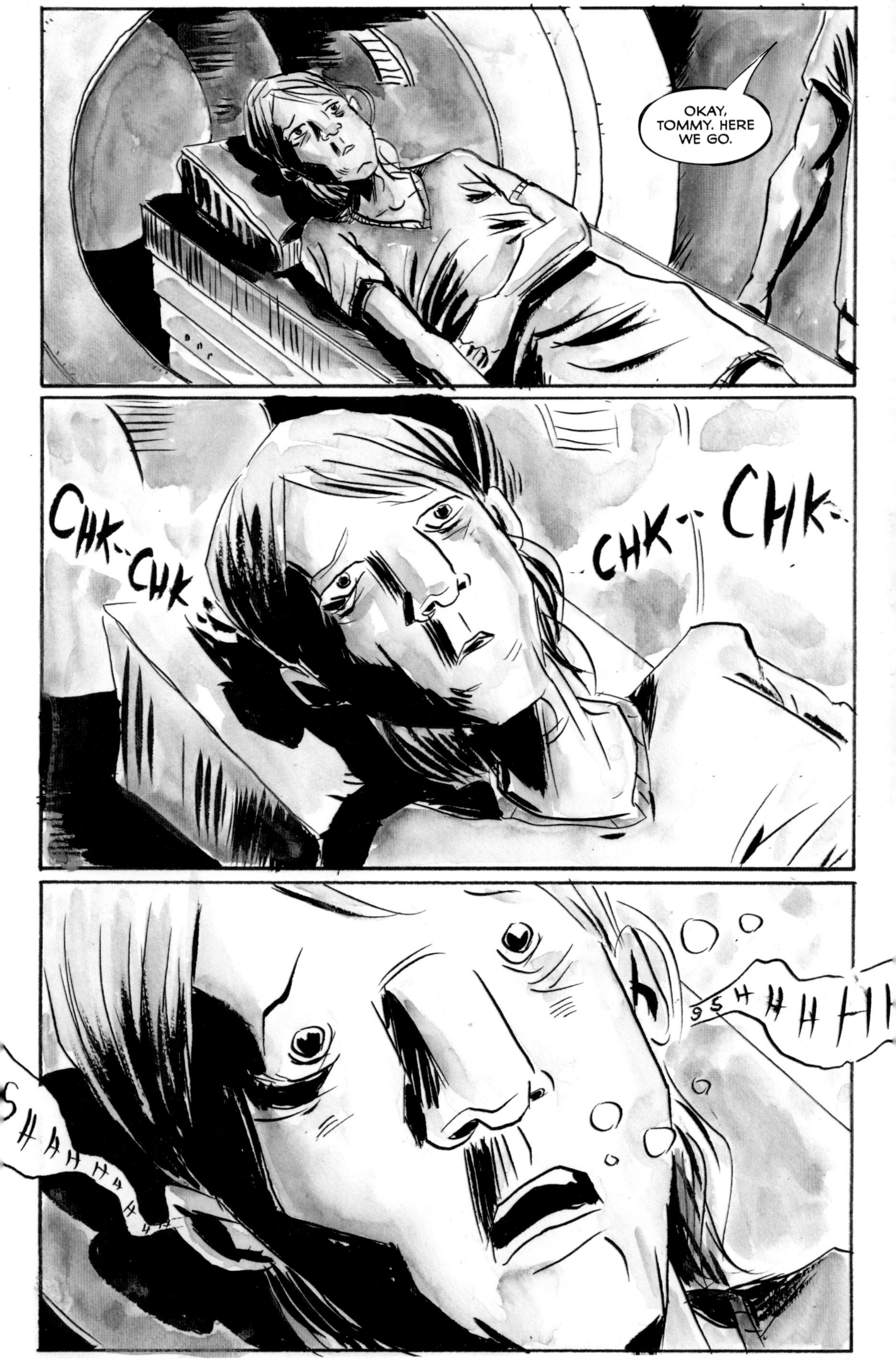
OKAY, TOMMY. HERE WE GO.
CHK--CHK--
--CHK--CHK--

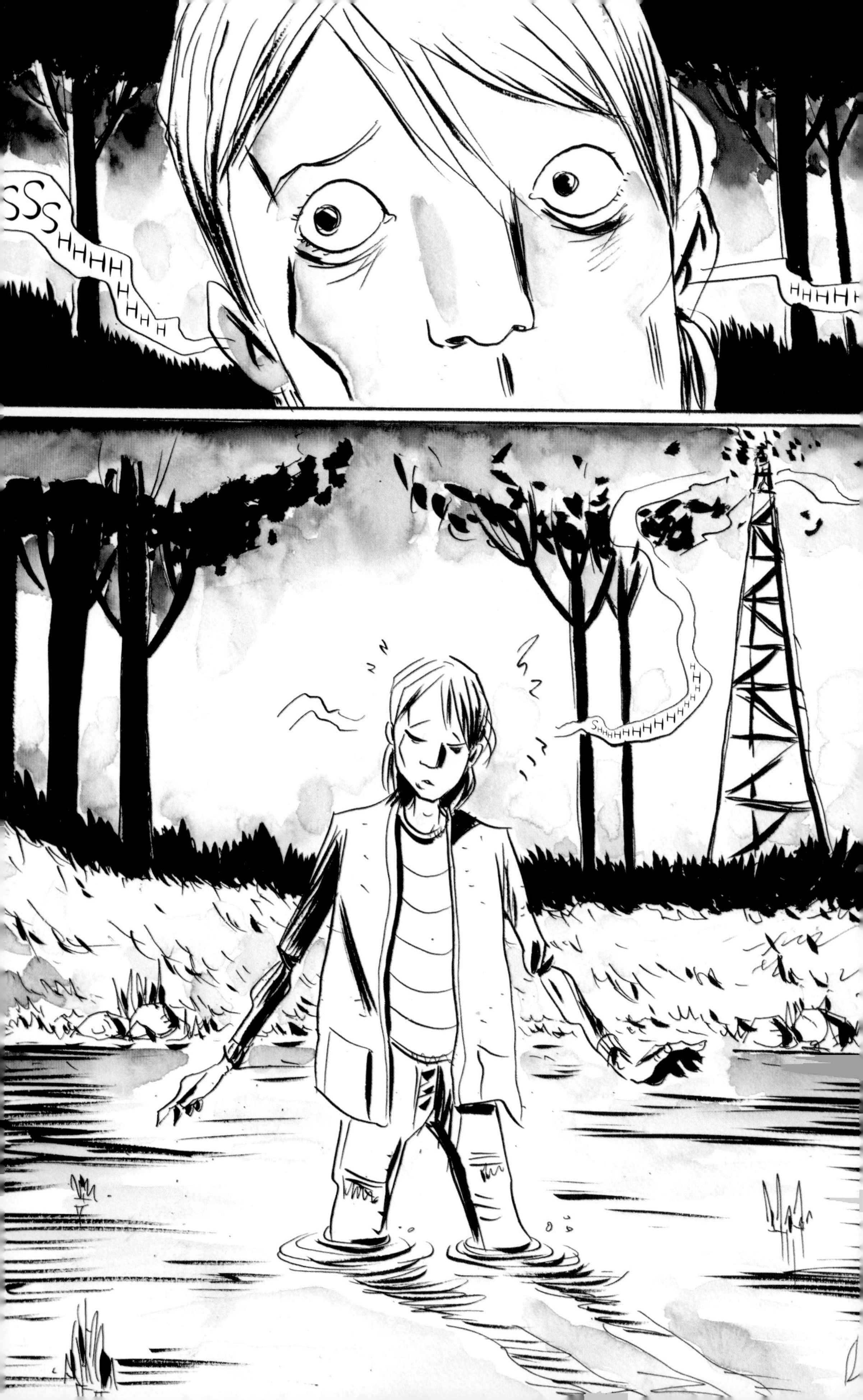
SSSHHHHHHHHH
HHHHH
SHHHHHHHHHHHHHHH

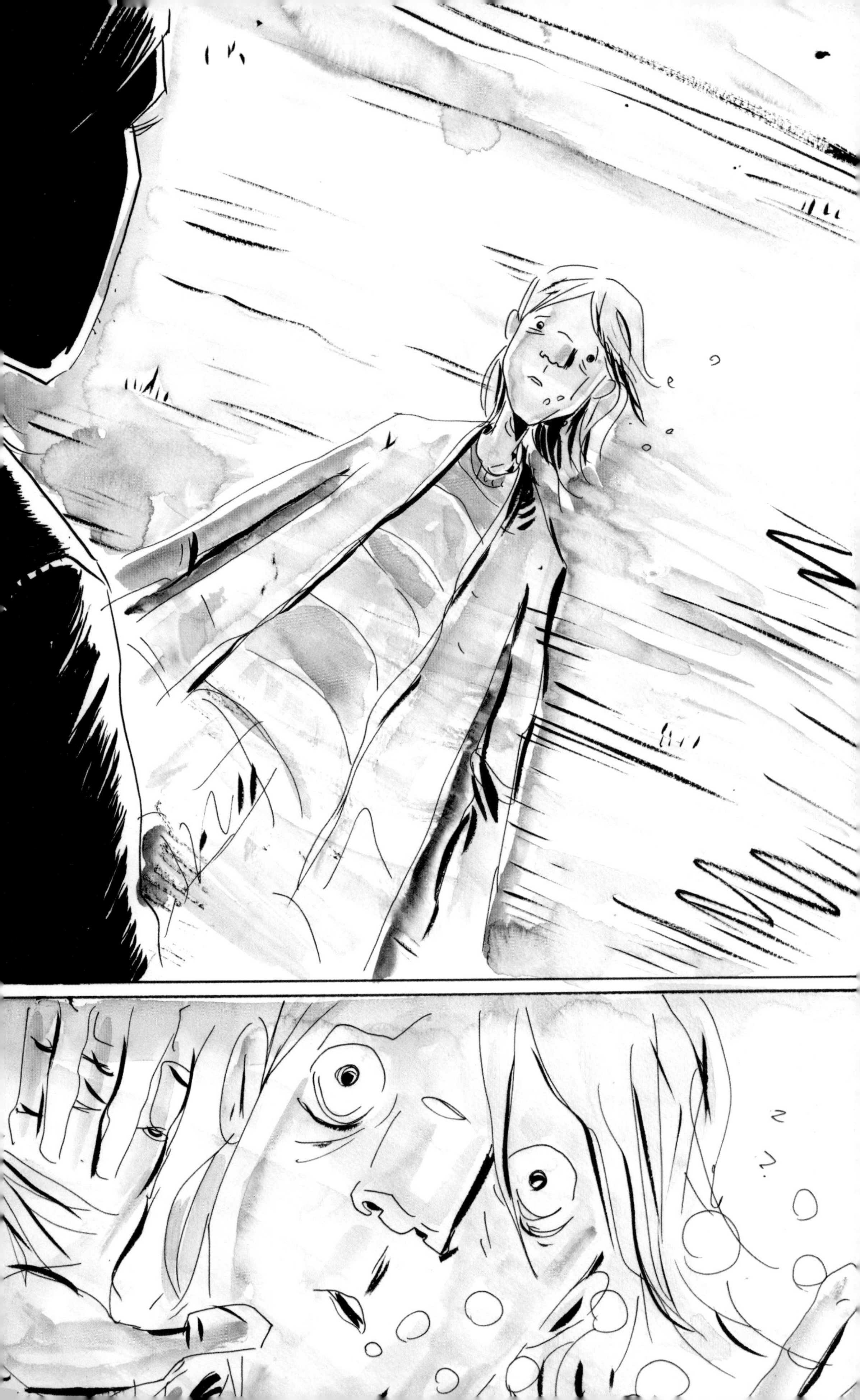

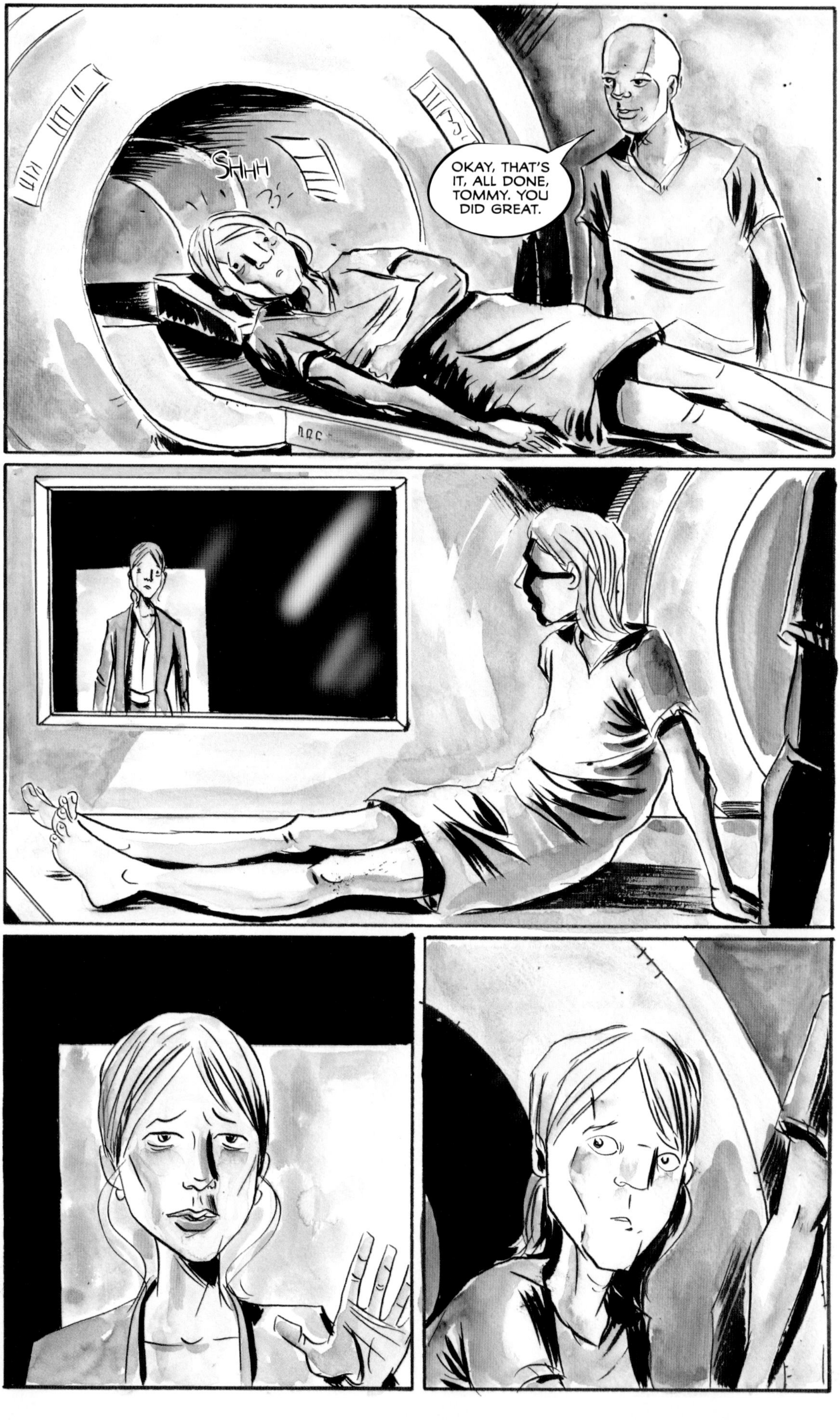
SHHH
OKAY, THAT'S IT, ALL DONE, TOMMY. YOU DID GREAT.

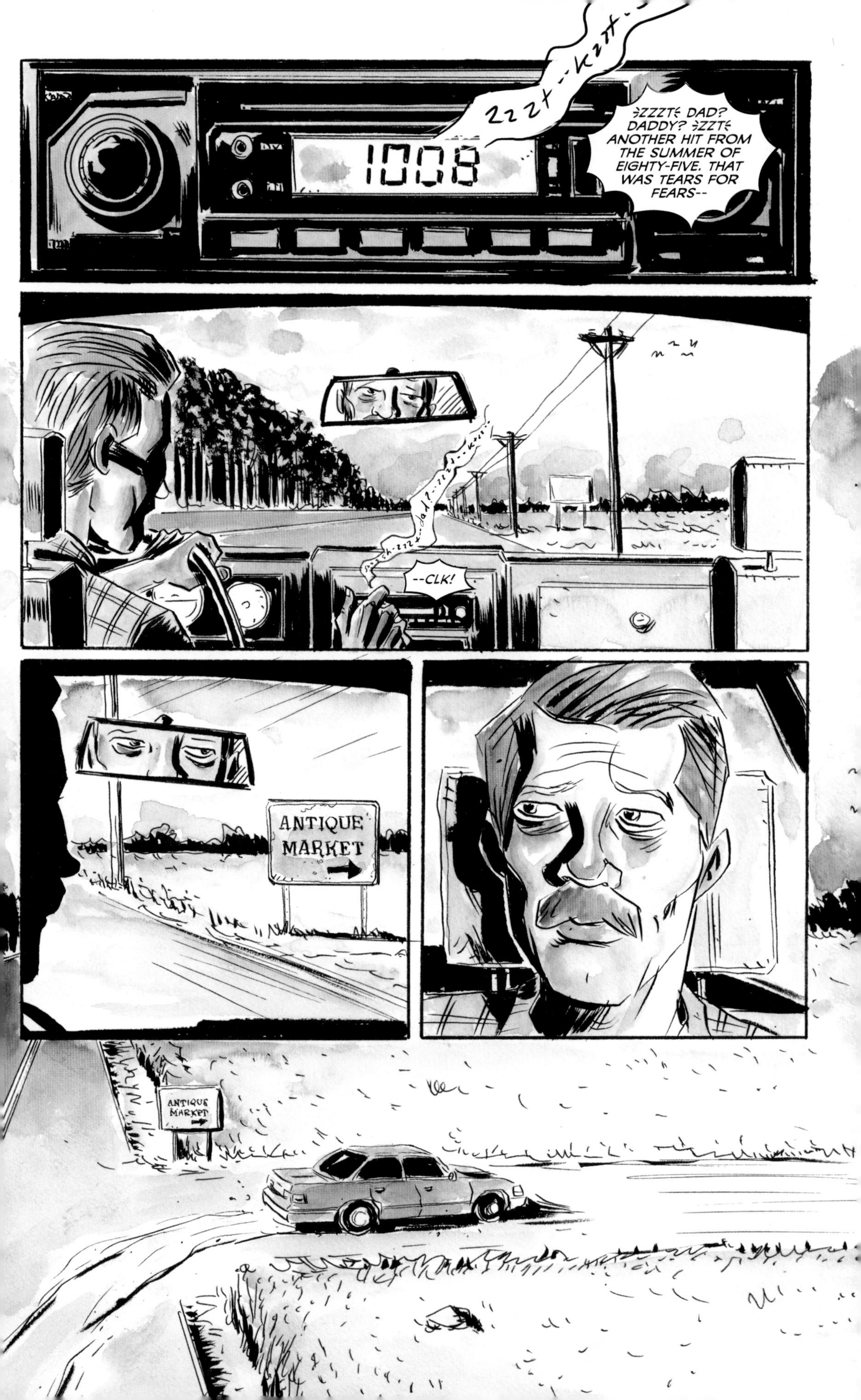
zzzt--kzzt--
ZZZZT DAD? DADDY? ZZZT ANOTHER HIT FROM THE SUMMER OF EIGHTY-FIVE. THAT WAS TEARS FOR FEARS--
--CLK!
ANTIQUE MARKET
ANTIQUE MARKET

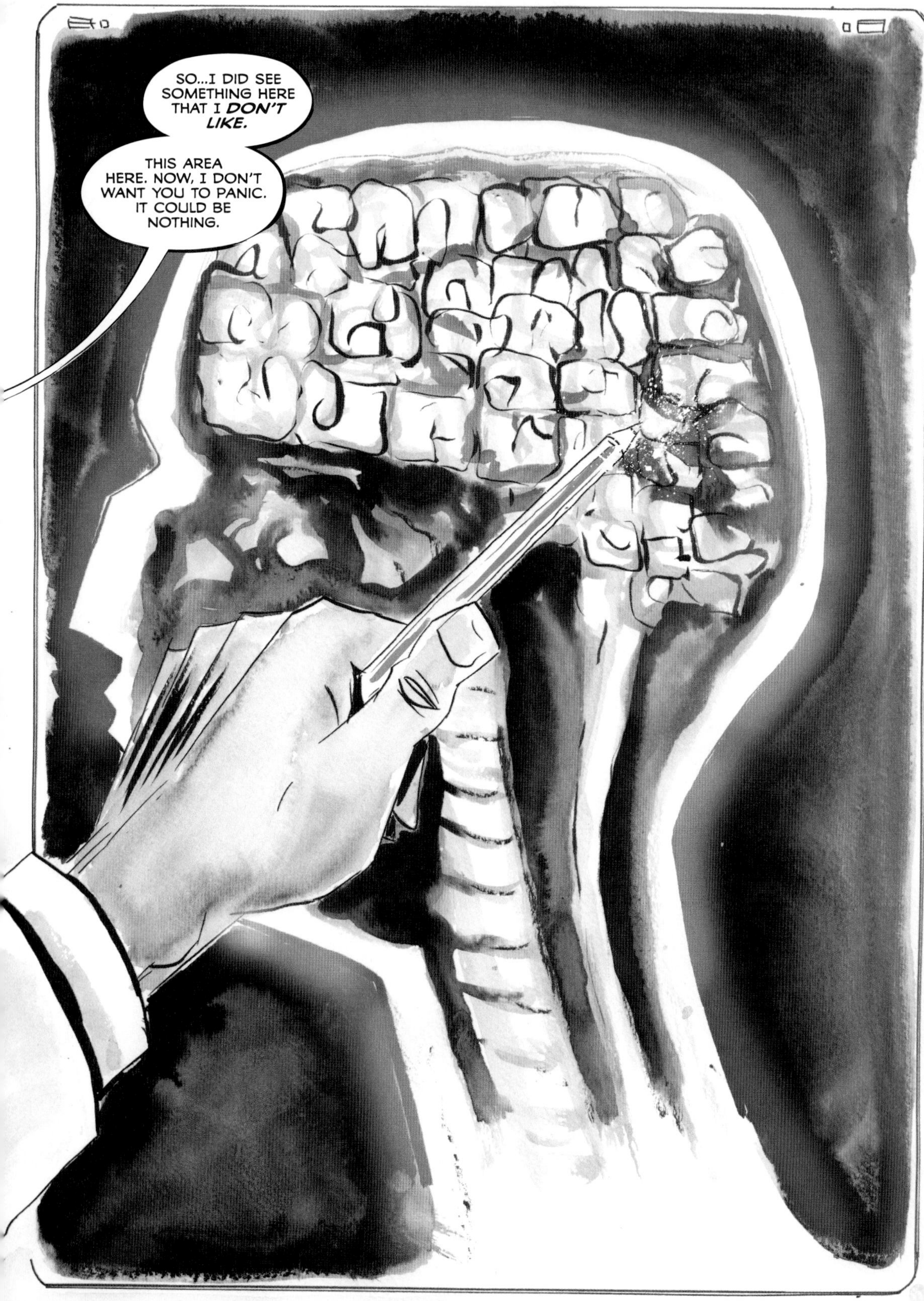
SO...I DID SEE SOMETHING HERE THAT I DON'T LIKE.
THIS AREA HERE. NOW, I DON'T WANT YOU TO PANIC. IT COULD BE NOTHING.

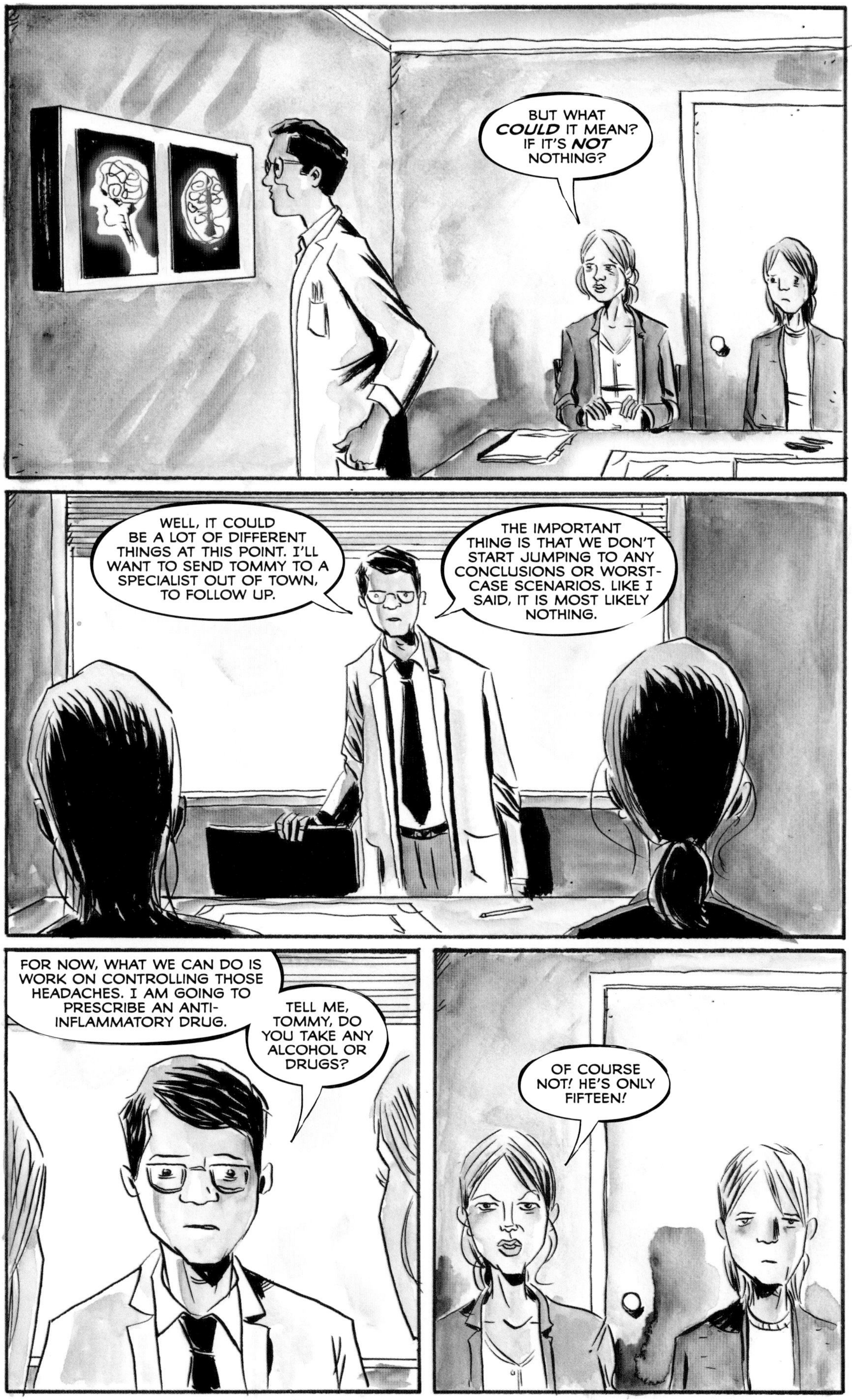
BUT WHAT *COULD* IT MEAN? IF IT'S *NOT* NOTHING?
WELL, IT COULD BE A LOT OF DIFFERENT THINGS AT THIS POINT. I'LL WANT TO SEND TOMMY TO A SPECIALIST OUT OF TOWN, TO FOLLOW UP.
THE IMPORTANT THING IS THAT WE DON'T START JUMPING TO ANY CONCLUSIONS OR WORST-CASE SCENARIOS. LIKE I SAID, IT IS MOST LIKELY NOTHING.
FOR NOW, WHAT WE CAN DO IS WORK ON CONTROLLING THOSE HEADACHES. I AM GOING TO PRESCRIBE AN ANTI-INFLAMMATORY DRUG.
TELL ME, TOMMY, DO YOU TAKE ANY ALCOHOL OR DRUGS?
OF COURSE NOT! HE'S ONLY FIFTEEN!

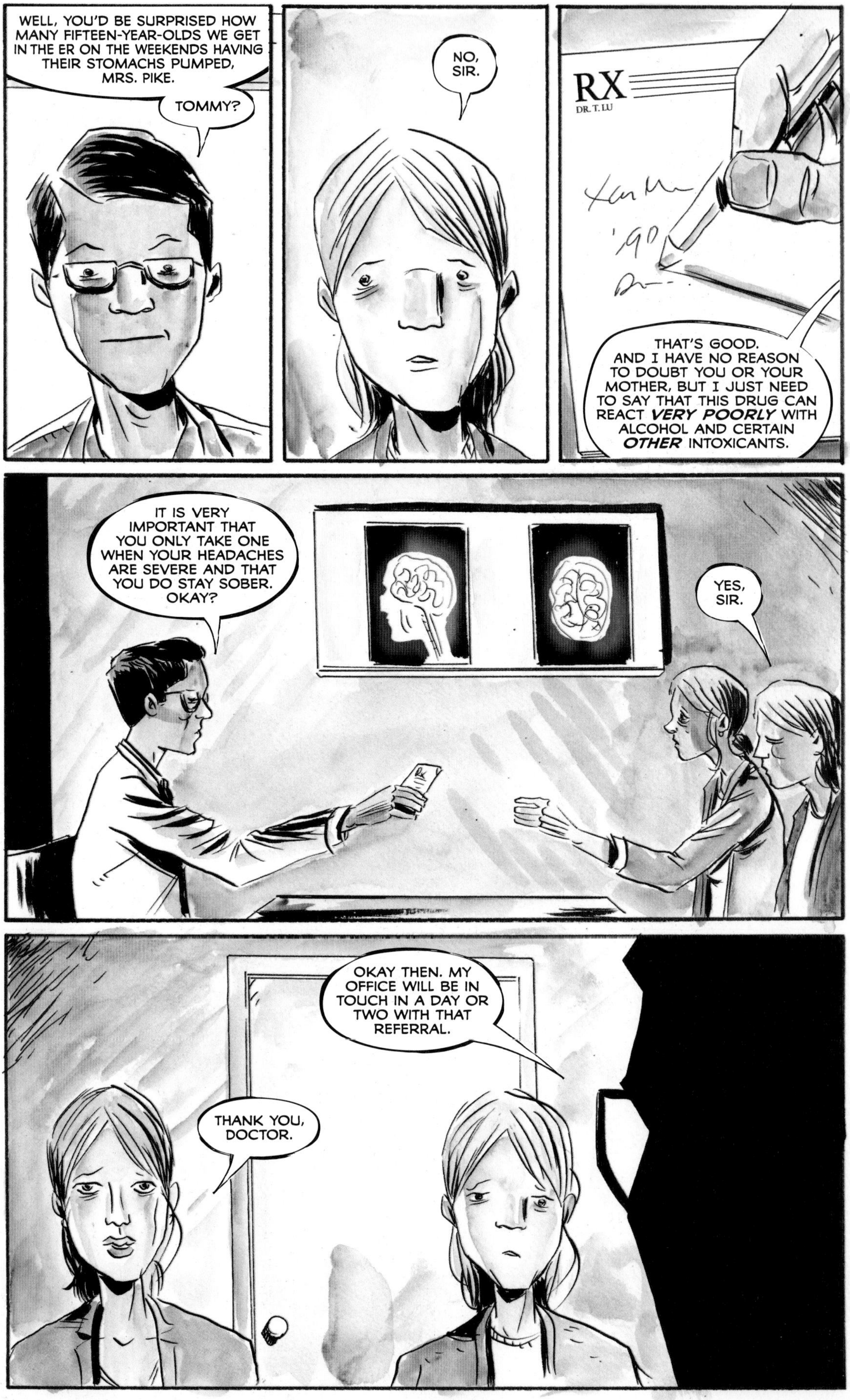
WELL, YOU'D BE SURPRISED HOW MANY FIFTEEN-YEAR-OLDS WE GET IN THE ER ON THE WEEKENDS HAVING THEIR STOMACHS PUMPED, MRS. PIKE.
TOMMY?
NO, SIR.
RX
DR. T. LU
THAT'S GOOD. AND I HAVE NO REASON TO DOUBT YOU OR YOUR MOTHER, BUT I JUST NEED TO SAY THAT THIS DRUG CAN REACT VERY POORLY WITH ALCOHOL AND CERTAIN OTHER INTOXICANTS.
IT IS VERY IMPORTANT THAT YOU ONLY TAKE ONE WHEN YOUR HEADACHES ARE SEVERE AND THAT YOU DO STAY SOBER. OKAY?
YES, SIR.
OKAY THEN. MY OFFICE WILL BE IN TOUCH IN A DAY OR TWO WITH THAT REFERRAL.
THANK YOU, DOCTOR.

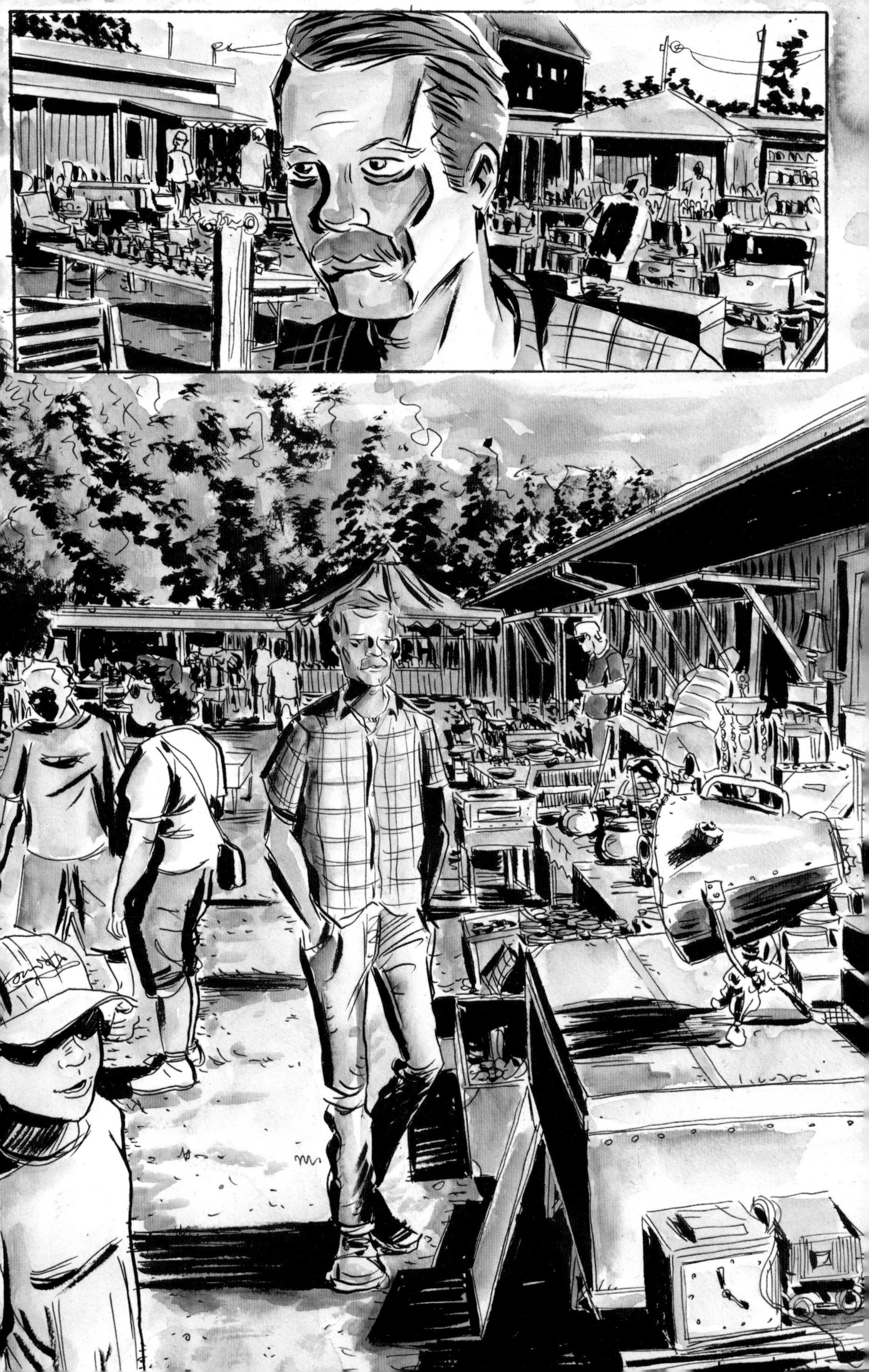

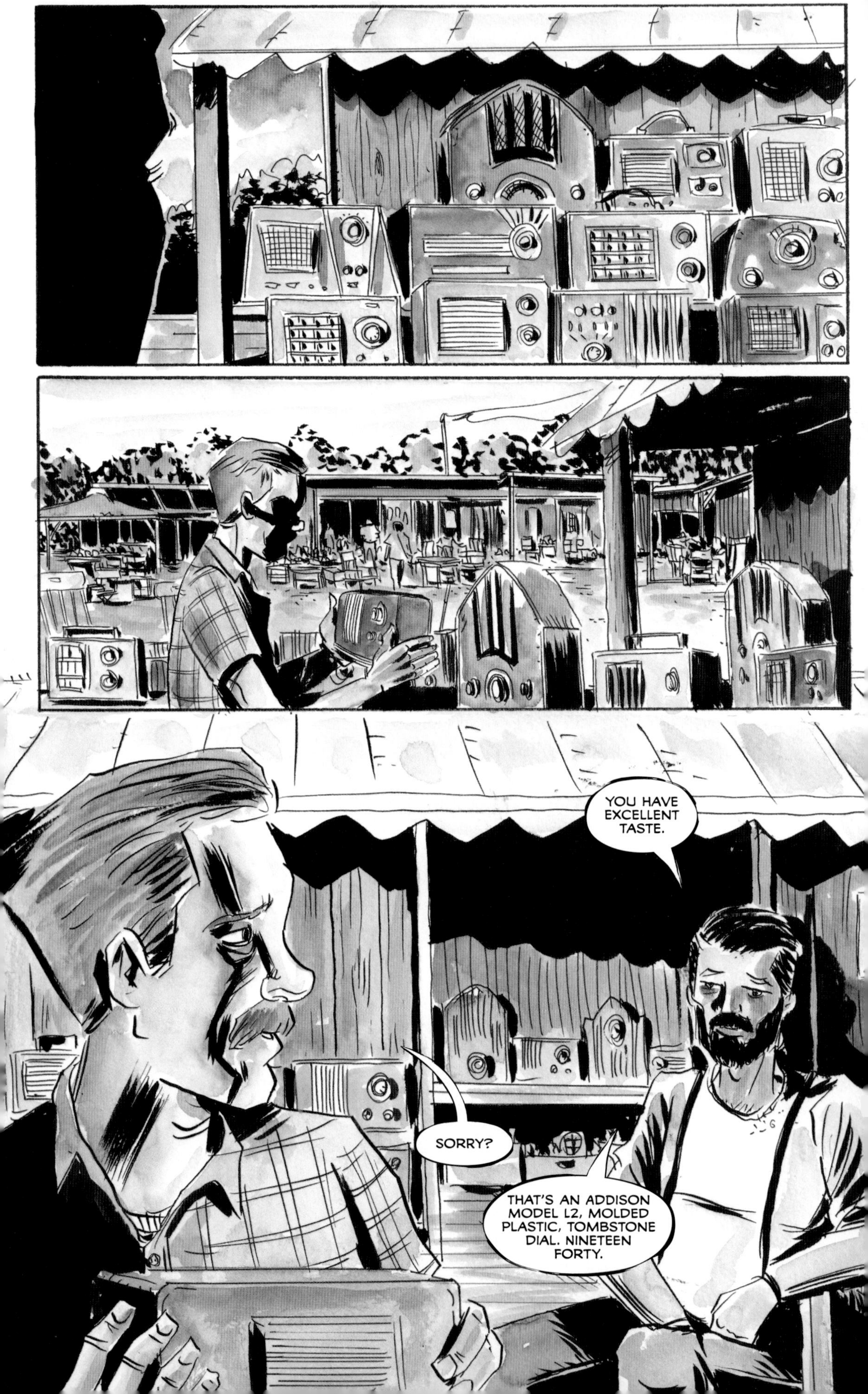
YOU HAVE EXCELLENT TASTE.
SORRY?
THAT'S AN ADDISON MODEL L2, MOLDED PLASTIC, TOMBSTONE DIAL. NINETEEN FORTY.

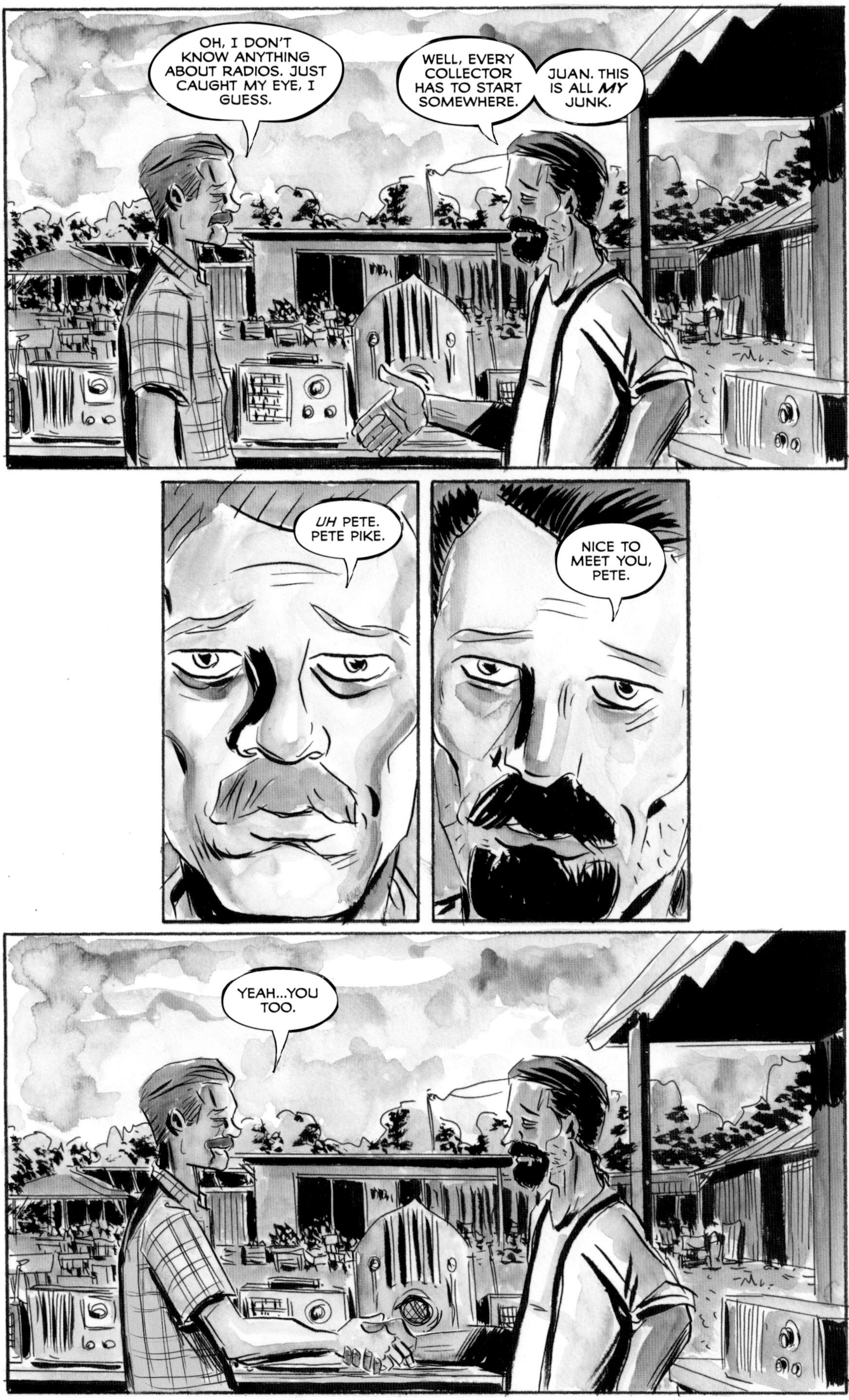
OH, I DON'T KNOW ANYTHING ABOUT RADIOS. JUST CAUGHT MY EYE, I GUESS.
WELL, EVERY COLLECTOR HAS TO START SOMEWHERE.
JUAN. THIS IS ALL *MY* JUNK.
UH PETE. PETE PIKE.
NICE TO MEET YOU, PETE.
YEAH...YOU TOO.

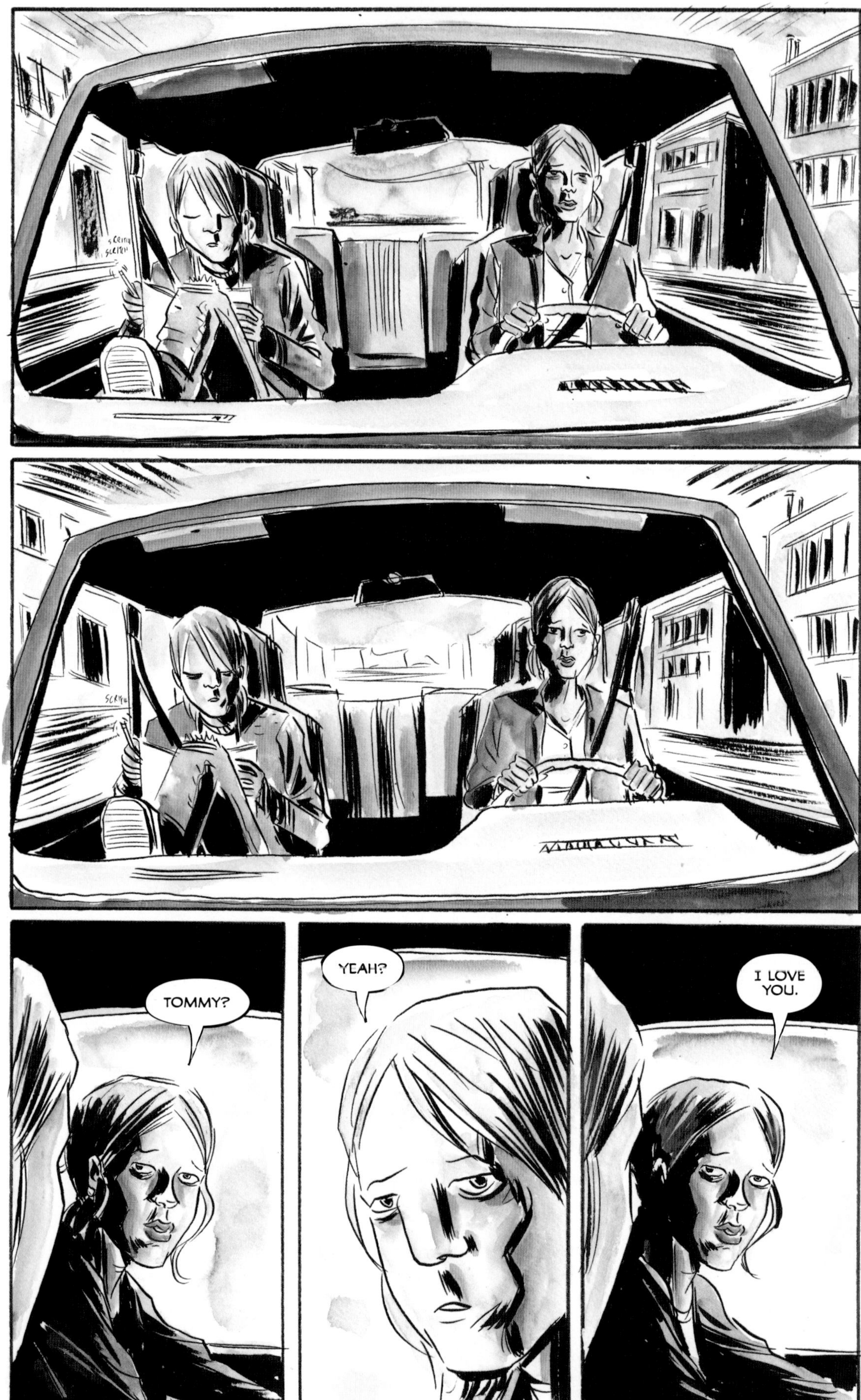
TOMMY?
YEAH?
I LOVE YOU.

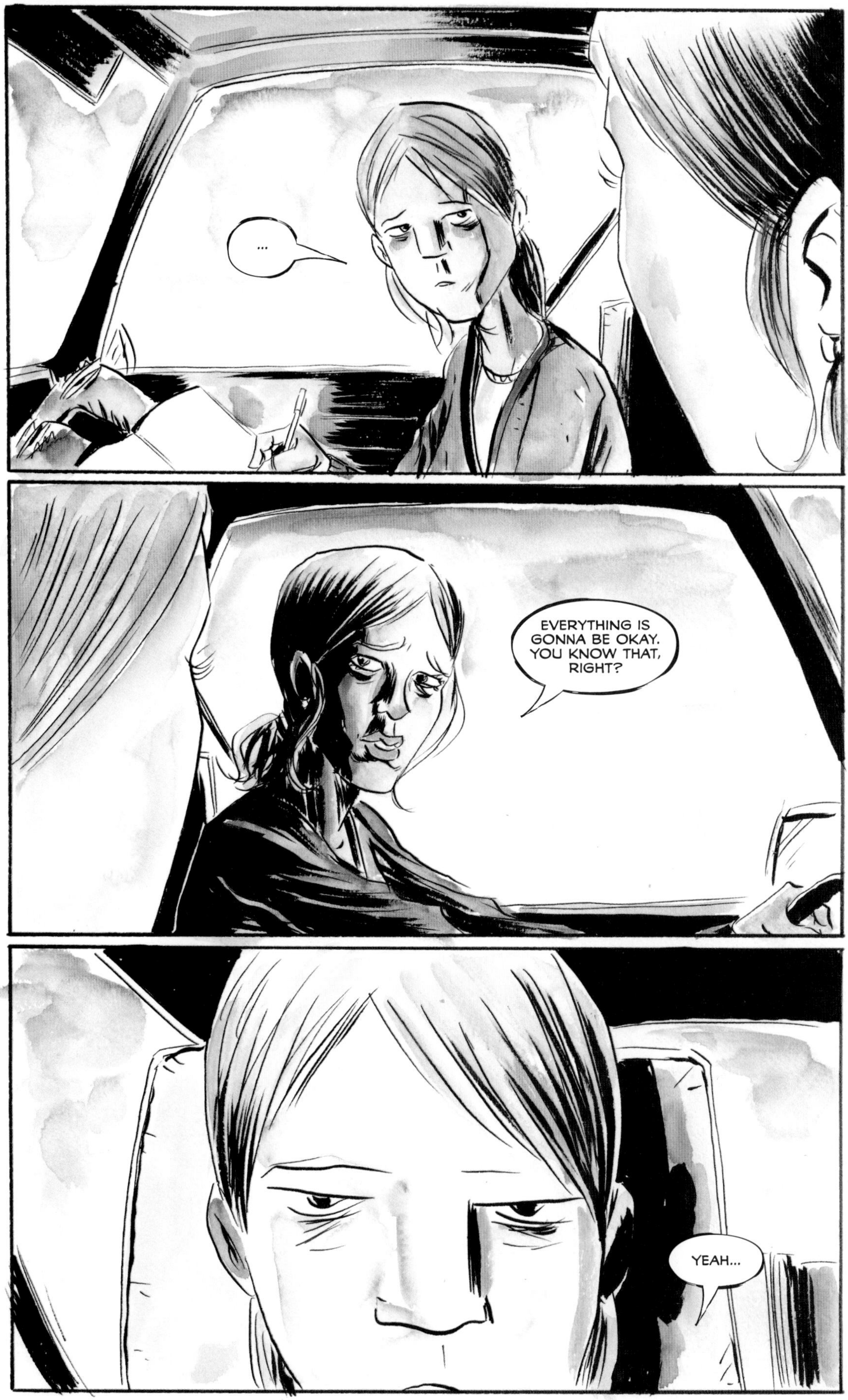
...
EVERYTHING IS GONNA BE OKAY. YOU KNOW THAT, RIGHT?
YEAH...

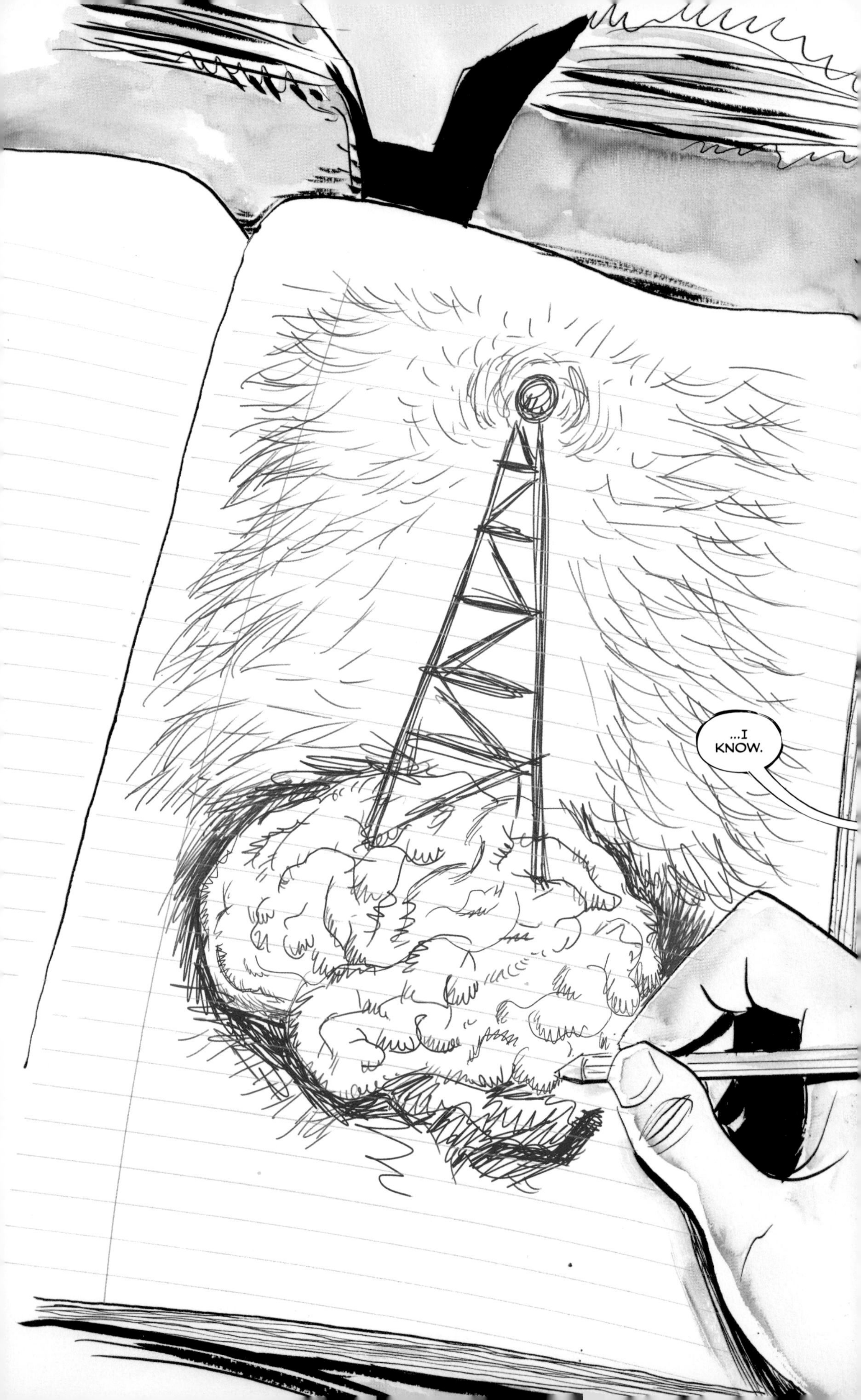
...I KNOW.

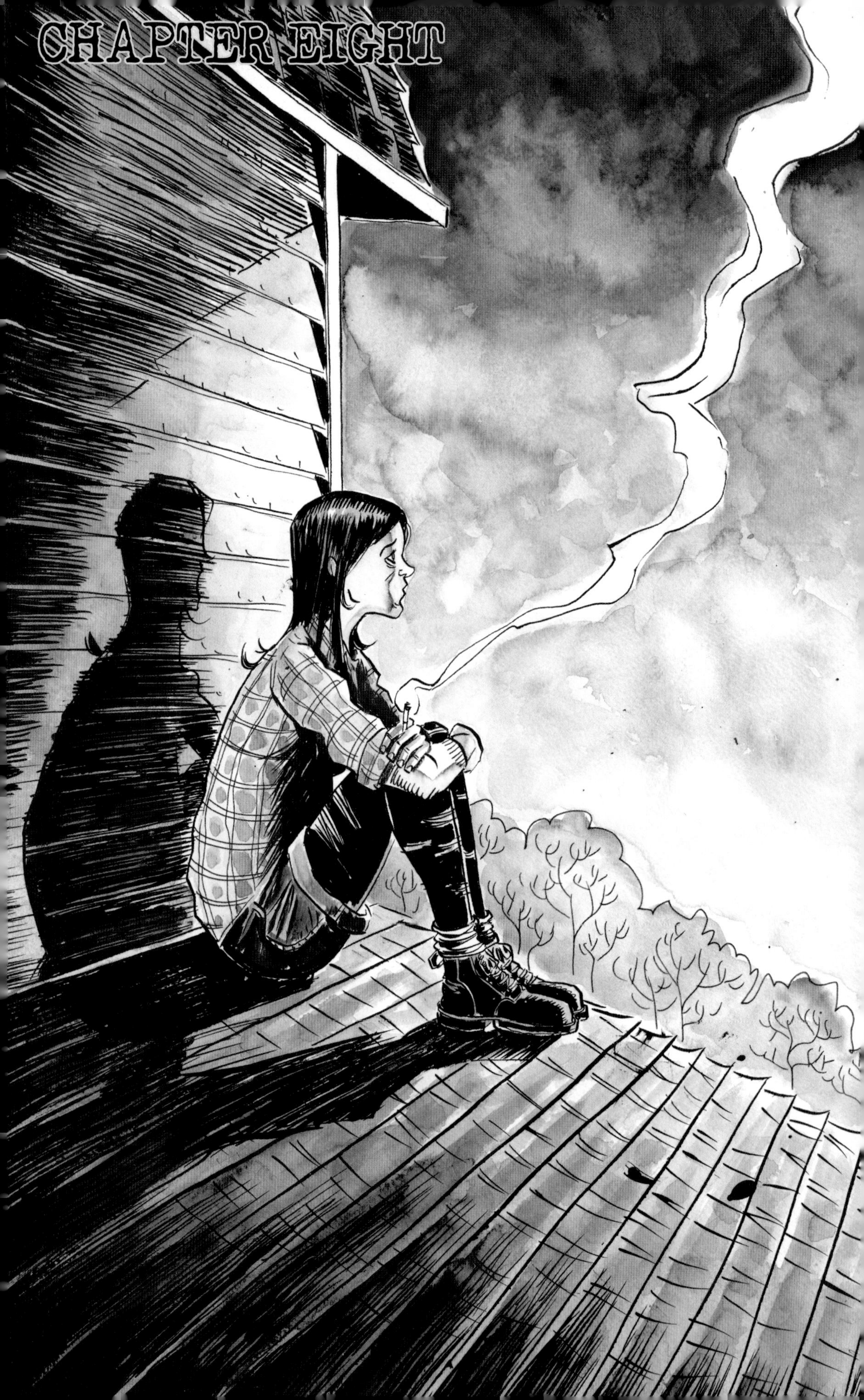
CHAPTER EIGHT

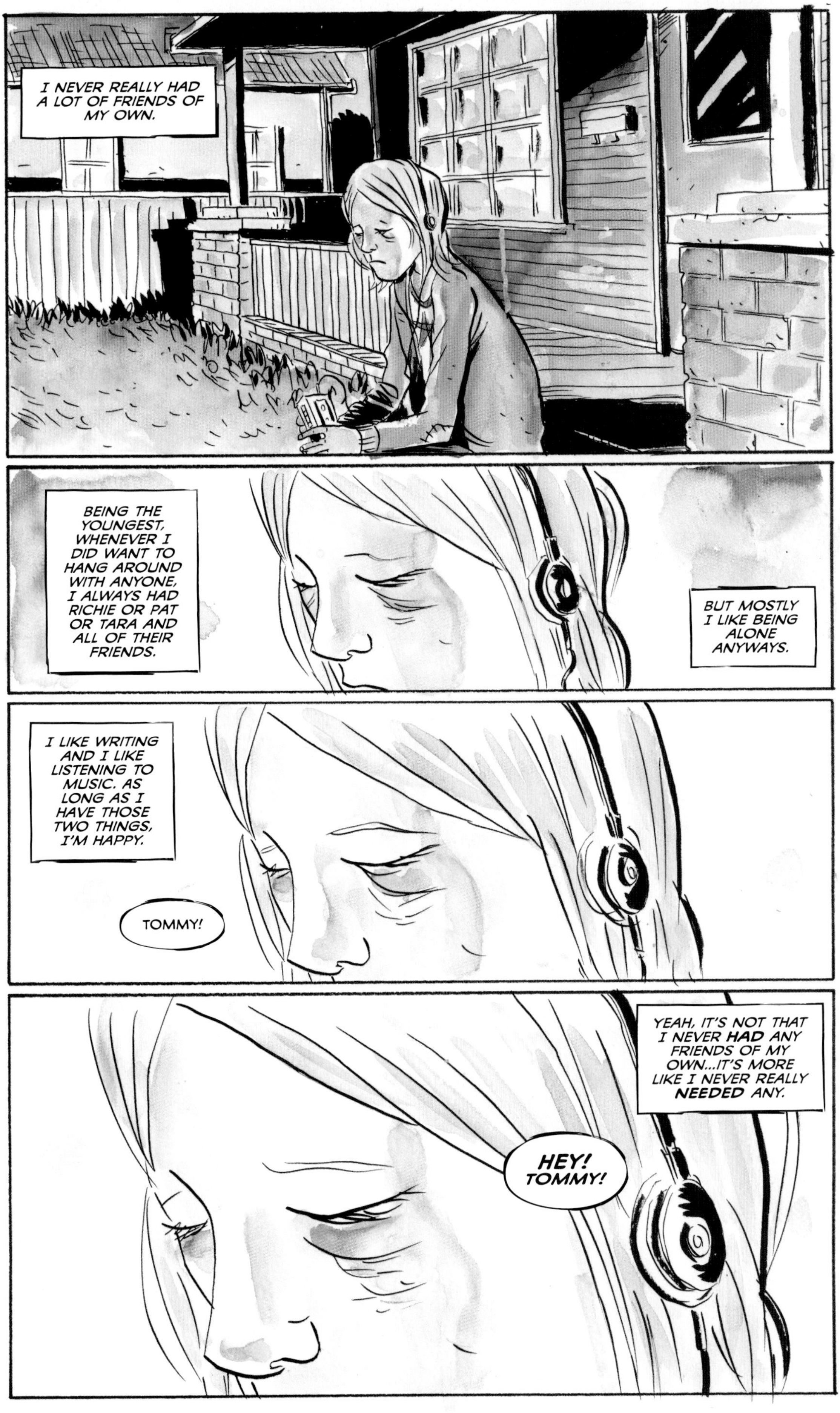
I NEVER REALLY HAD A LOT OF FRIENDS OF MY OWN.
BEING THE YOUNGEST, WHENEVER I DID WANT TO HANG AROUND WITH ANYONE, I ALWAYS HAD RICHIE OR PAT OR TARA AND ALL OF THEIR FRIENDS.
BUT MOSTLY I LIKE BEING ALONE ANYWAYS.
I LIKE WRITING AND I LIKE LISTENING TO MUSIC. AS LONG AS I HAVE THOSE TWO THINGS, I'M HAPPY.
TOMMY!
YEAH, IT'S NOT THAT I NEVER HAD ANY FRIENDS OF MY OWN...IT'S MORE LIKE I NEVER REALLY NEEDED ANY.
HEY! TOMMY!

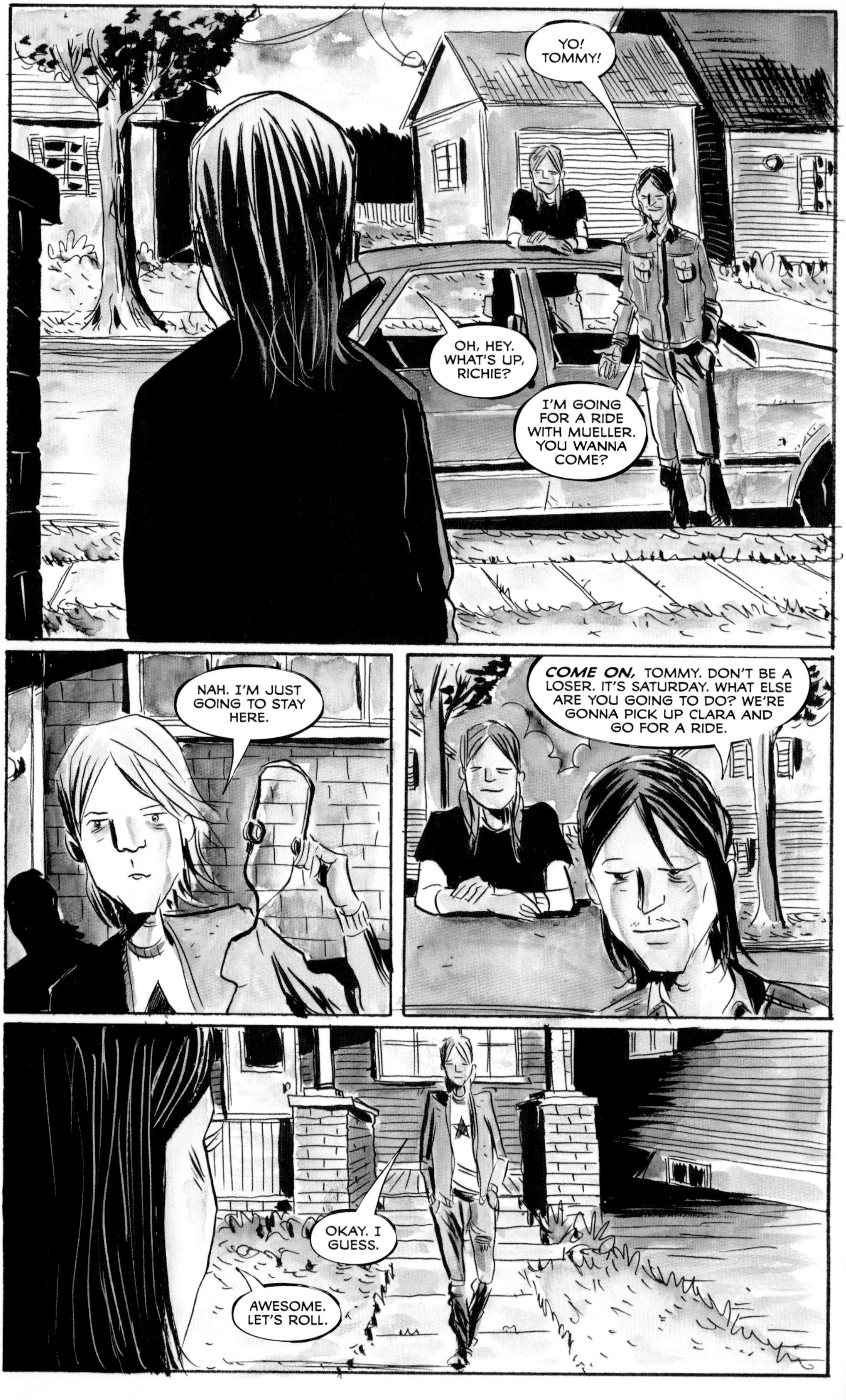
YO! TOMMY!
OH, HEY. WHAT'S UP, RICHIE?
I'M GOING FOR A RIDE WITH MUELLER. YOU WANNA COME?
NAH. I'M JUST GOING TO STAY HERE.
COME ON, TOMMY. DON'T BE A LOSER. IT'S SATURDAY. WHAT ELSE ARE YOU GOING TO DO? WE'RE GONNA PICK UP CLARA AND GO FOR A RIDE.
OKAY. I GUESS.
AWESOME. LET'S ROLL.

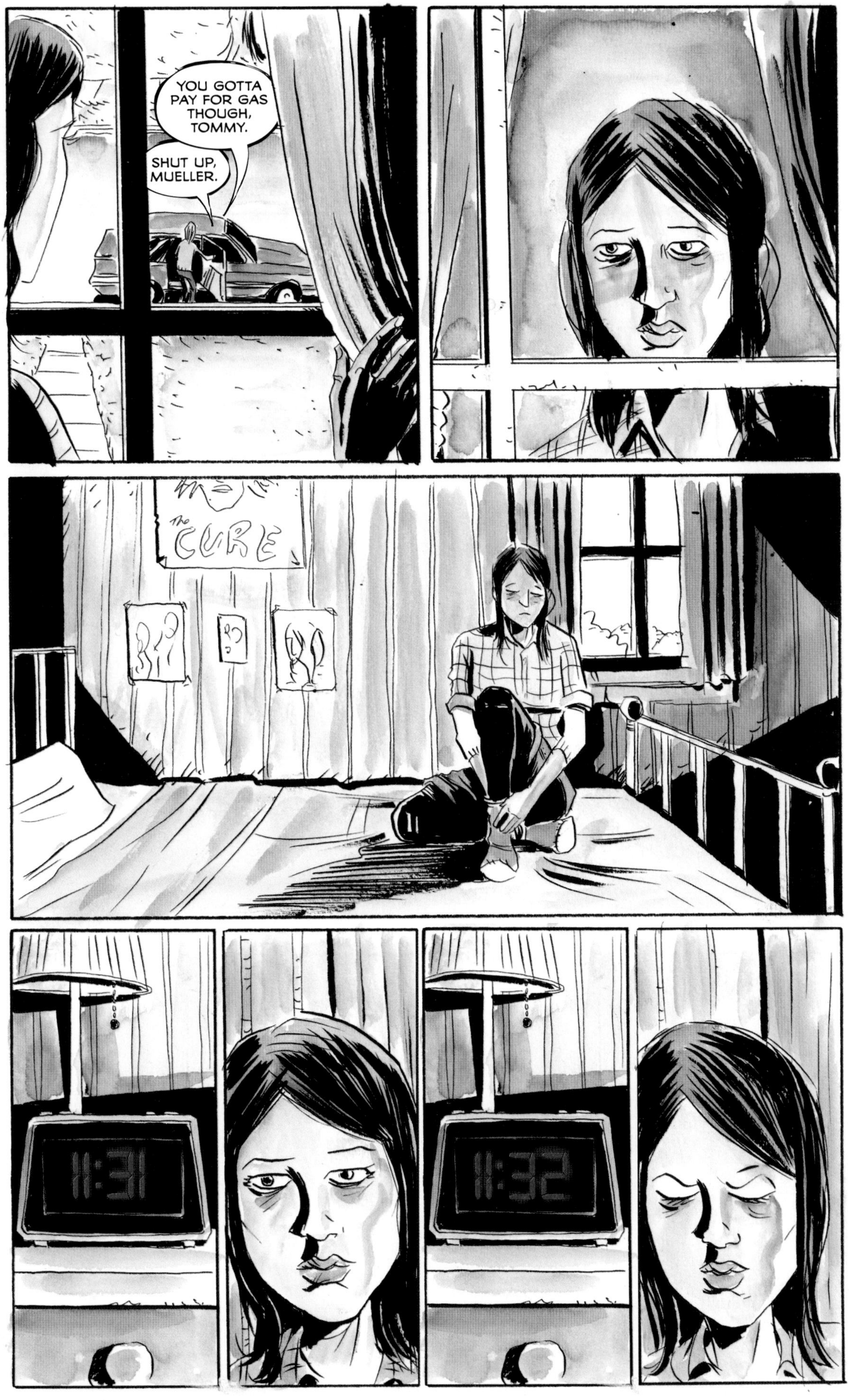
YOU GOTTA PAY FOR GAS THOUGH, TOMMY.
SHUT UP, MUELLER.
The CURE
11:31
11:32

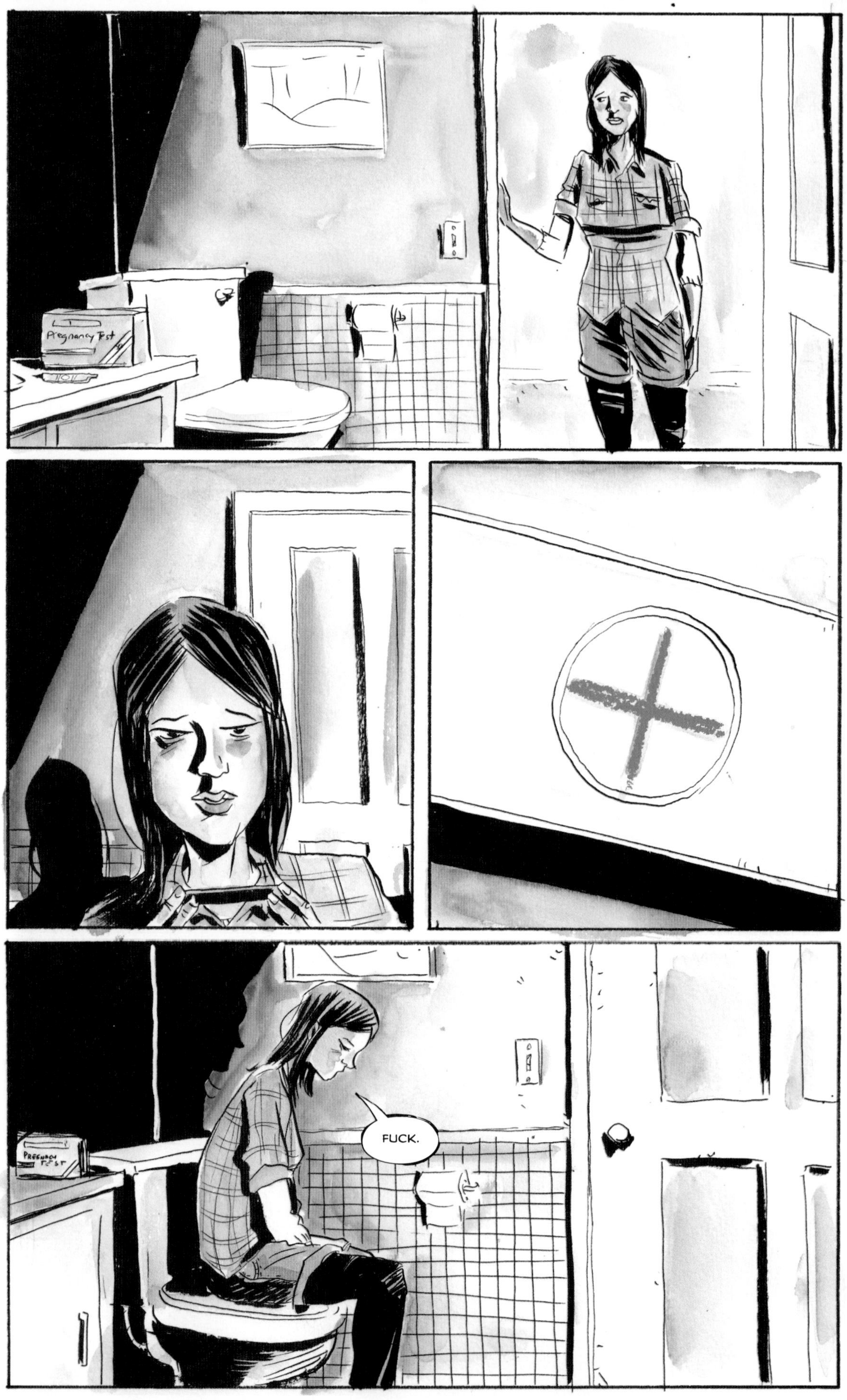
Pregnancy Test
FUCK.

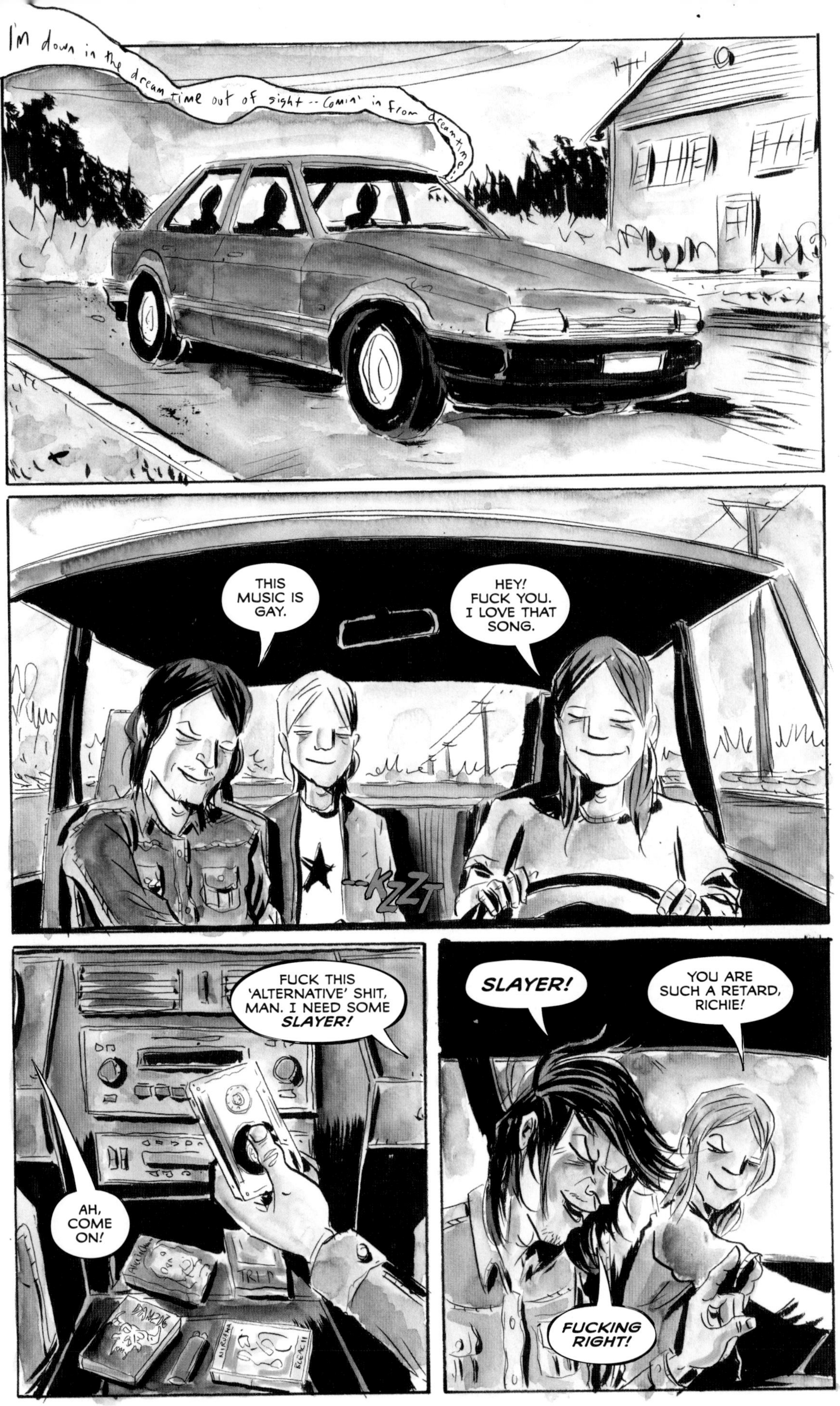
I'm down in the dream time out of sight -- Comin' in from dreamtime...
THIS MUSIC IS GAY.
HEY! FUCK YOU. I LOVE THAT SONG.
KZZZT
FUCK THIS 'ALTERNATIVE' SHIT, MAN. I NEED SOME ***SLAYER!***
AH, COME ON!
SLAYER!
YOU ARE SUCH A RETARD, RICHIE!
FUCKING RIGHT!

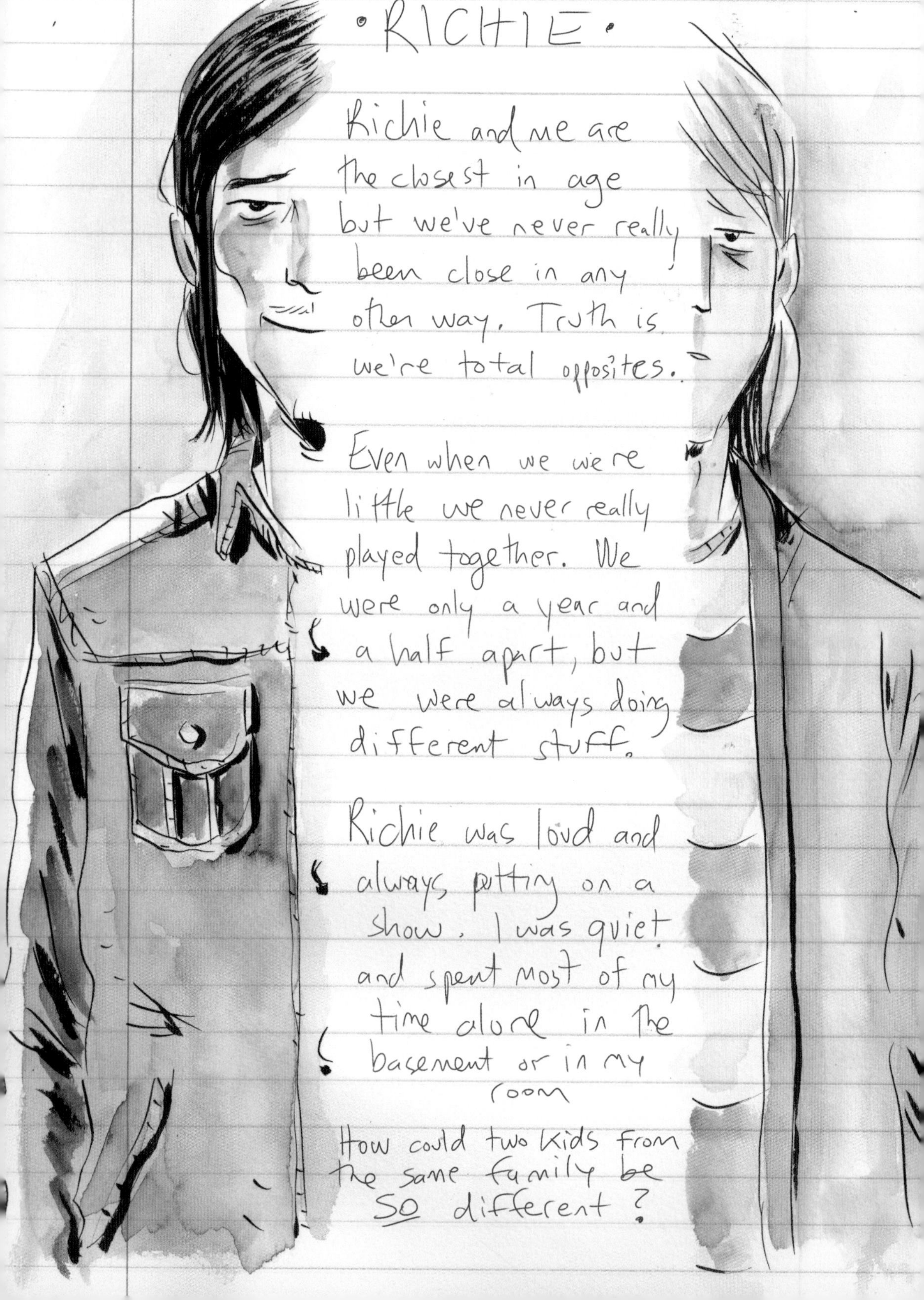

•RICHIE•
Richie and me are the closest in age but we've never really been close in any other way. Truth is we're total opposites.
Even when we were little we never really played together. We were only a year and a half apart, but we were always doing different stuff.
Richie was loud and always putting on a show. I was quiet and spent most of my time alone in the basement or in my room
How could two kids from the same family be SO different?

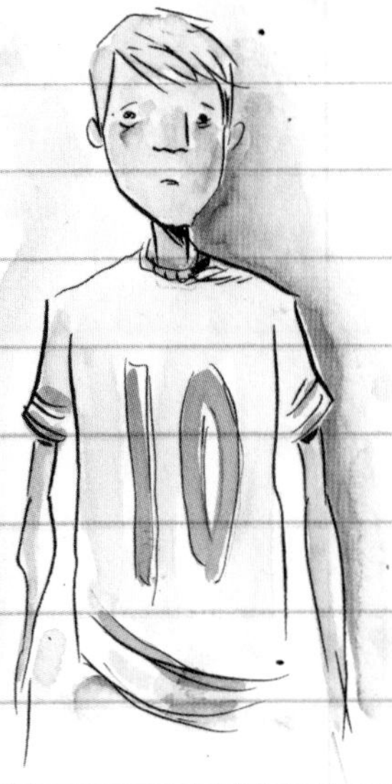
10

The wierd part is, even Though Richie can be totally obnoxious, I sort of admire him too.
I mean, he always has lots of friends and he can make every on laugh all the time.

And lately he's been asking me to do more stuff with him... hang out with his friends and stuff. It's okay, I guess, but sometimes I think it's just because he feels sorry for me.

Or maybe it's just me. Maybe I'm just being paranoid and self-conscious and overthinking everything as usual?

Richie never overthinks anything.

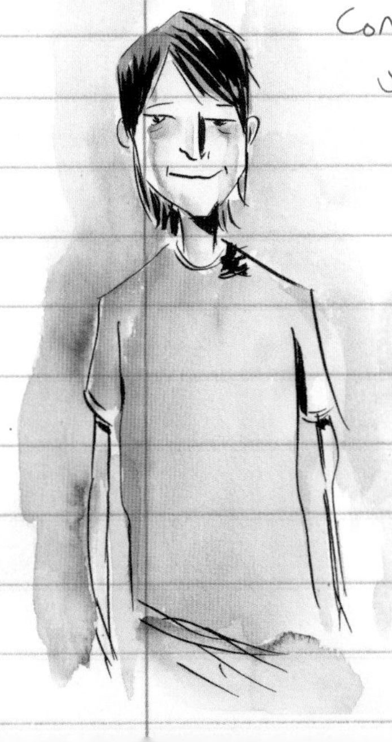

Richie doesn't give a shit what anyone thinks about him. I wish I could be more like That.

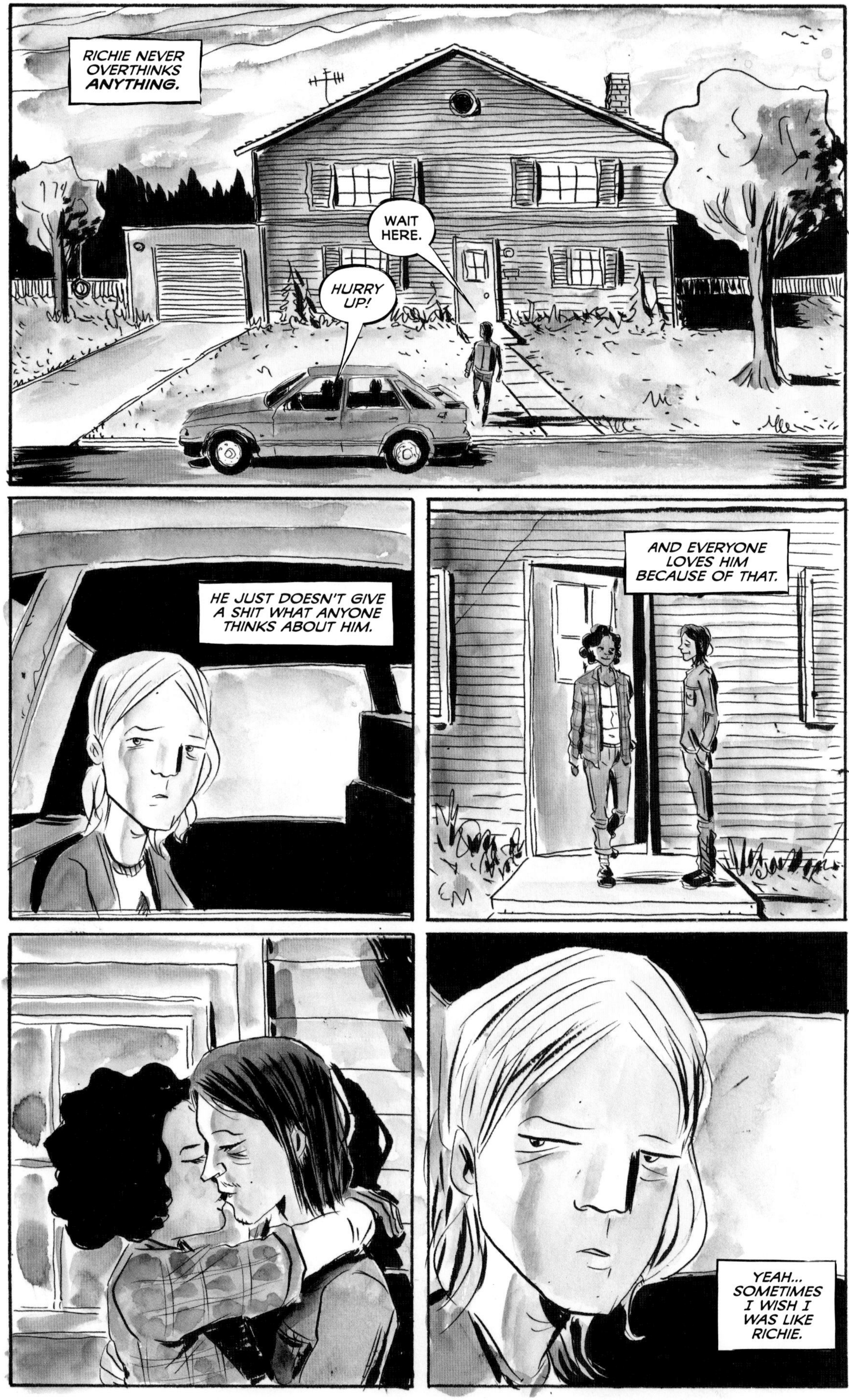
RICHIE NEVER OVERTHINKS ANYTHING.
WAIT HERE.
HURRY UP!
HE JUST DOESN'T GIVE A SHIT WHAT ANYONE THINKS ABOUT HIM.
AND EVERYONE LOVES HIM BECAUSE OF THAT.
YEAH... SOMETIMES I WISH I WAS LIKE RICHIE.

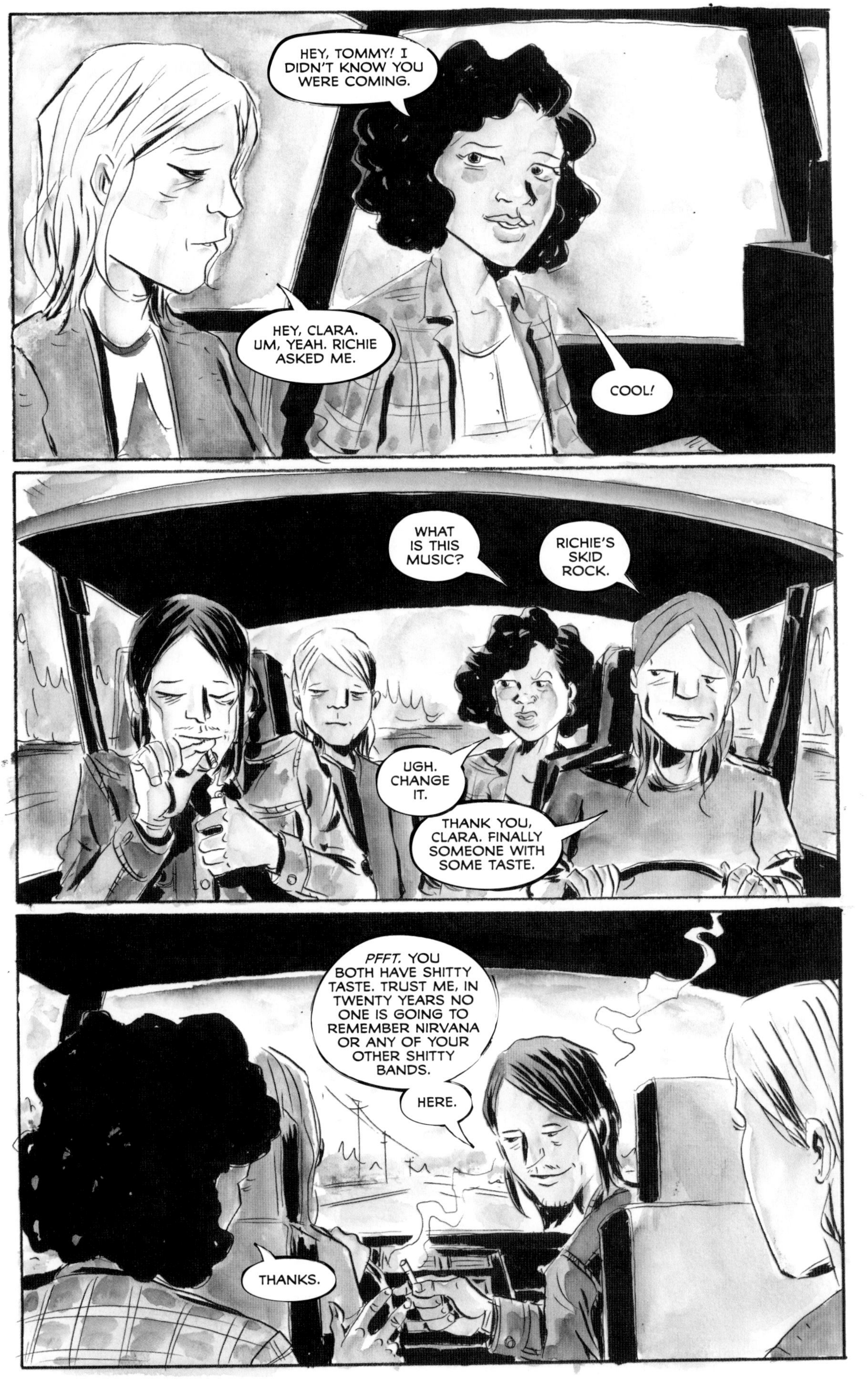
HEY, TOMMY! I DIDN'T KNOW YOU WERE COMING.
HEY, CLARA. UM, YEAH. RICHIE ASKED ME.
COOL!
WHAT IS THIS MUSIC?
RICHIE'S SKID ROCK.
UGH. CHANGE IT.
THANK YOU, CLARA. FINALLY SOMEONE WITH SOME TASTE.
PFFT. YOU BOTH HAVE SHITTY TASTE. TRUST ME, IN TWENTY YEARS NO ONE IS GOING TO REMEMBER NIRVANA OR ANY OF YOUR OTHER SHITTY BANDS.
HERE.
THANKS.

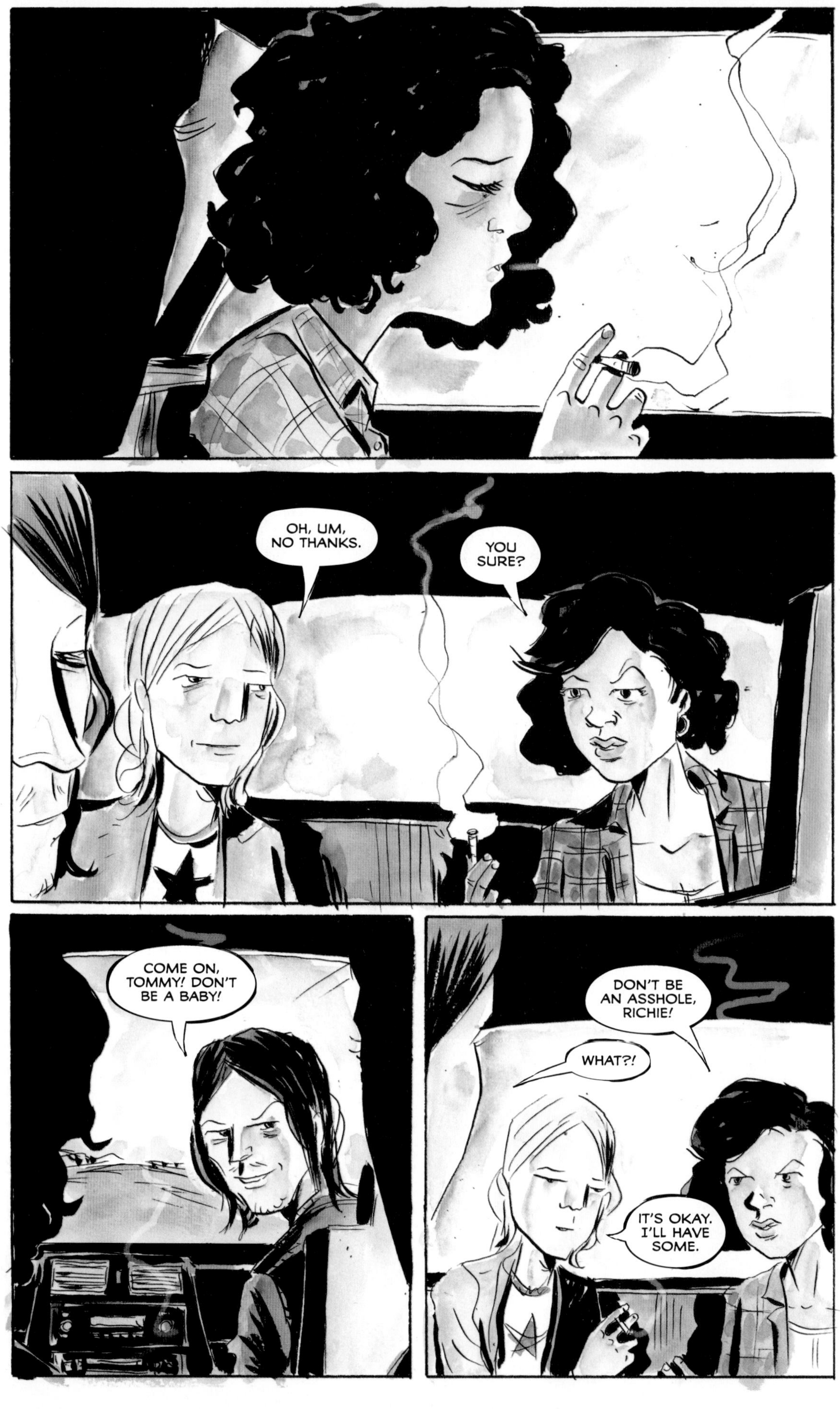
OH, UM, NO THANKS.
YOU SURE?
COME ON, TOMMY! DON'T BE A BABY!
DON'T BE AN ASSHOLE, RICHIE!
WHAT?!
IT'S OKAY. I'LL HAVE SOME.

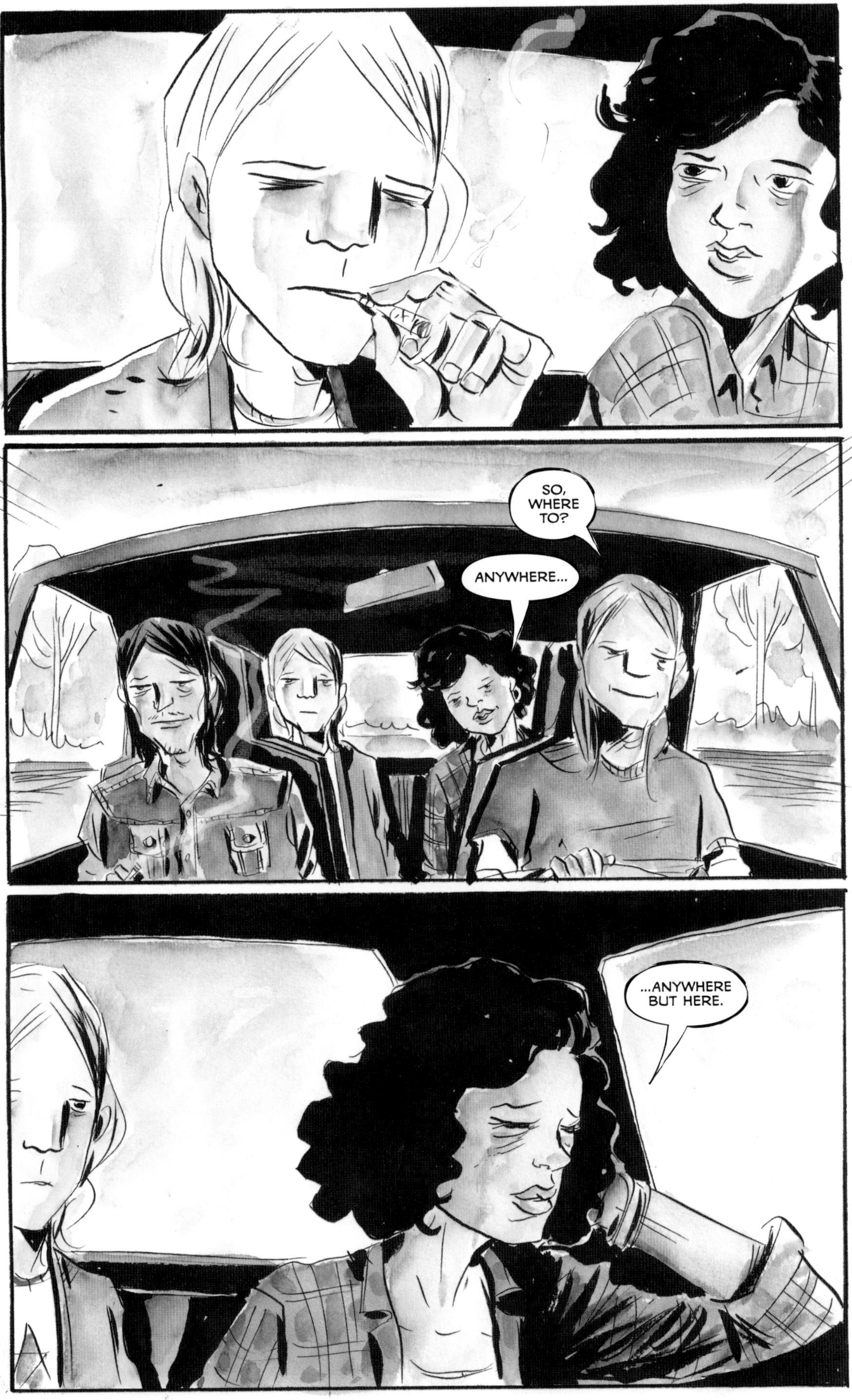
SO, WHERE TO?
ANYWHERE...
...ANYWHERE BUT HERE.

YEAH, RICHIE JUST GOES WITH THINGS. HE NEVER OBSESSES OVER THE DETAILS LIKE I ALWAYS DO.

DETAILS.

SITTING IN THE BACK SEAT WITH CLARA. SO CLOSE I CAN SMELL HER SKIN. HER HAIR.

DETAILS: THE WAY MY EYES LOOK DISTORTED IN THE REARVIEW.

DETAILS: THE HISS BEFORE THE NEW FRANK BLACK ALBUM STARTS WHEN RICHIE FLIPS THE TAPE OVER.

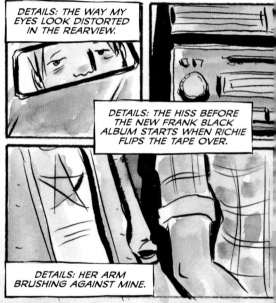

DETAILS: HER ARM BRUSHING AGAINST MINE.

DETAILS.

MY OLDER BROTHER ALWAYS LAUGHING. THE MUSIC SO LOUD I CAN'T HEAR WHAT HE'S SAYING, JUST FRANK BLACK'S VOICE COMING FROM THE RADIO INSTEAD.

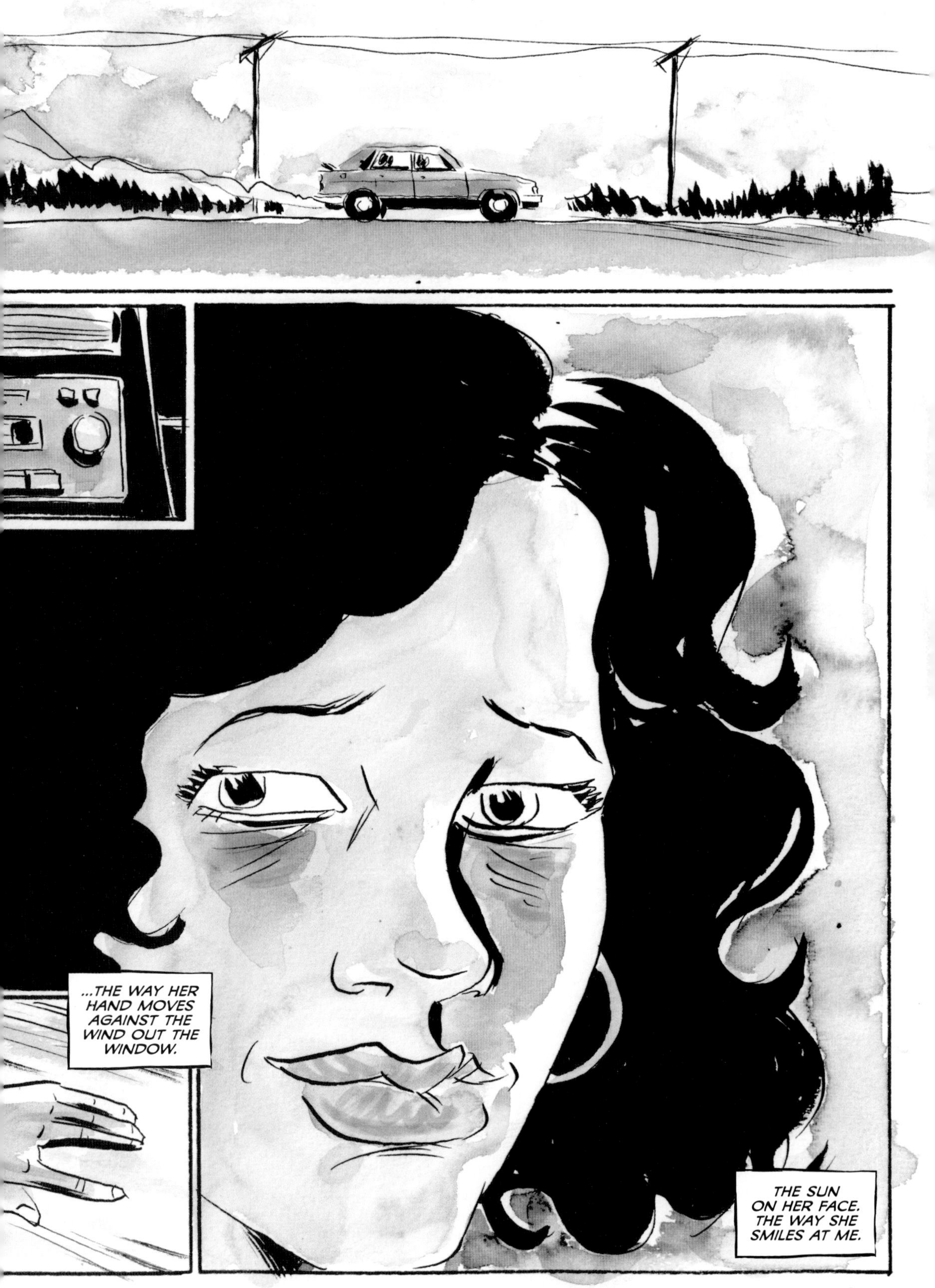
...THE WAY HER HAND MOVES AGAINST THE WIND OUT THE WINDOW.
THE SUN ON HER FACE. THE WAY SHE SMILES AT ME.

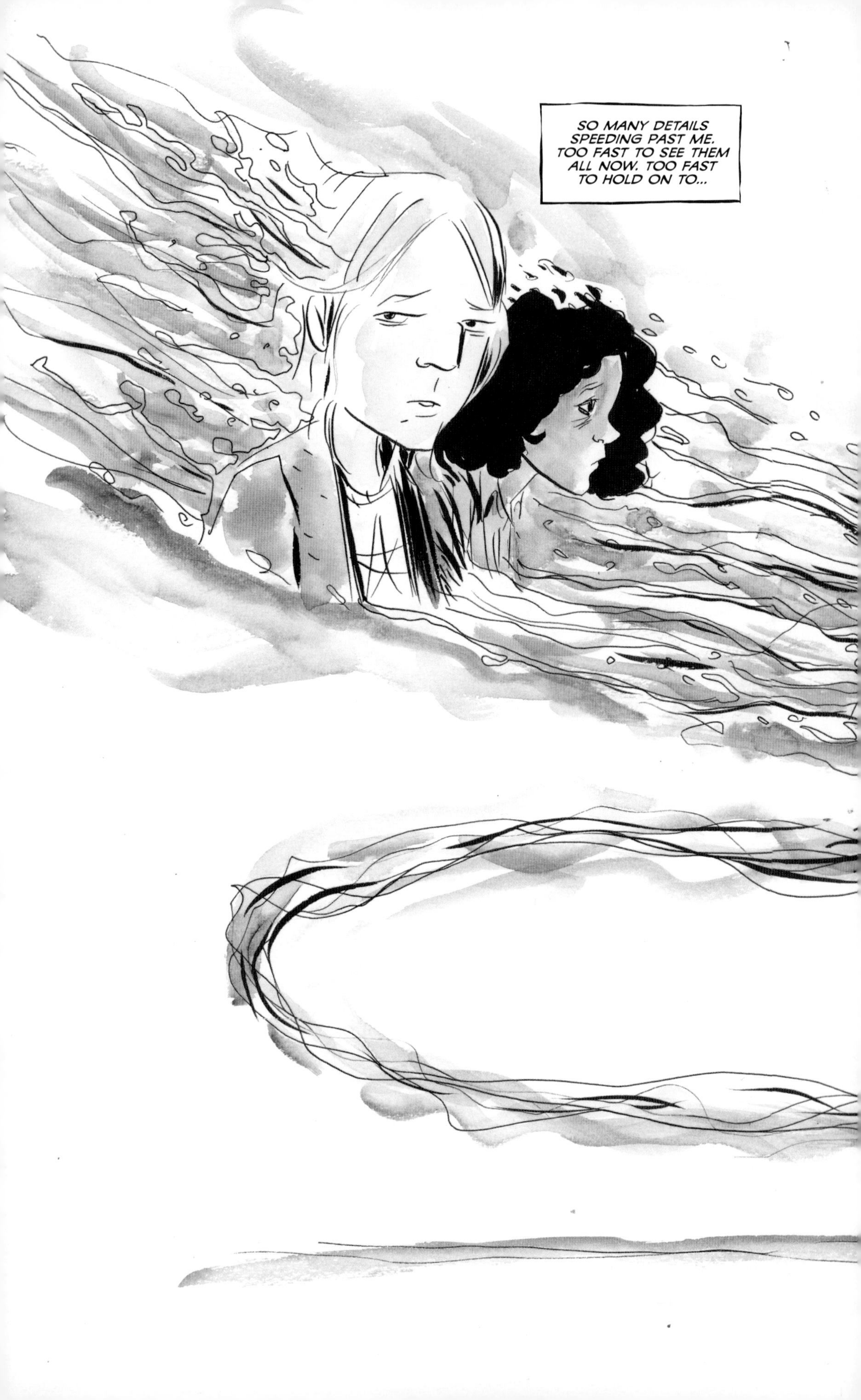
SO MANY DETAILS SPEEDING PAST ME. TOO FAST TO SEE THEM ALL NOW. TOO FAST TO HOLD ON TO...

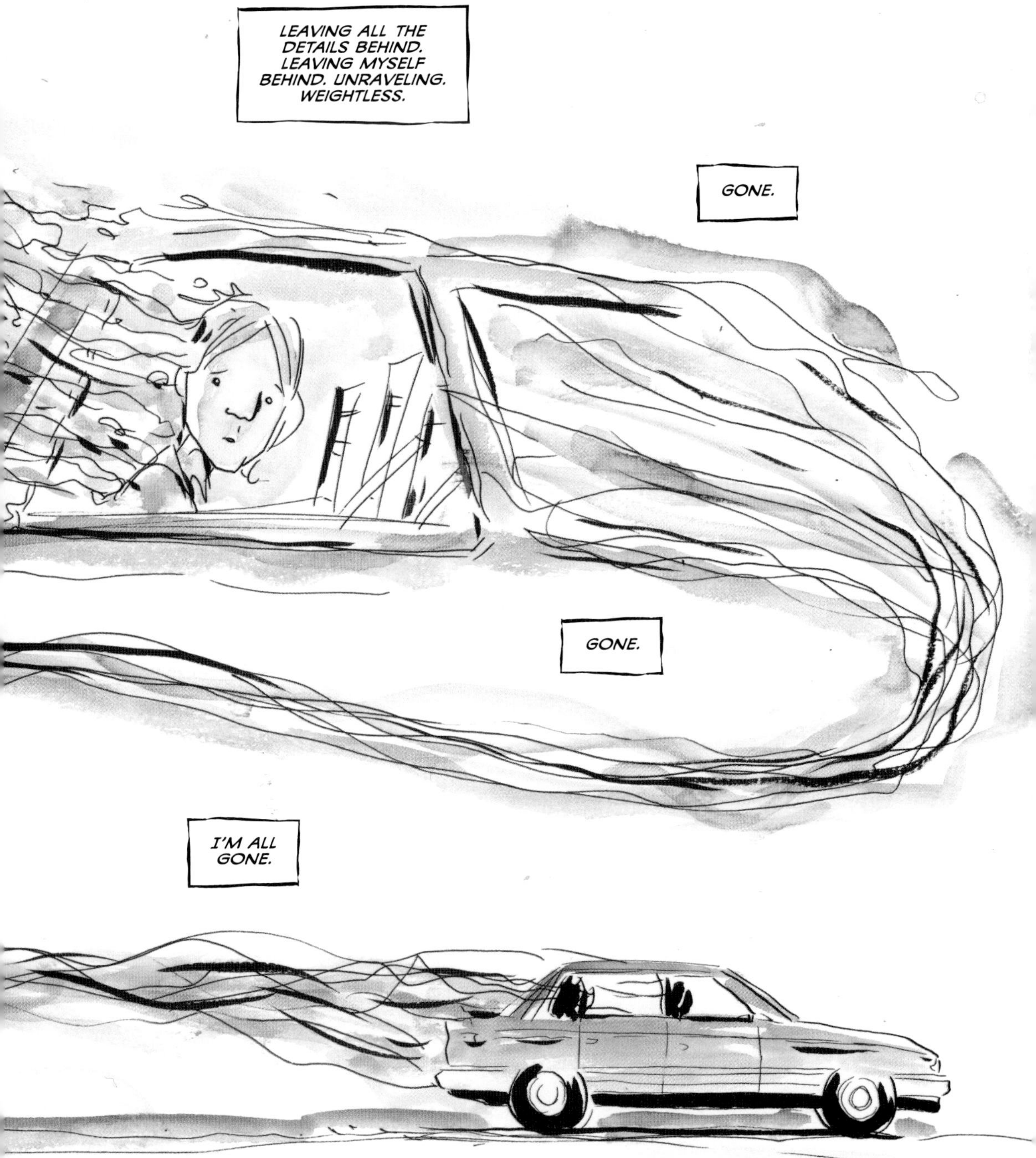
LEAVING ALL THE DETAILS BEHIND. LEAVING MYSELF BEHIND. UNRAVELING. WEIGHTLESS.
GONE.
GONE.
I'M ALL GONE.

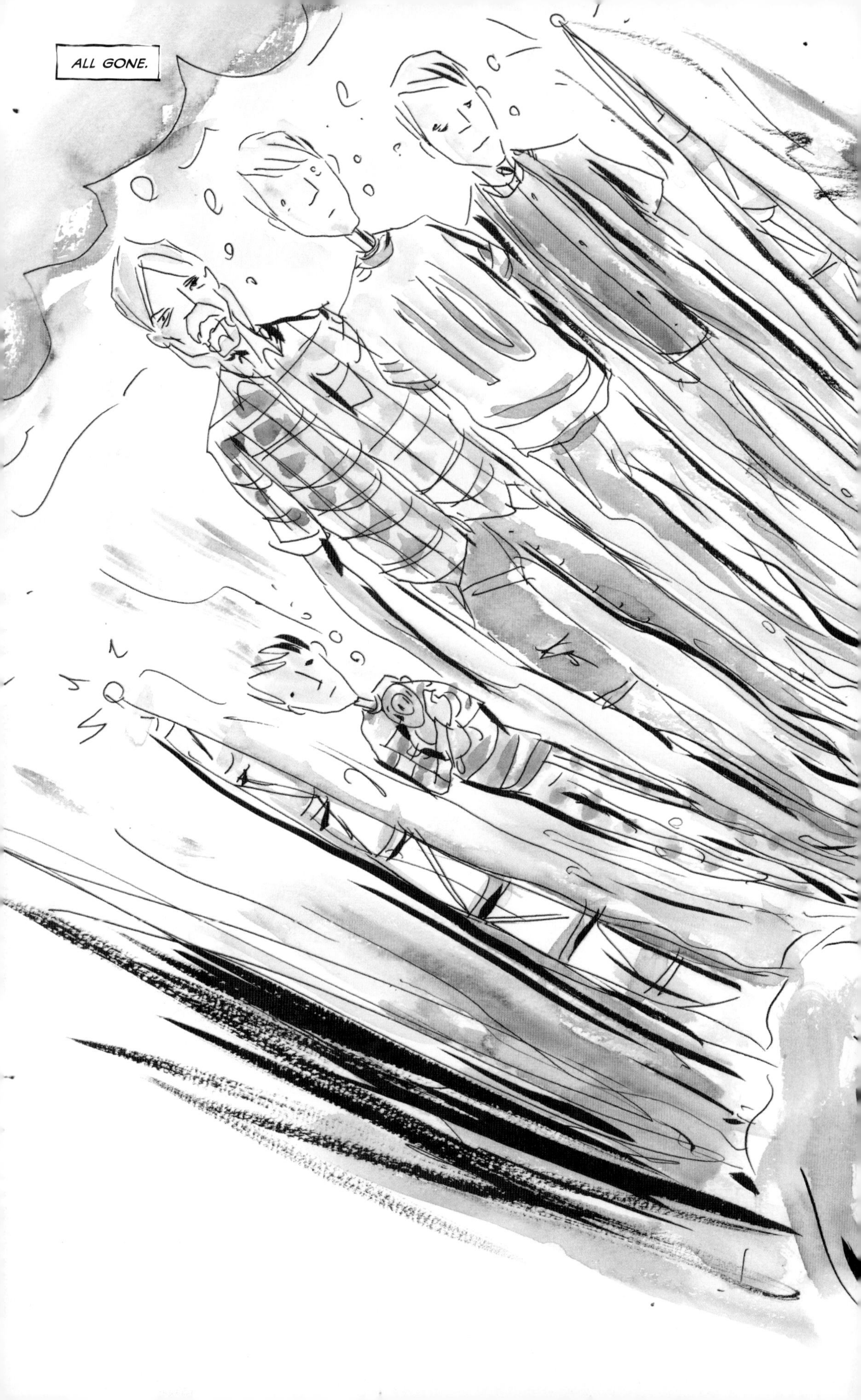
ALL GONE.

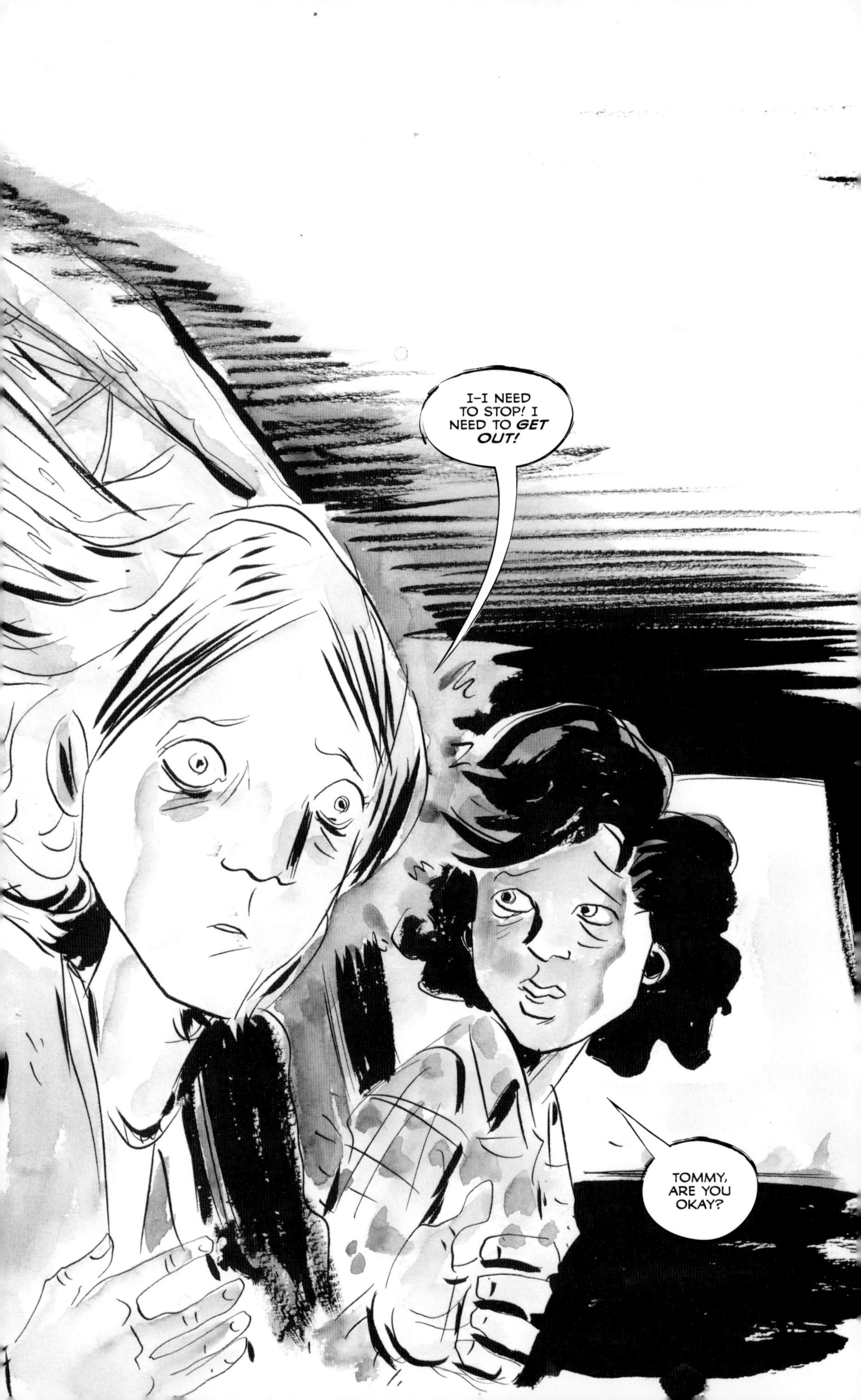
I–I NEED TO STOP! I NEED TO *GET OUT!*
TOMMY, ARE YOU OKAY?

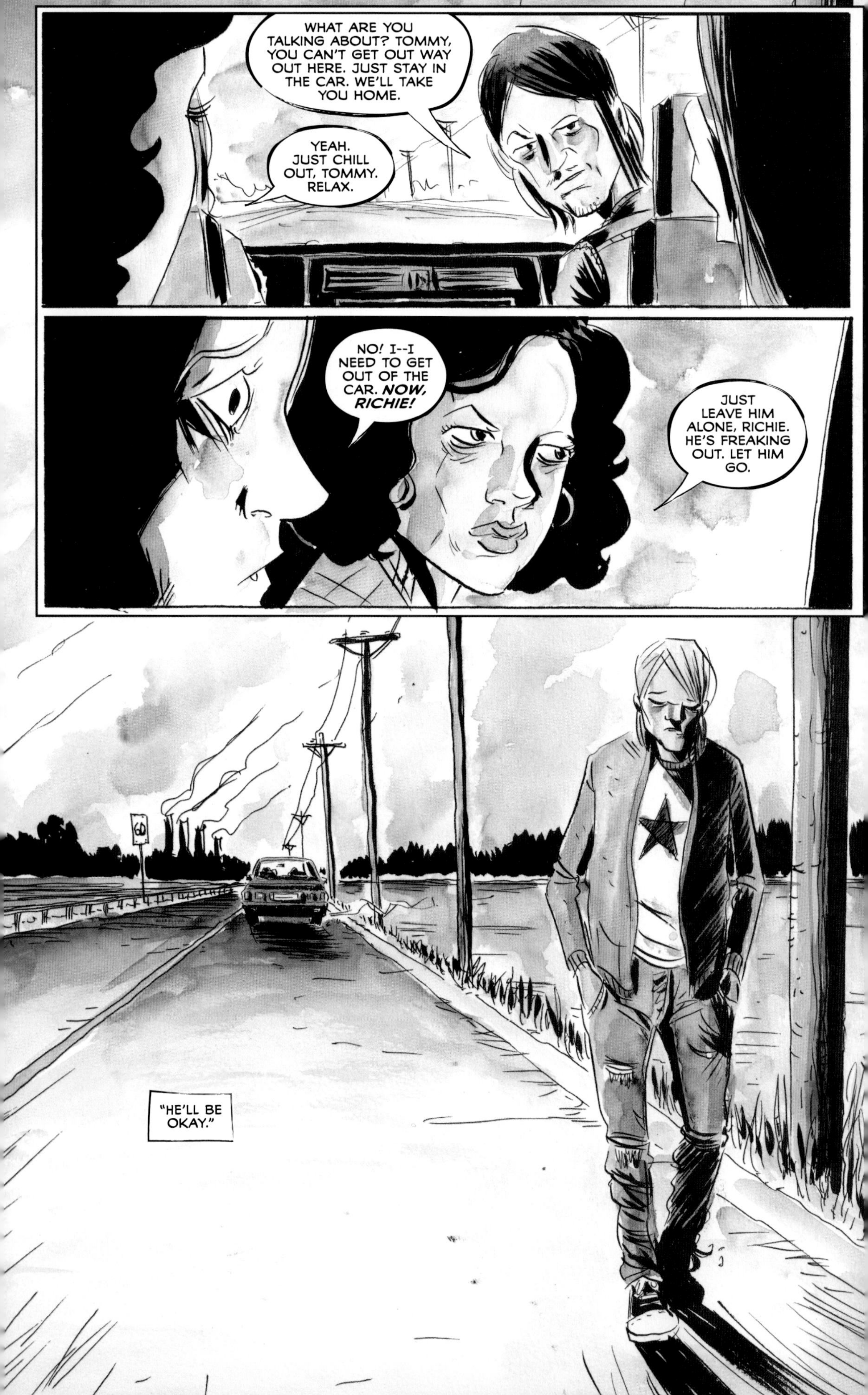
WHAT ARE YOU TALKING ABOUT? TOMMY, YOU CAN'T GET OUT WAY OUT HERE. JUST STAY IN THE CAR. WE'LL TAKE YOU HOME.
YEAH. JUST CHILL OUT, TOMMY. RELAX.
NO! I--I NEED TO GET OUT OF THE CAR. NOW, RICHIE!
JUST LEAVE HIM ALONE, RICHIE. HE'S FREAKING OUT. LET HIM GO.
60
"HE'LL BE OKAY."

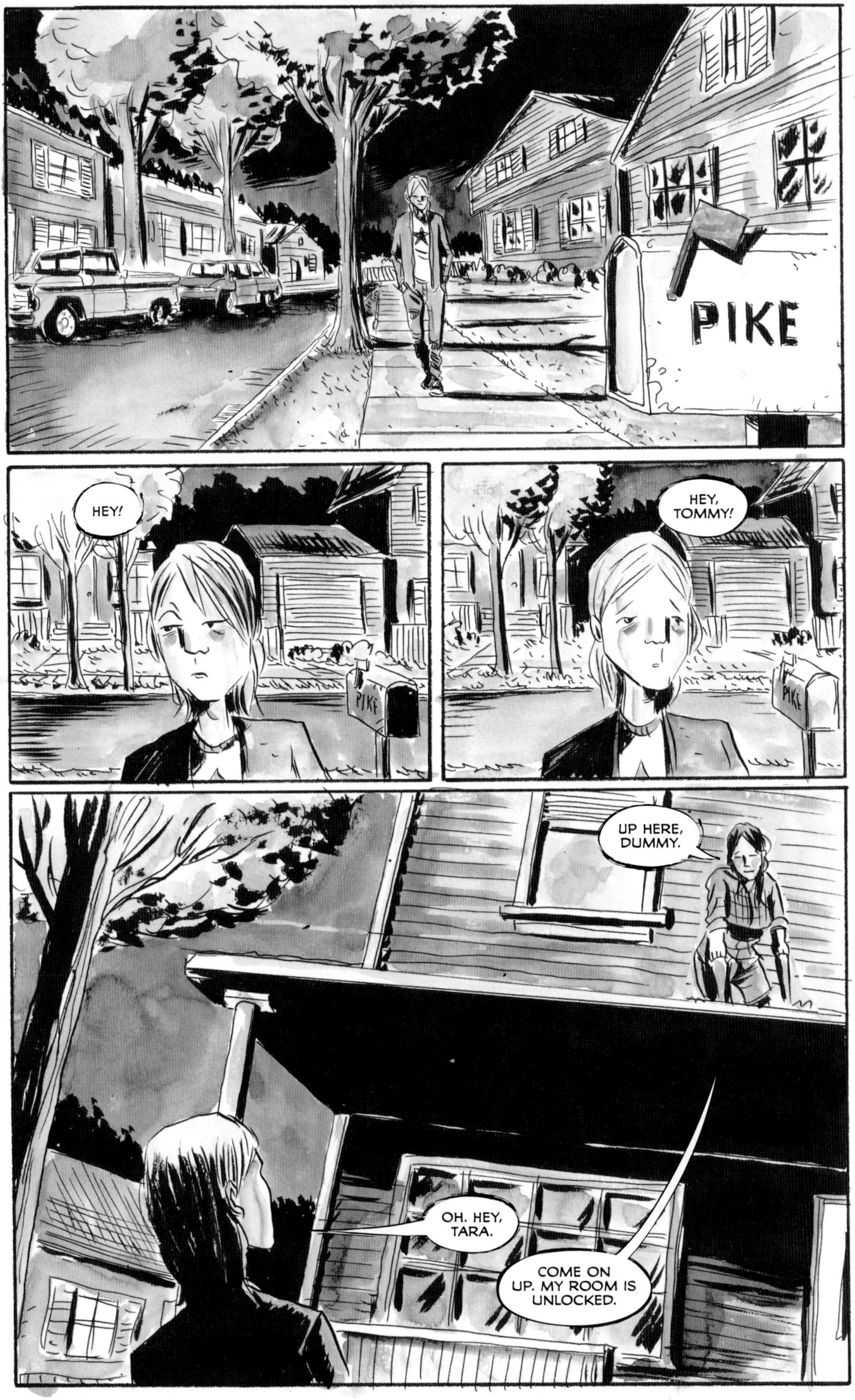
PIKE
HEY!
PIKE
HEY, TOMMY!
PIKE
UP HERE, DUMMY.
OH. HEY, TARA.
COME ON UP. MY ROOM IS UNLOCKED.

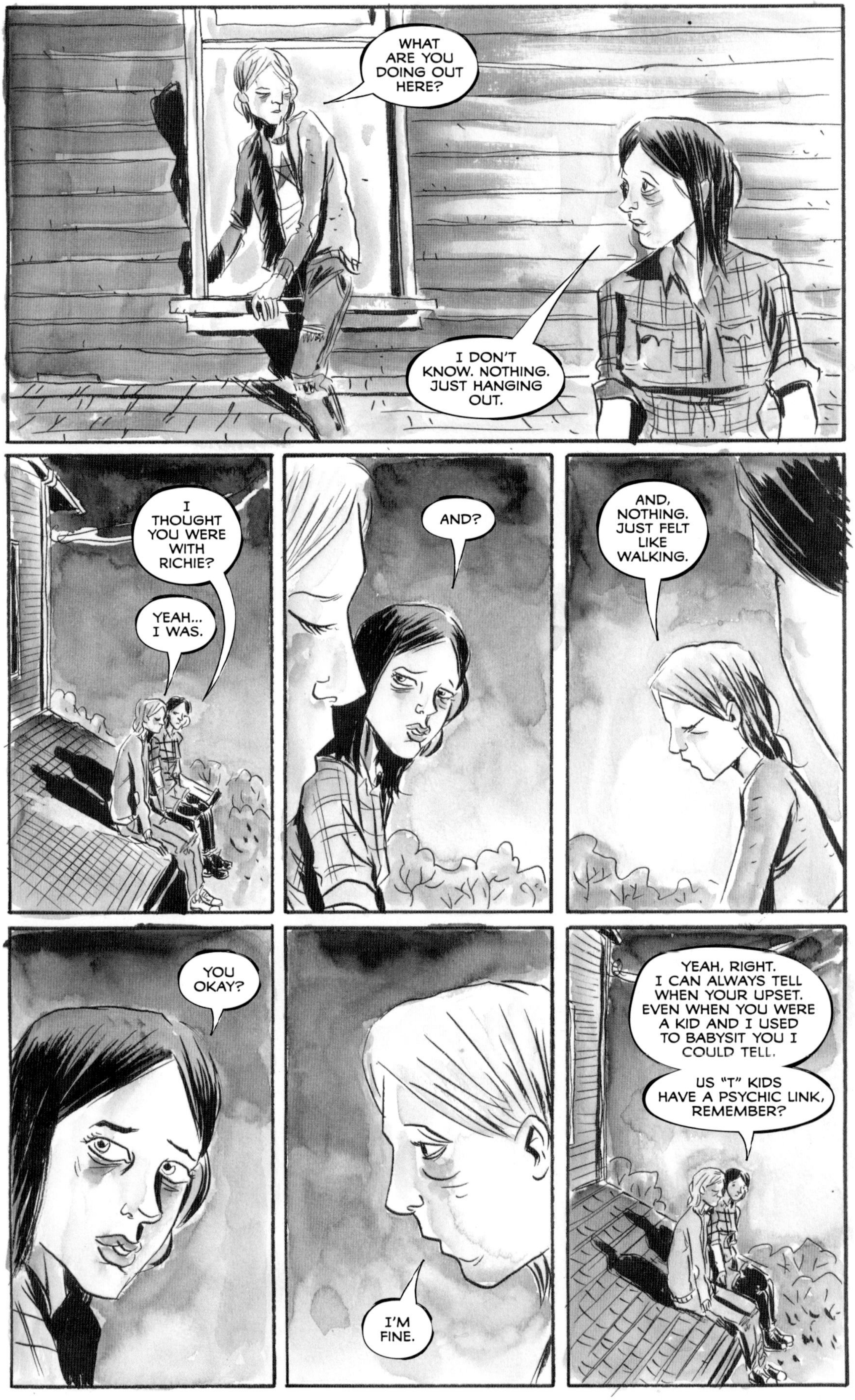
WHAT ARE YOU DOING OUT HERE?
I DON'T KNOW. NOTHING. JUST HANGING OUT.
I THOUGHT YOU WERE WITH RICHIE?
YEAH... I WAS.
AND?
AND, NOTHING. JUST FELT LIKE WALKING.
YOU OKAY?
I'M FINE.
YEAH, RIGHT. I CAN ALWAYS TELL WHEN YOUR UPSET. EVEN WHEN YOU WERE A KID AND I USED TO BABYSIT YOU I COULD TELL.
US "T" KIDS HAVE A PSYCHIC LINK, REMEMBER?

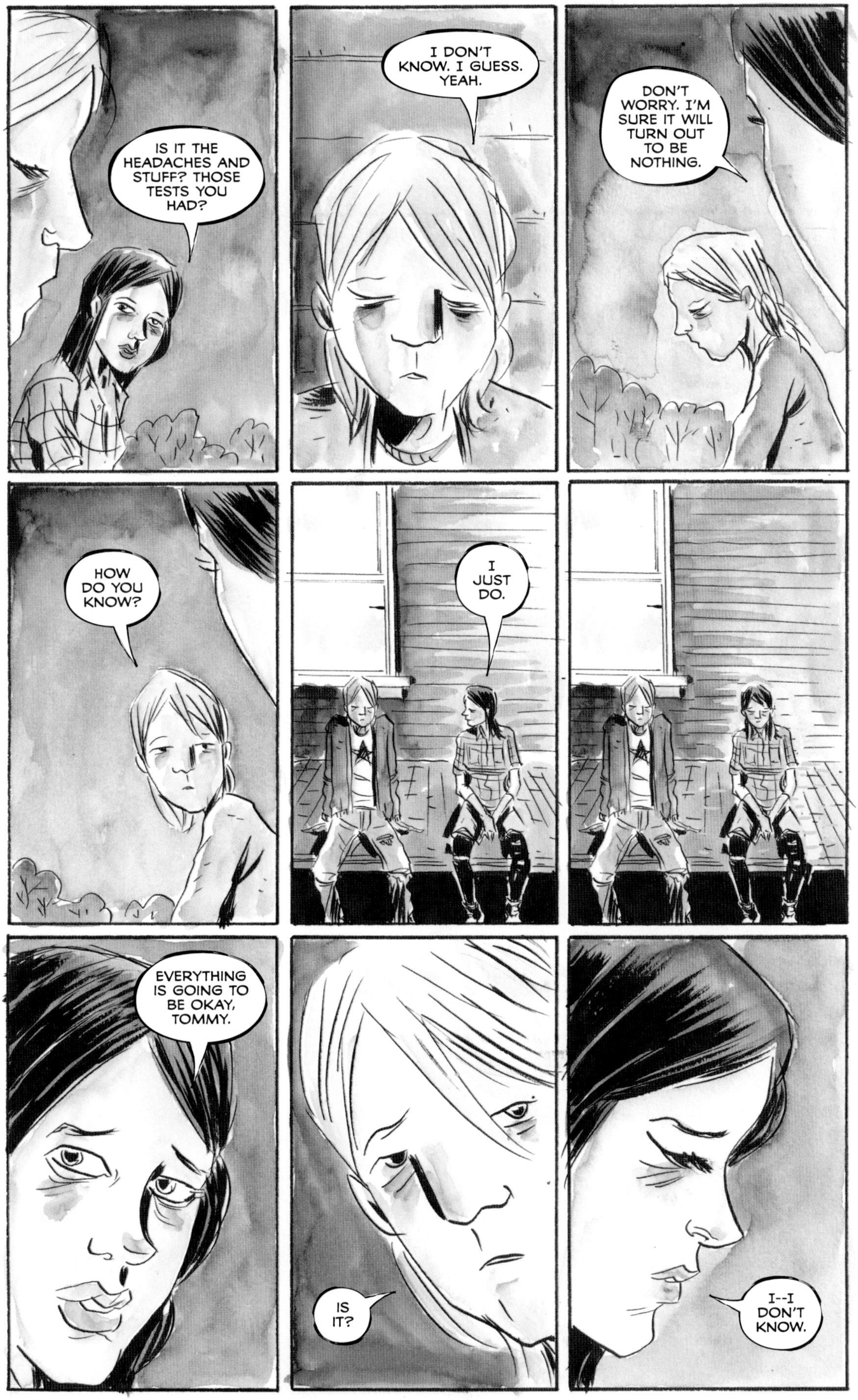
IS IT THE HEADACHES AND STUFF? THOSE TESTS YOU HAD?
I DON'T KNOW. I GUESS. YEAH.
DON'T WORRY. I'M SURE IT WILL TURN OUT TO BE NOTHING.
HOW DO YOU KNOW?
I JUST DO.
EVERYTHING IS GOING TO BE OKAY, TOMMY.
IS IT?
I--I DON'T KNOW.

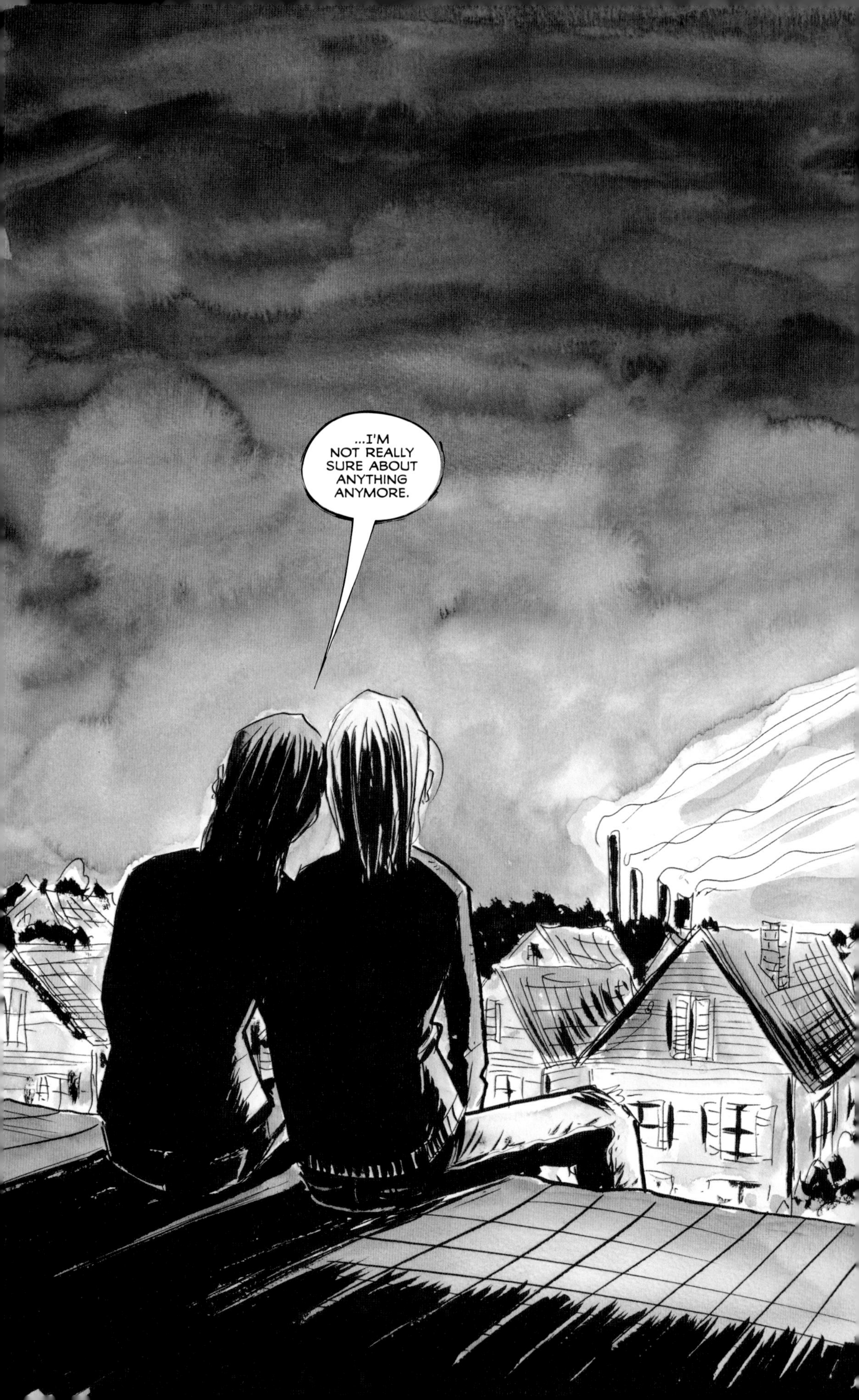
...I'M NOT REALLY SURE ABOUT ANYTHING ANYMORE.

CHAPTER NINE

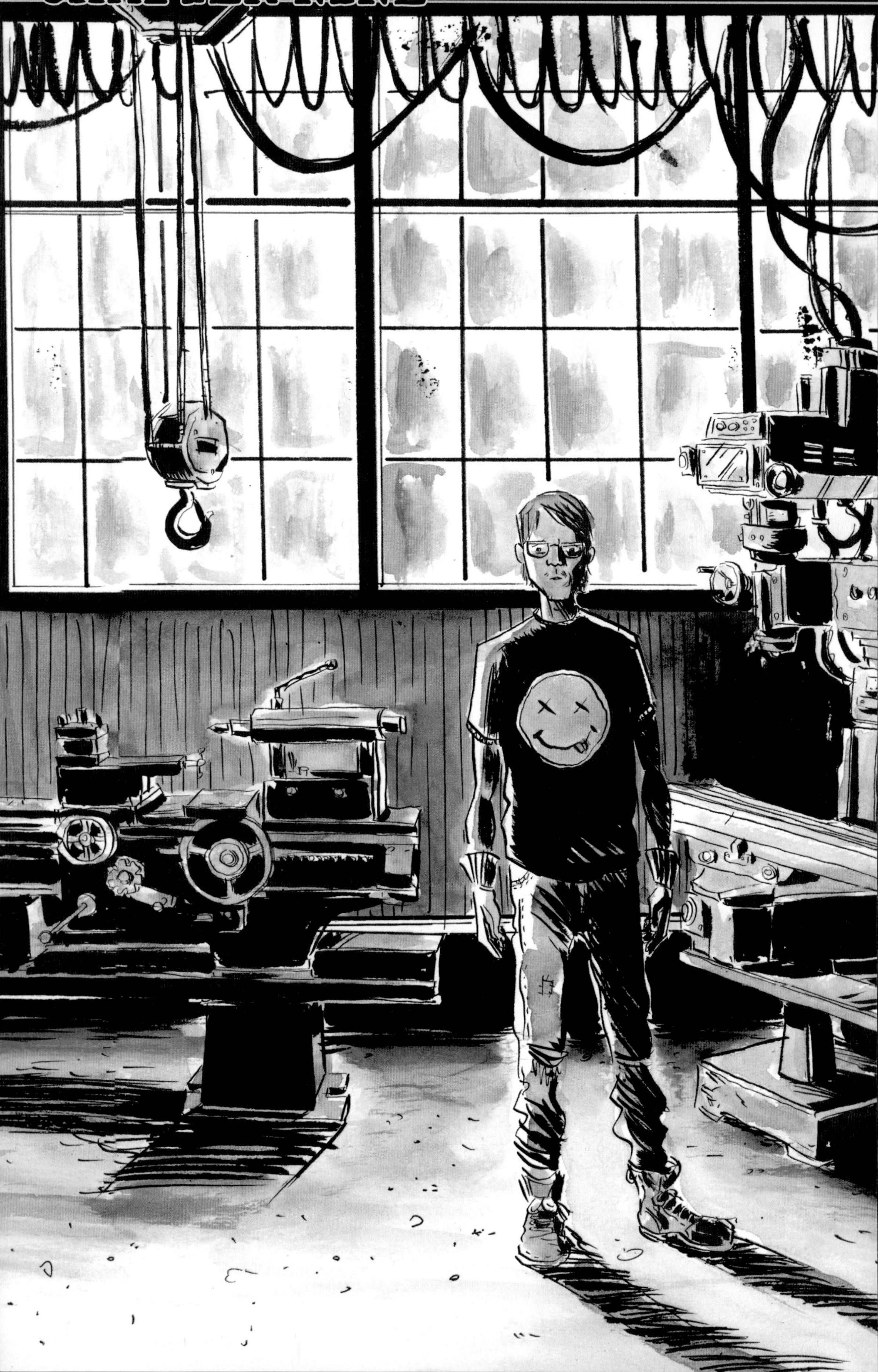

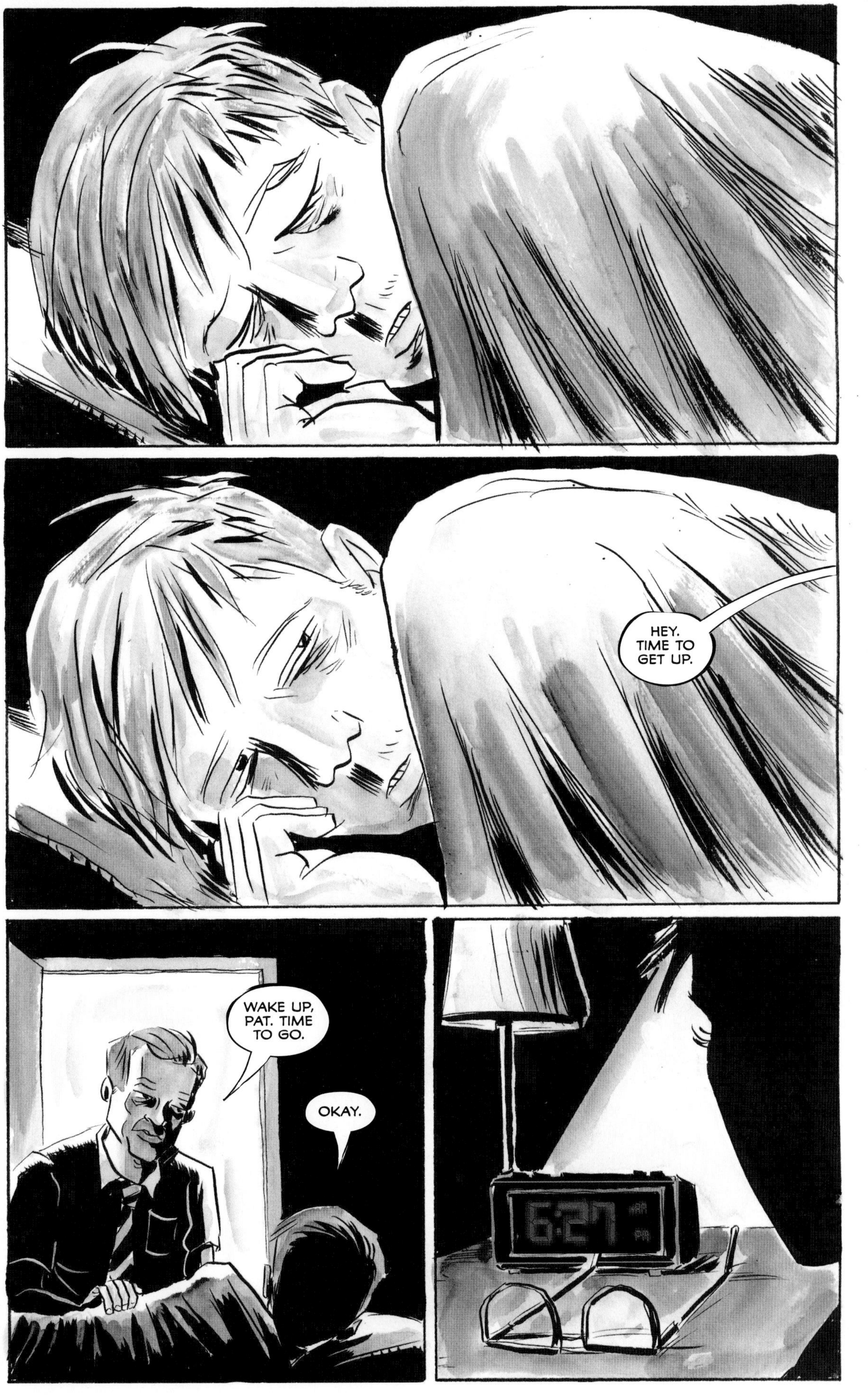
HEY. TIME TO GET UP.
WAKE UP, PAT. TIME TO GO.
OKAY.

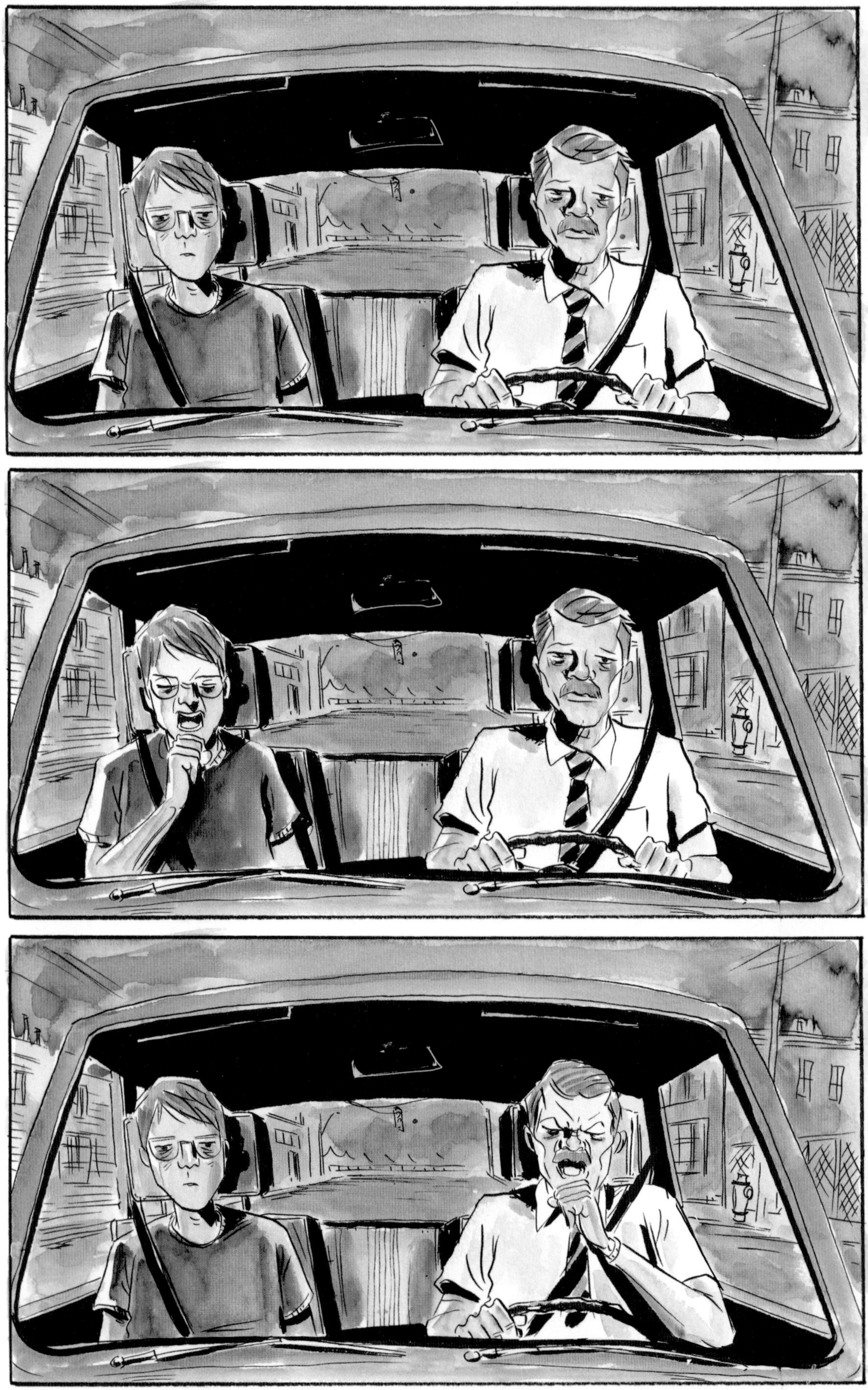

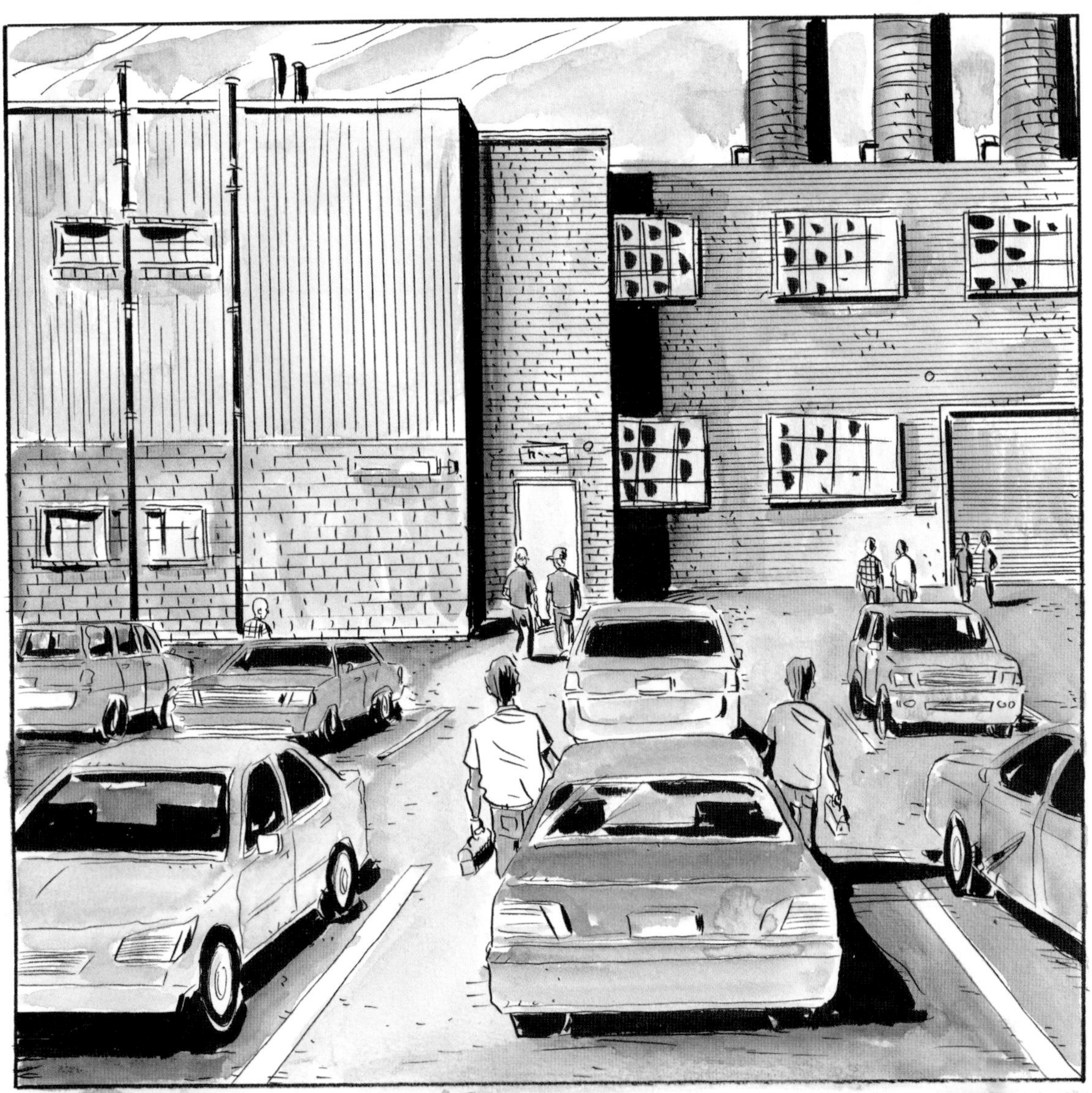

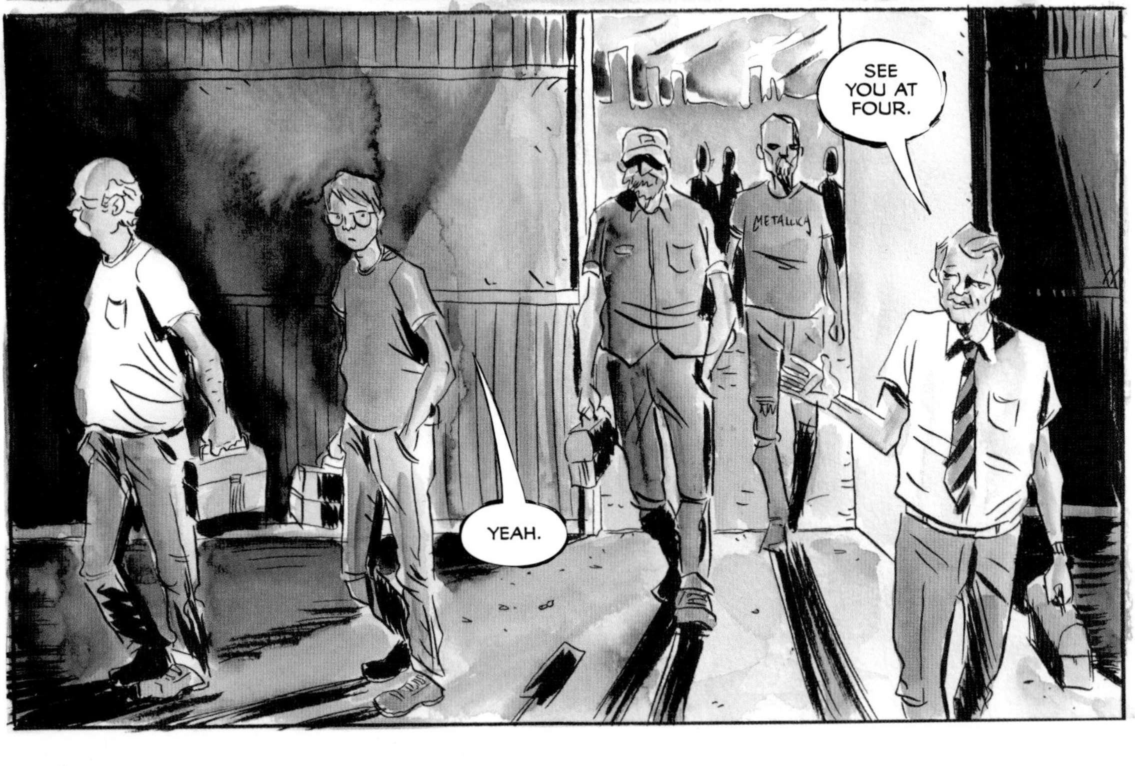
SEE YOU AT FOUR.
YEAH.
METALLICA

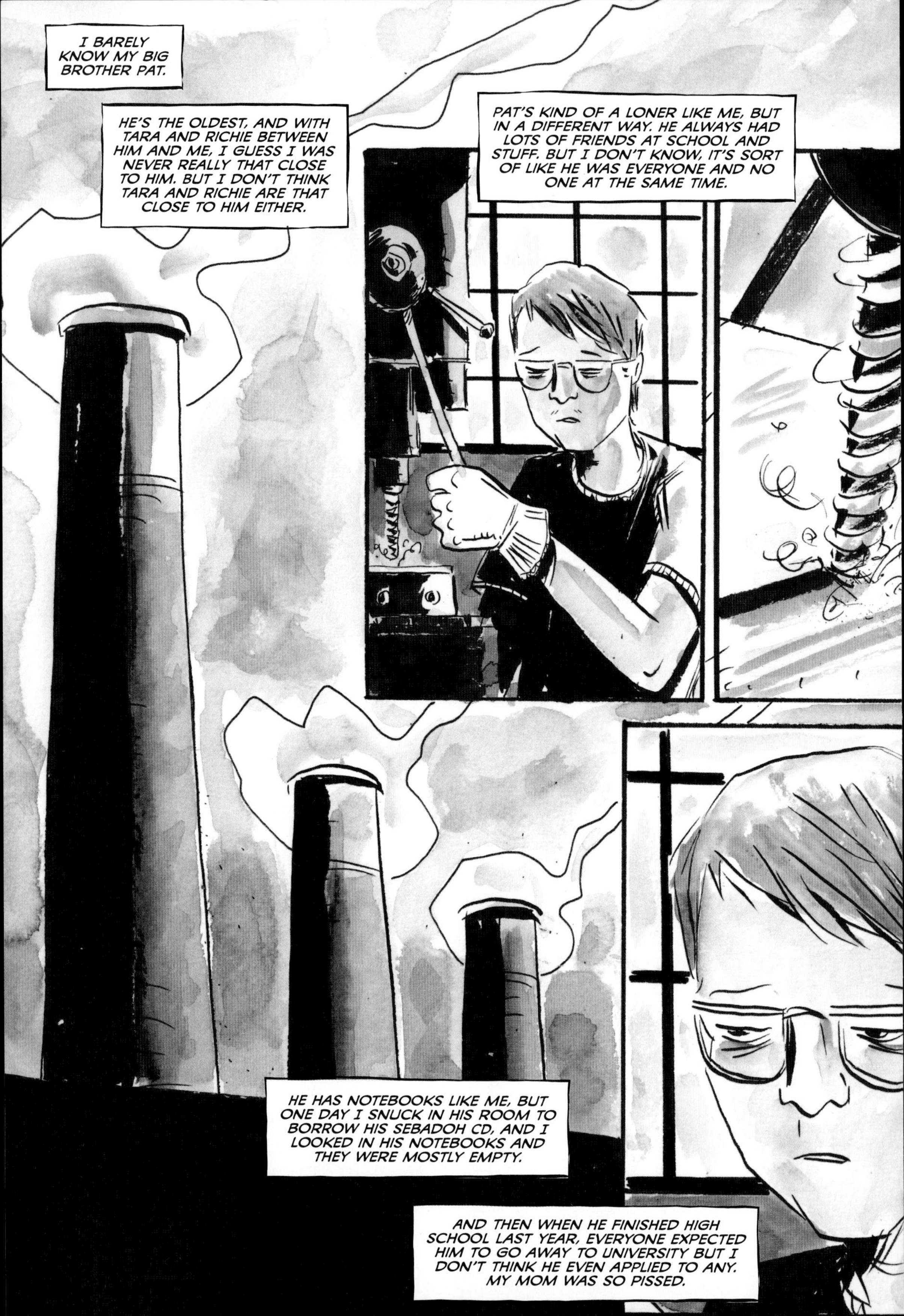
I BARELY KNOW MY BIG BROTHER PAT.
HE'S THE OLDEST, AND WITH TARA AND RICHIE BETWEEN HIM AND ME, I GUESS I WAS NEVER REALLY THAT CLOSE TO HIM. BUT I DON'T THINK TARA AND RICHIE ARE THAT CLOSE TO HIM EITHER.
PAT'S KIND OF A LONER LIKE ME, BUT IN A DIFFERENT WAY. HE ALWAYS HAD LOTS OF FRIENDS AT SCHOOL AND STUFF. BUT I DON'T KNOW, IT'S SORT OF LIKE HE WAS EVERYONE AND NO ONE AT THE SAME TIME.
HE HAS NOTEBOOKS LIKE ME, BUT ONE DAY I SNUCK IN HIS ROOM TO BORROW HIS SEBADOH CD, AND I LOOKED IN HIS NOTEBOOKS AND THEY WERE MOSTLY EMPTY.
AND THEN WHEN HE FINISHED HIGH SCHOOL LAST YEAR, EVERYONE EXPECTED HIM TO GO AWAY TO UNIVERSITY BUT I DON'T THINK HE EVEN APPLIED TO ANY. MY MOM WAS SO PISSED.

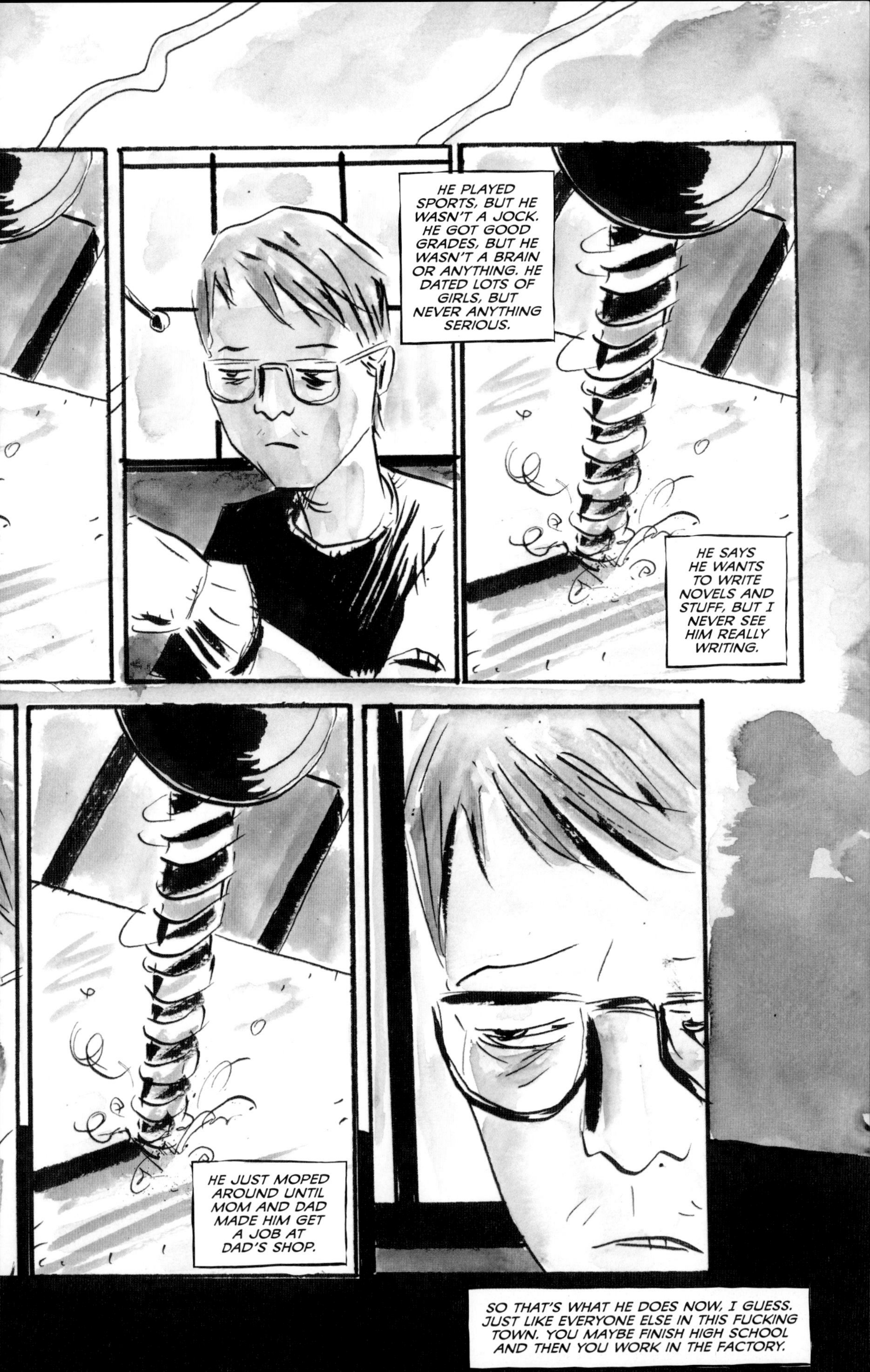
HE PLAYED SPORTS, BUT HE WASN'T A JOCK. HE GOT GOOD GRADES, BUT HE WASN'T A BRAIN OR ANYTHING. HE DATED LOTS OF GIRLS, BUT NEVER ANYTHING SERIOUS.
HE SAYS HE WANTS TO WRITE NOVELS AND STUFF, BUT I NEVER SEE HIM REALLY WRITING.
HE JUST MOPED AROUND UNTIL MOM AND DAD MADE HIM GET A JOB AT DAD'S SHOP.
SO THAT'S WHAT HE DOES NOW, I GUESS. JUST LIKE EVERYONE ELSE IN THIS FUCKING TOWN. YOU MAYBE FINISH HIGH SCHOOL AND THEN YOU WORK IN THE FACTORY.

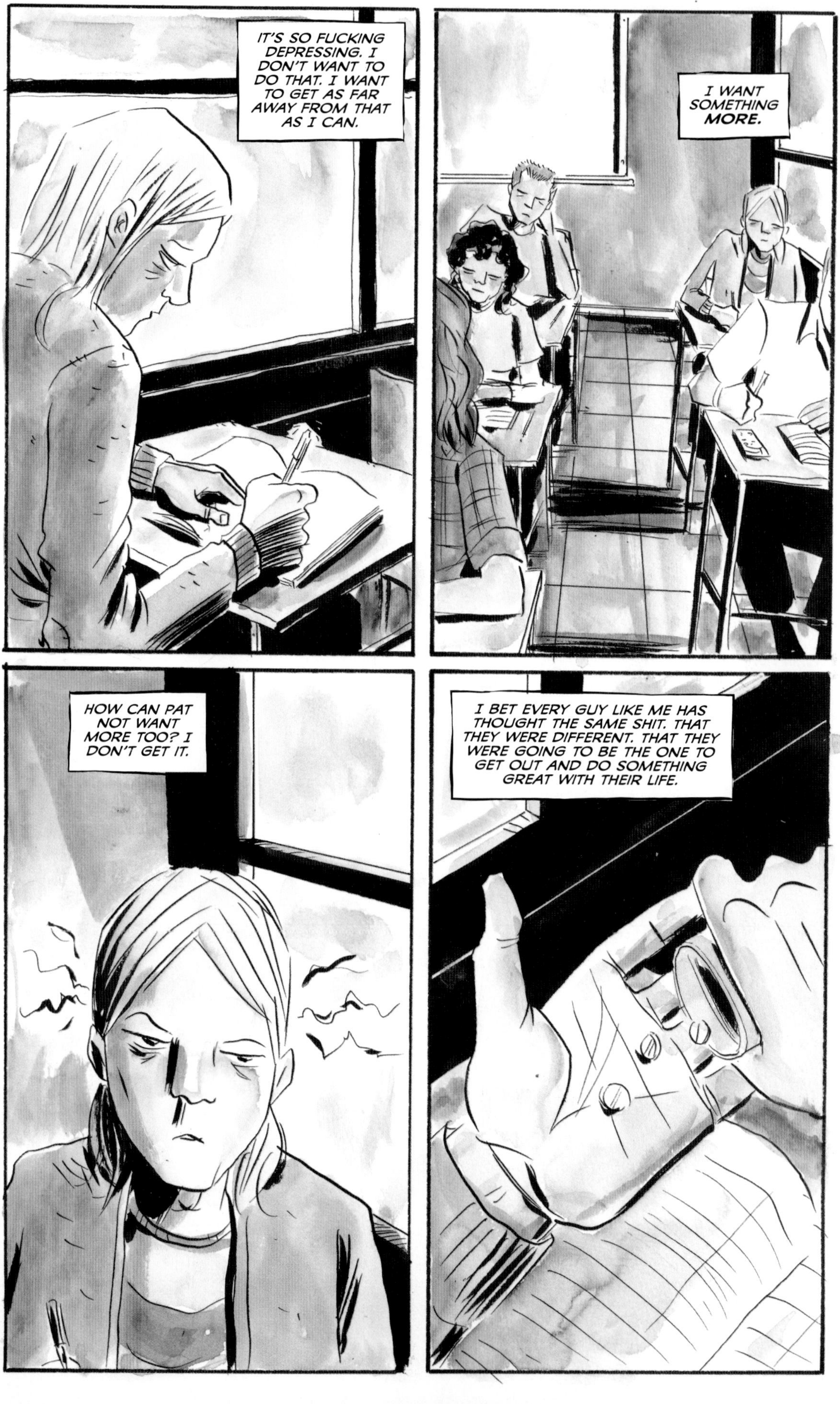
IT'S SO FUCKING DEPRESSING. I DON'T WANT TO DO THAT. I WANT TO GET AS FAR AWAY FROM THAT AS I CAN.
I WANT SOMETHING MORE.
HOW CAN PAT NOT WANT MORE TOO? I DON'T GET IT.
I BET EVERY GUY LIKE ME HAS THOUGHT THE SAME SHIT. THAT THEY WERE DIFFERENT. THAT THEY WERE GOING TO BE THE ONE TO GET OUT AND DO SOMETHING GREAT WITH THEIR LIFE.

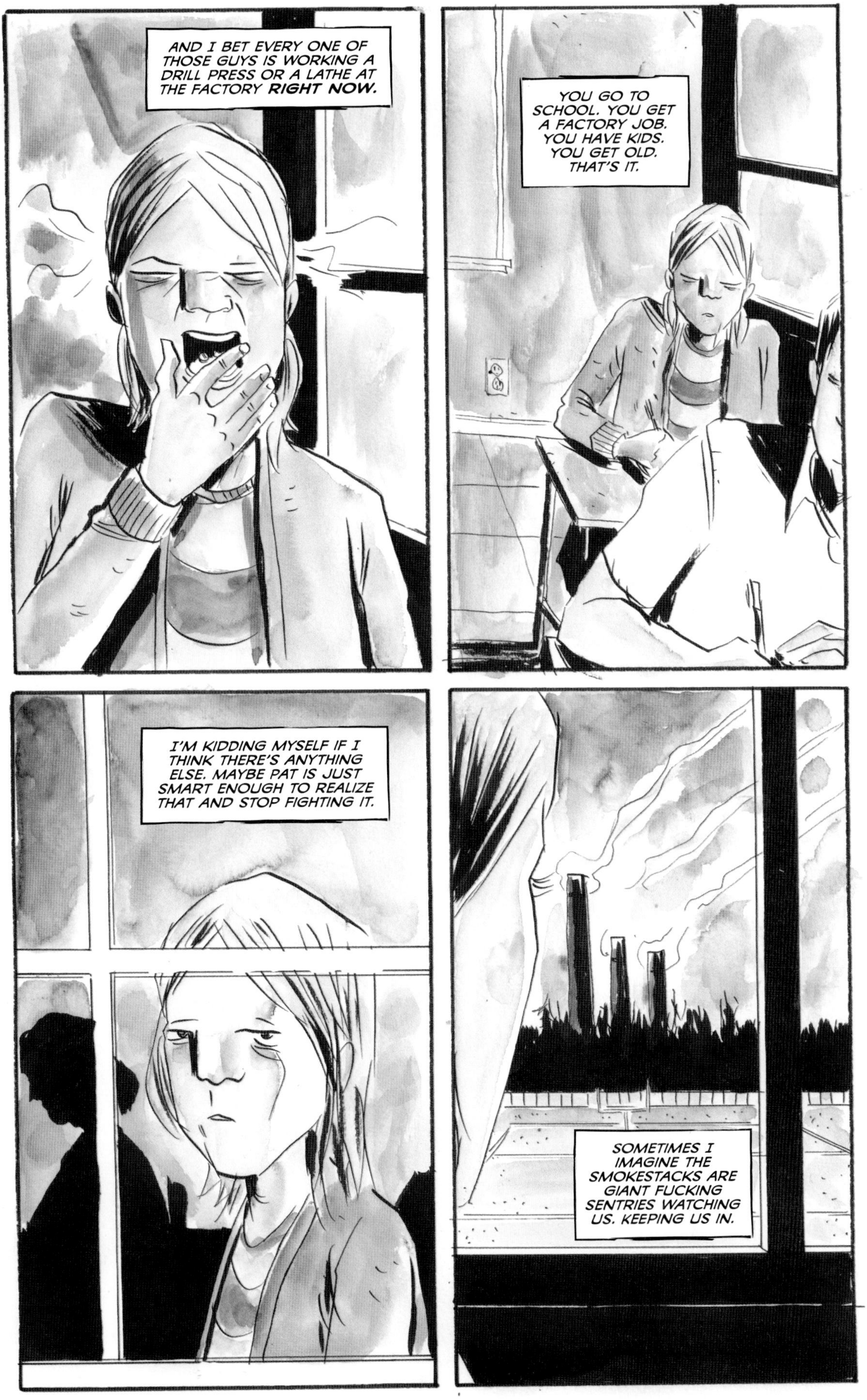
AND I BET EVERY ONE OF THOSE GUYS IS WORKING A DRILL PRESS OR A LATHE AT THE FACTORY **RIGHT NOW.**
YOU GO TO SCHOOL. YOU GET A FACTORY JOB. YOU HAVE KIDS. YOU GET OLD. THAT'S IT.
I'M KIDDING MYSELF IF I THINK THERE'S ANYTHING ELSE. MAYBE PAT IS JUST SMART ENOUGH TO REALIZE THAT AND STOP FIGHTING IT.
SOMETIMES I IMAGINE THE SMOKESTACKS ARE GIANT FUCKING SENTRIES WATCHING US. KEEPING US IN.

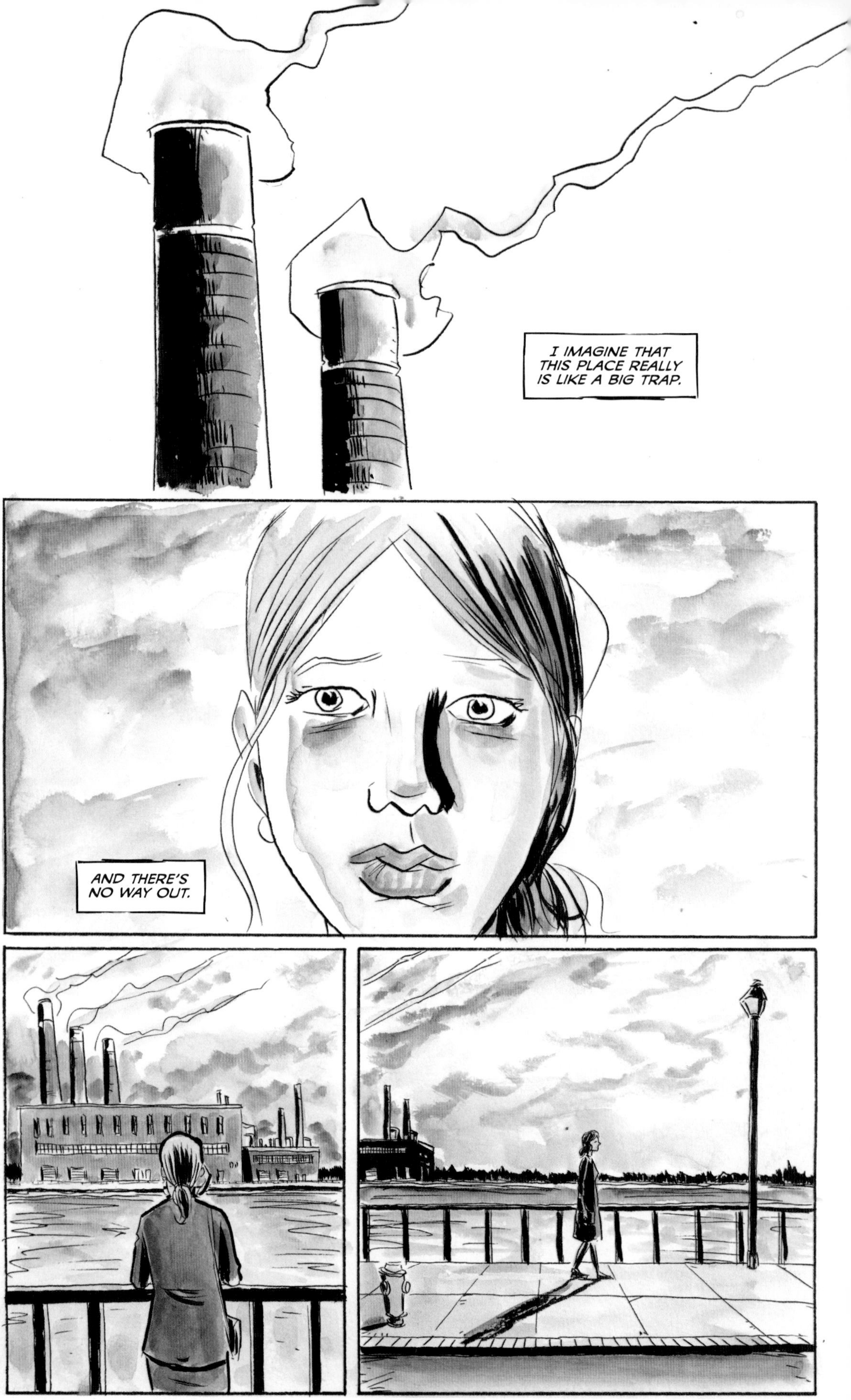
I IMAGINE THAT THIS PLACE REALLY IS LIKE A BIG TRAP.
AND THERE'S NO WAY OUT.

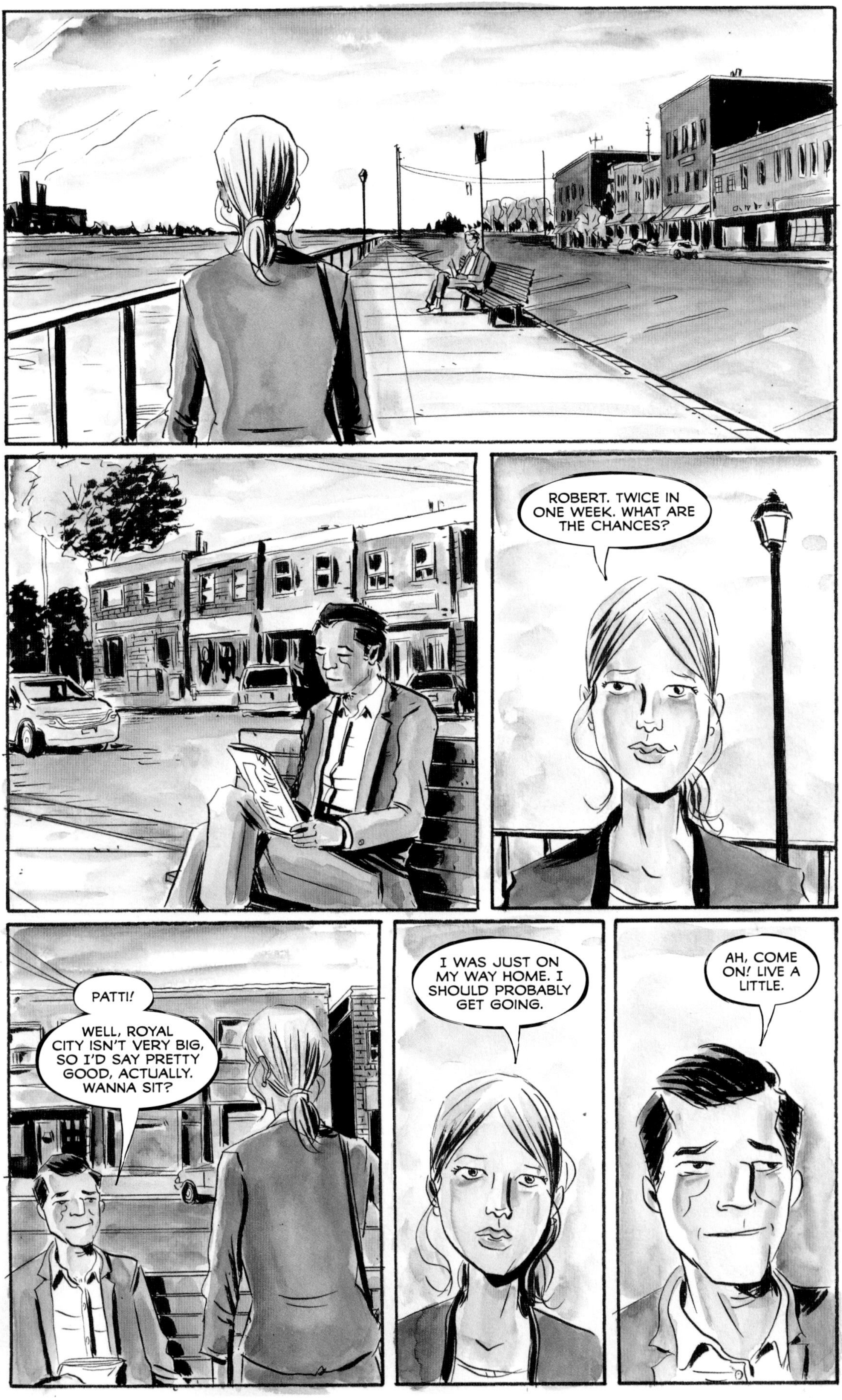
ROBERT. TWICE IN ONE WEEK. WHAT ARE THE CHANCES?
PATTI!
WELL, ROYAL CITY ISN'T VERY BIG, SO I'D SAY PRETTY GOOD, ACTUALLY. WANNA SIT?
I WAS JUST ON MY WAY HOME. I SHOULD PROBABLY GET GOING.
AH, COME ON! LIVE A LITTLE.

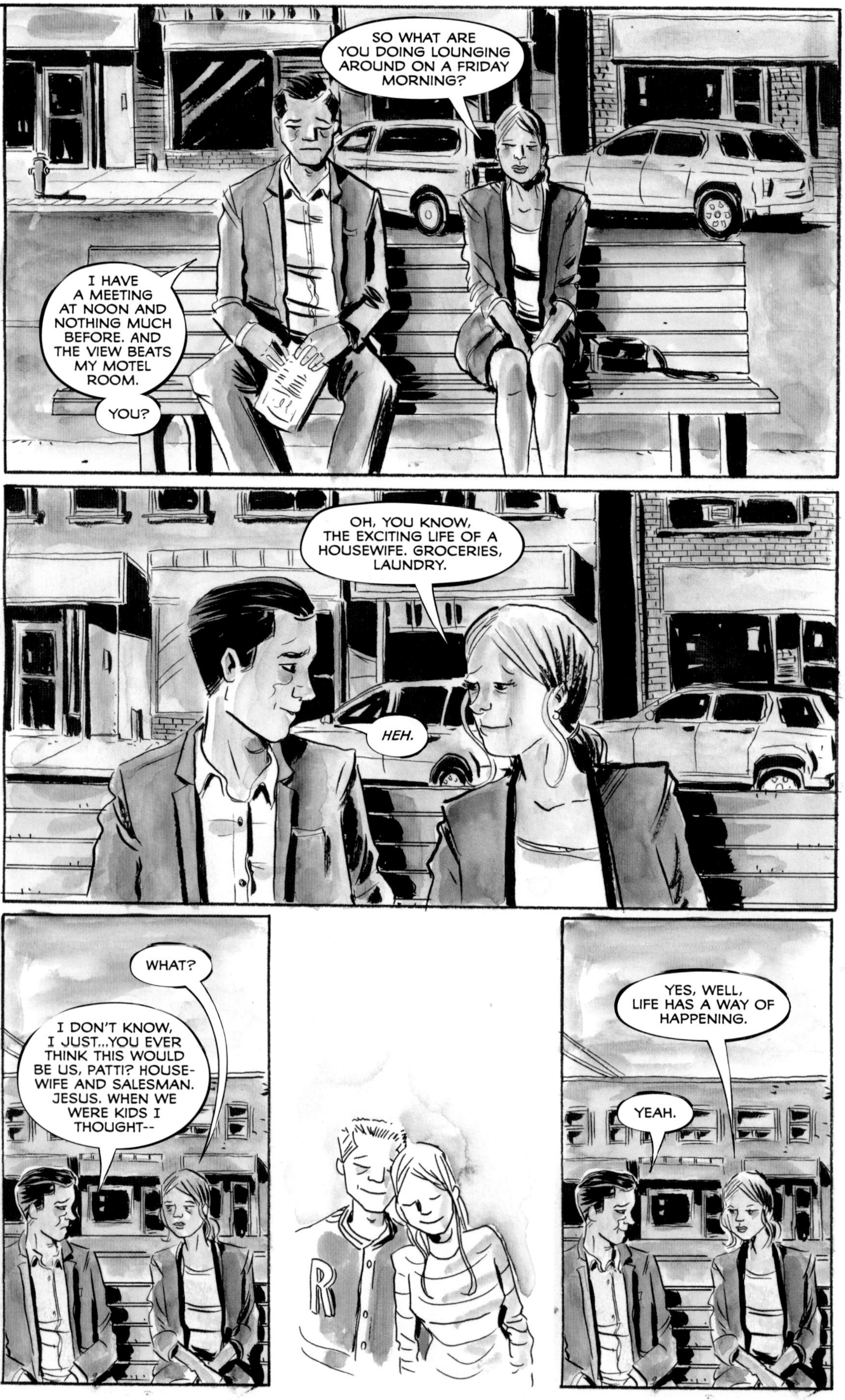
SO WHAT ARE YOU DOING LOUNGING AROUND ON A FRIDAY MORNING?
I HAVE A MEETING AT NOON AND NOTHING MUCH BEFORE. AND THE VIEW BEATS MY MOTEL ROOM.
YOU?
OH, YOU KNOW, THE EXCITING LIFE OF A HOUSEWIFE. GROCERIES, LAUNDRY.
HEH.
I DON'T KNOW, I JUST...YOU EVER THINK THIS WOULD BE US, PATTI? HOUSE-WIFE AND SALESMAN. JESUS. WHEN WE WERE KIDS I THOUGHT--
WHAT?
R
YES, WELL, LIFE HAS A WAY OF HAPPENING.
YEAH.

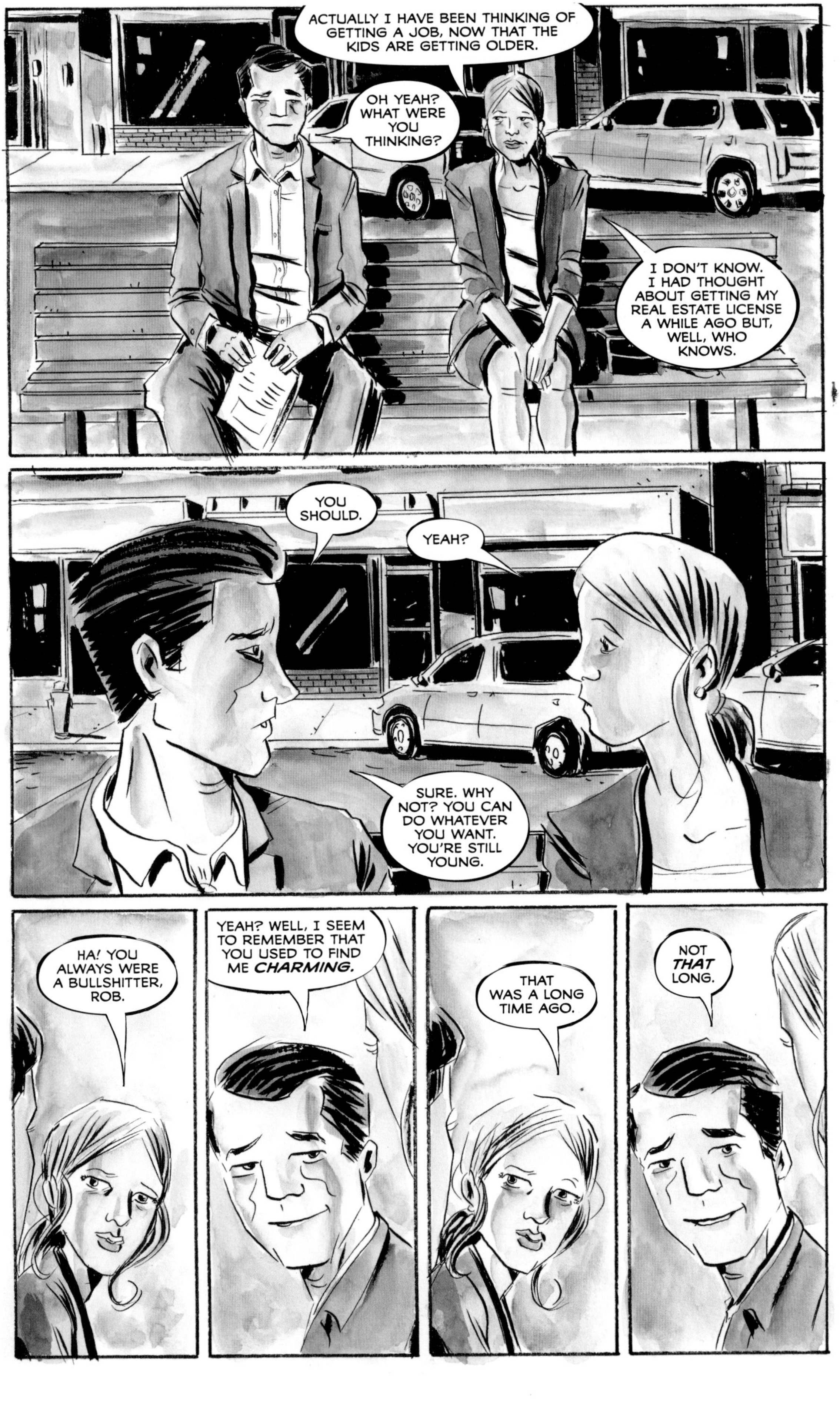
ACTUALLY I HAVE BEEN THINKING OF GETTING A JOB, NOW THAT THE KIDS ARE GETTING OLDER.
OH YEAH? WHAT WERE YOU THINKING?
I DON'T KNOW. I HAD THOUGHT ABOUT GETTING MY REAL ESTATE LICENSE A WHILE AGO BUT, WELL, WHO KNOWS.
YOU SHOULD.
YEAH?
SURE. WHY NOT? YOU CAN DO WHATEVER YOU WANT. YOU'RE STILL YOUNG.
HA! YOU ALWAYS WERE A BULLSHITTER, ROB.
YEAH? WELL, I SEEM TO REMEMBER THAT YOU USED TO FIND ME CHARMING.
THAT WAS A LONG TIME AGO.
NOT THAT LONG.

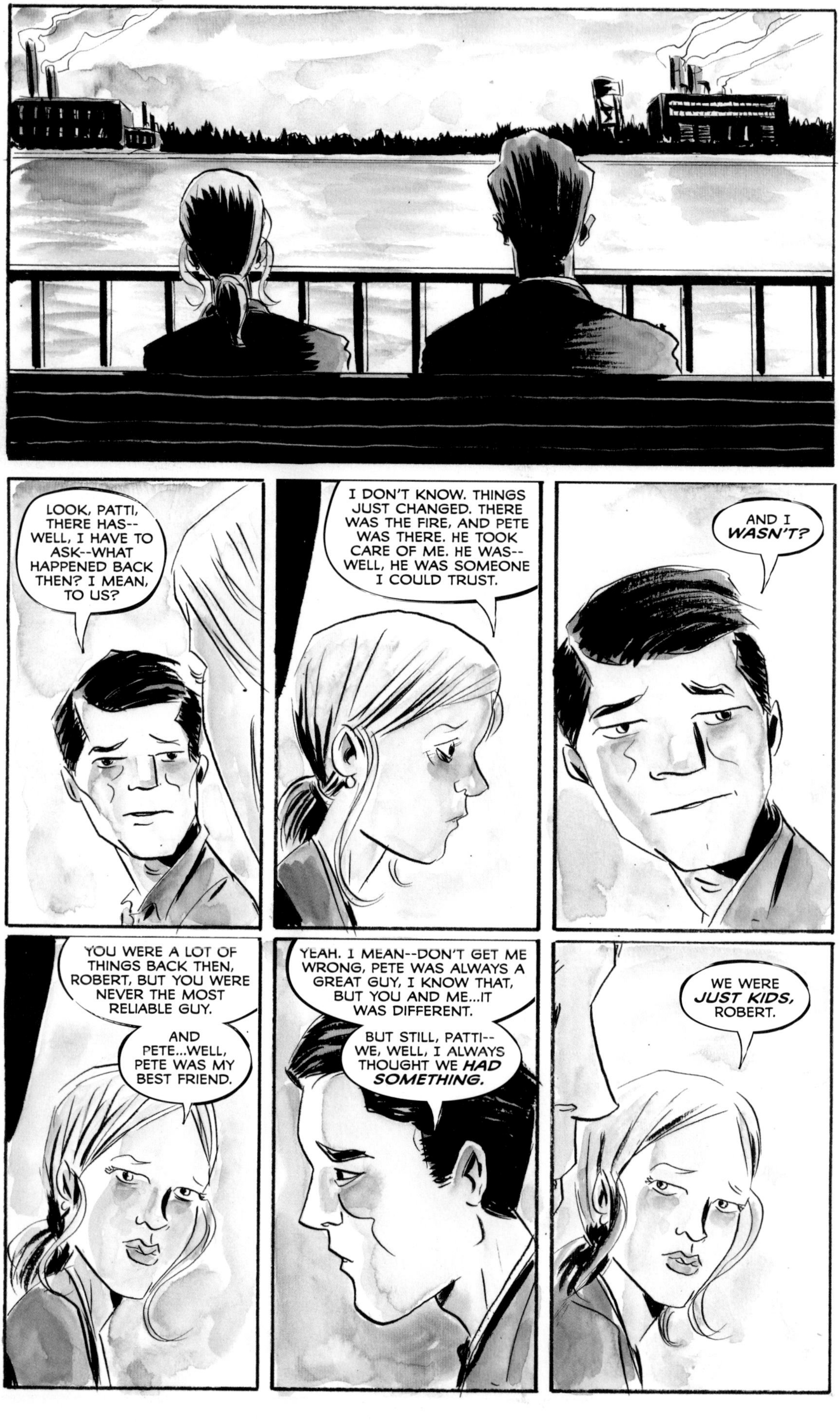
LOOK, PATTI, THERE HAS--WELL, I HAVE TO ASK--WHAT HAPPENED BACK THEN? I MEAN, TO US?
I DON'T KNOW. THINGS JUST CHANGED. THERE WAS THE FIRE, AND PETE WAS THERE. HE TOOK CARE OF ME. HE WAS--WELL, HE WAS SOMEONE I COULD TRUST.
AND I *WASN'T?*
YOU WERE A LOT OF THINGS BACK THEN, ROBERT, BUT YOU WERE NEVER THE MOST RELIABLE GUY.
AND PETE...WELL, PETE WAS MY BEST FRIEND.
YEAH. I MEAN--DON'T GET ME WRONG, PETE WAS ALWAYS A GREAT GUY, I KNOW THAT, BUT YOU AND ME...IT WAS DIFFERENT.
BUT STILL, PATTI--WE, WELL, I ALWAYS THOUGHT WE *HAD SOMETHING.*
WE WERE *JUST KIDS,* ROBERT.

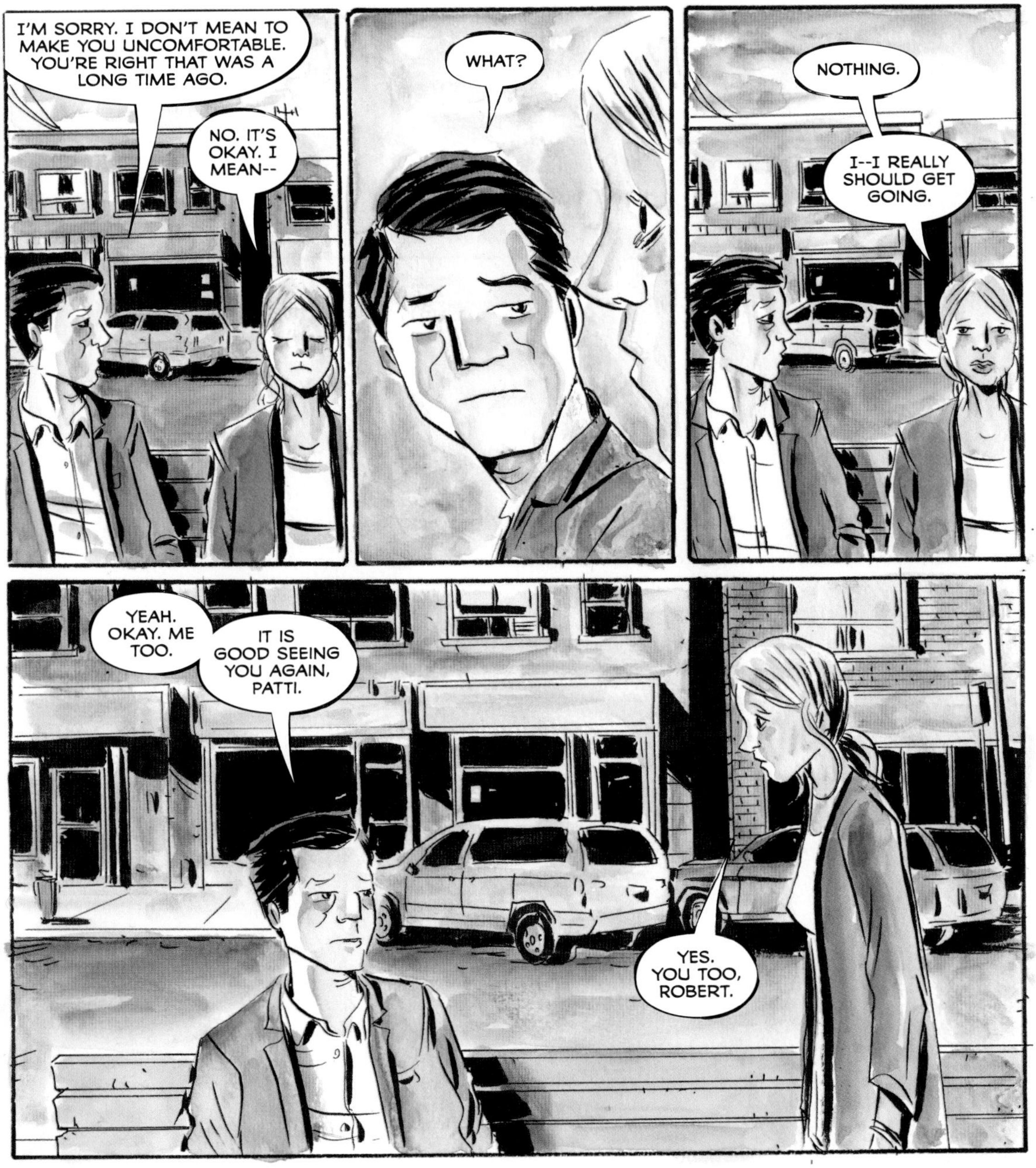
I'M SORRY. I DON'T MEAN TO MAKE YOU UNCOMFORTABLE. YOU'RE RIGHT THAT WAS A LONG TIME AGO.
NO. IT'S OKAY. I MEAN--
WHAT?
NOTHING.
I--I REALLY SHOULD GET GOING.
YEAH. OKAY. ME TOO.
IT IS GOOD SEEING YOU AGAIN, PATTI.
YES. YOU TOO, ROBERT.

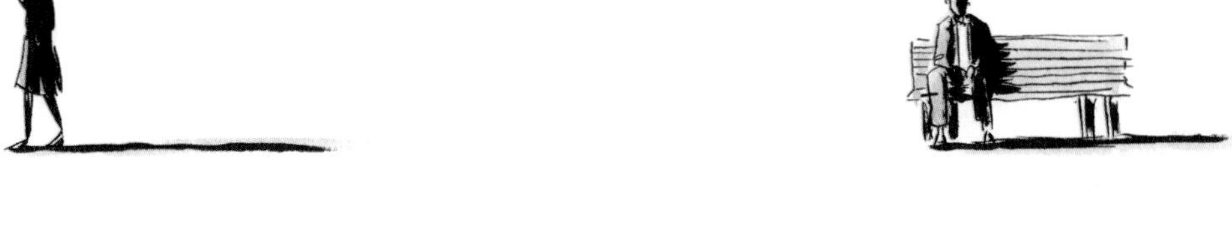

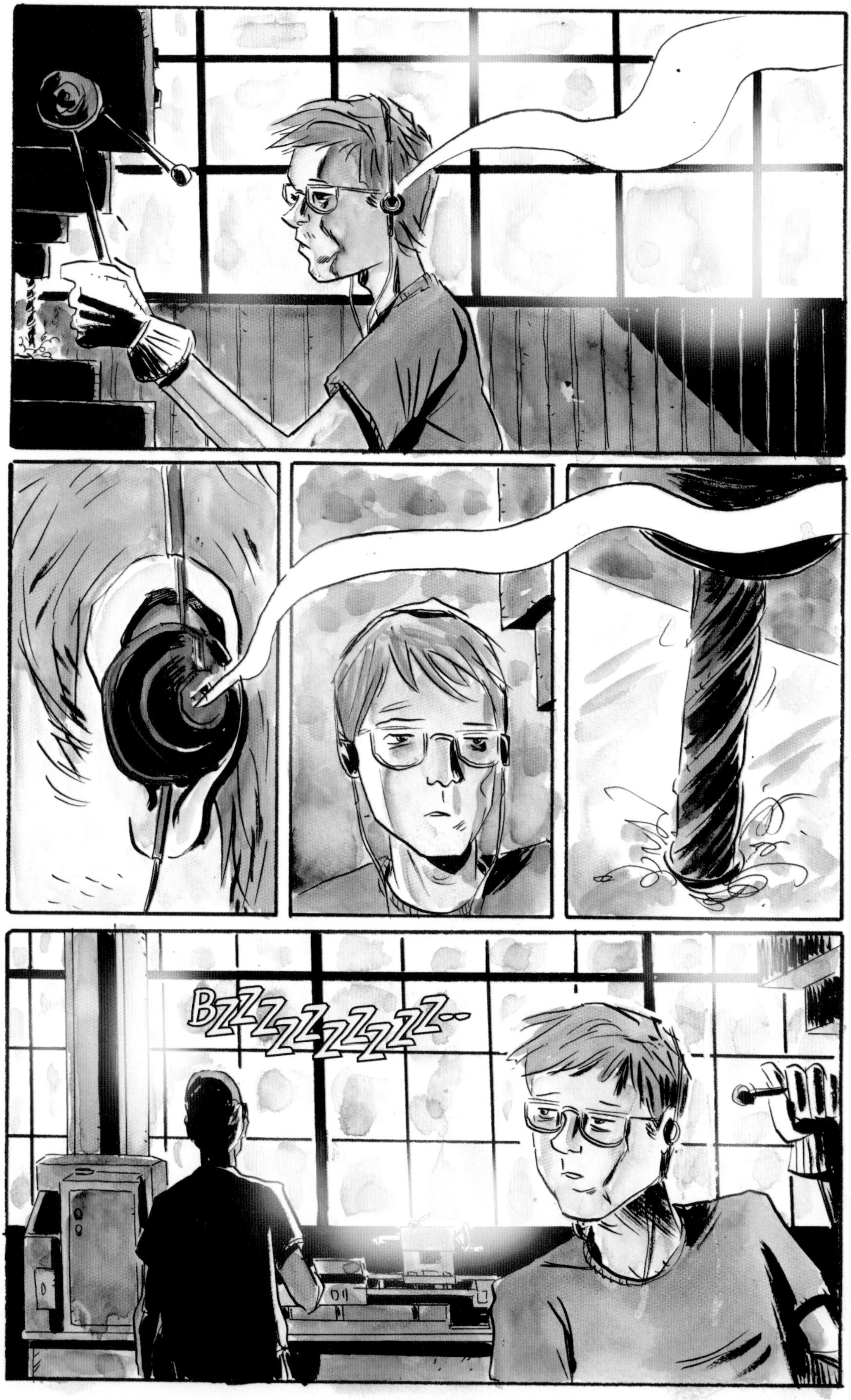
BZZZZZZZZZZ--

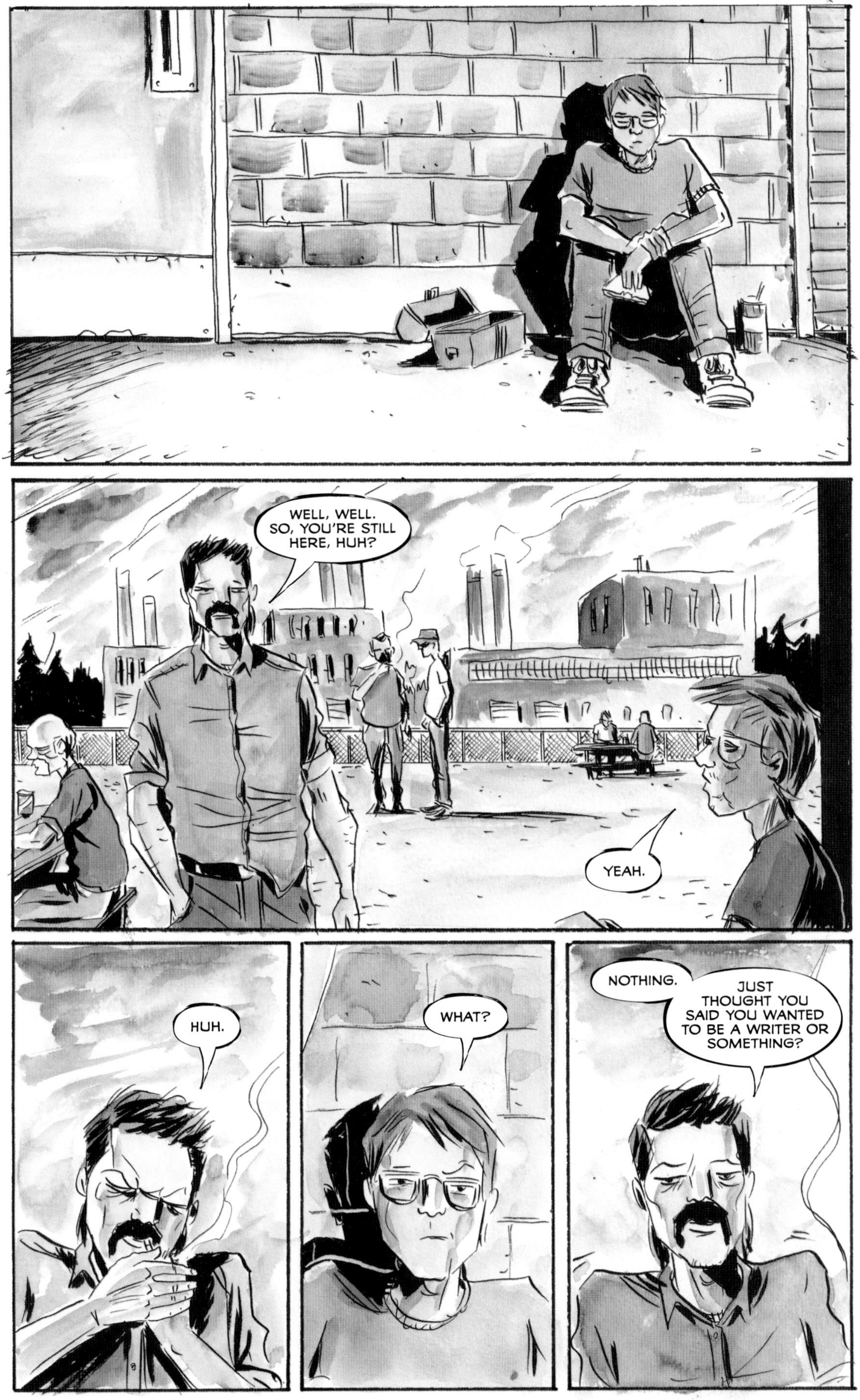
WELL, WELL. SO, YOU'RE STILL HERE, HUH?
YEAH.
HUH.
WHAT?
NOTHING.
JUST THOUGHT YOU SAID YOU WANTED TO BE A WRITER OR SOMETHING?

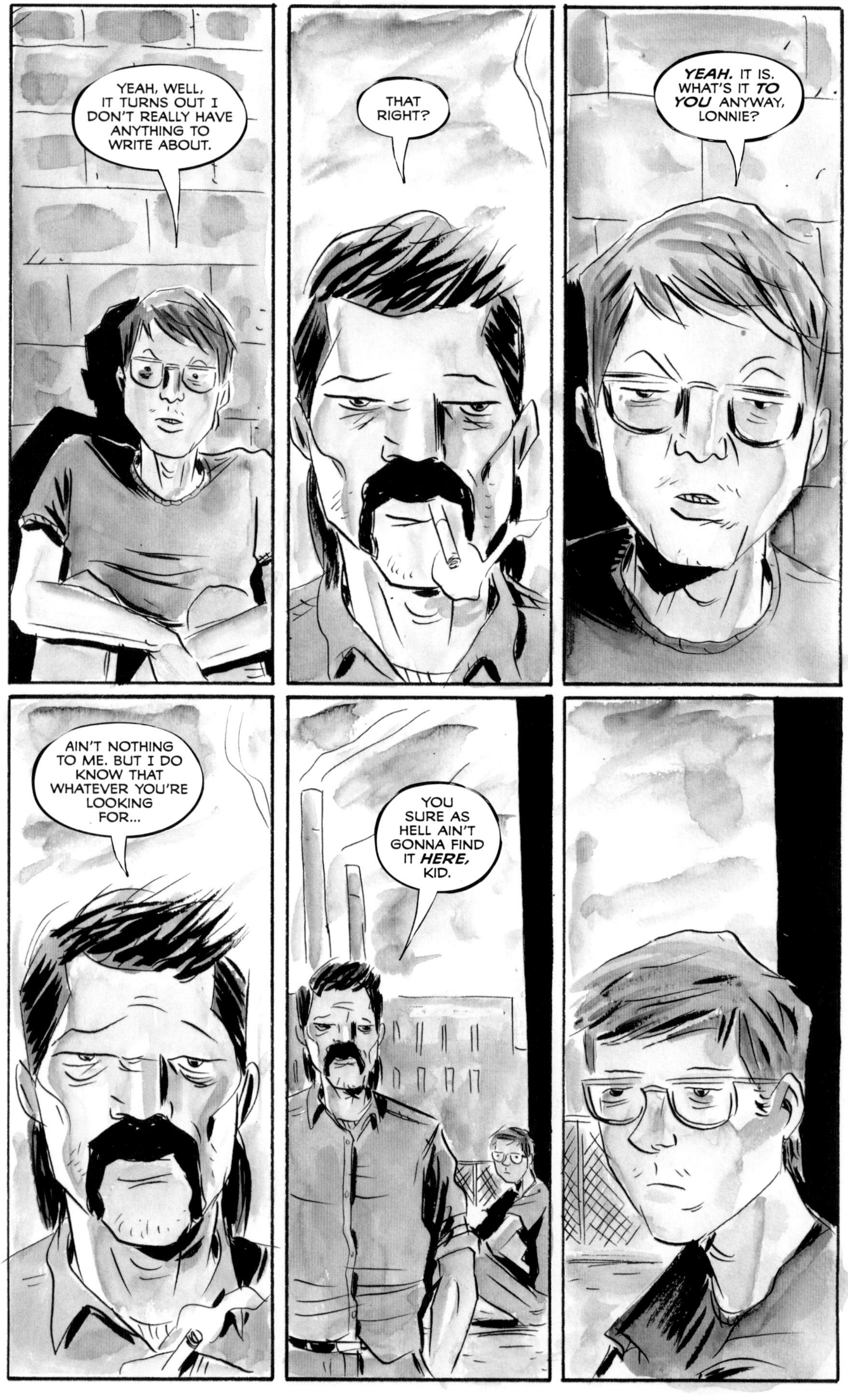
YEAH, WELL, IT TURNS OUT I DON'T REALLY HAVE ANYTHING TO WRITE ABOUT.
THAT RIGHT?
YEAH. IT IS. WHAT'S IT TO YOU ANYWAY, LONNIE?
AIN'T NOTHING TO ME. BUT I DO KNOW THAT WHATEVER YOU'RE LOOKING FOR...
YOU SURE AS HELL AIN'T GONNA FIND IT HERE, KID.

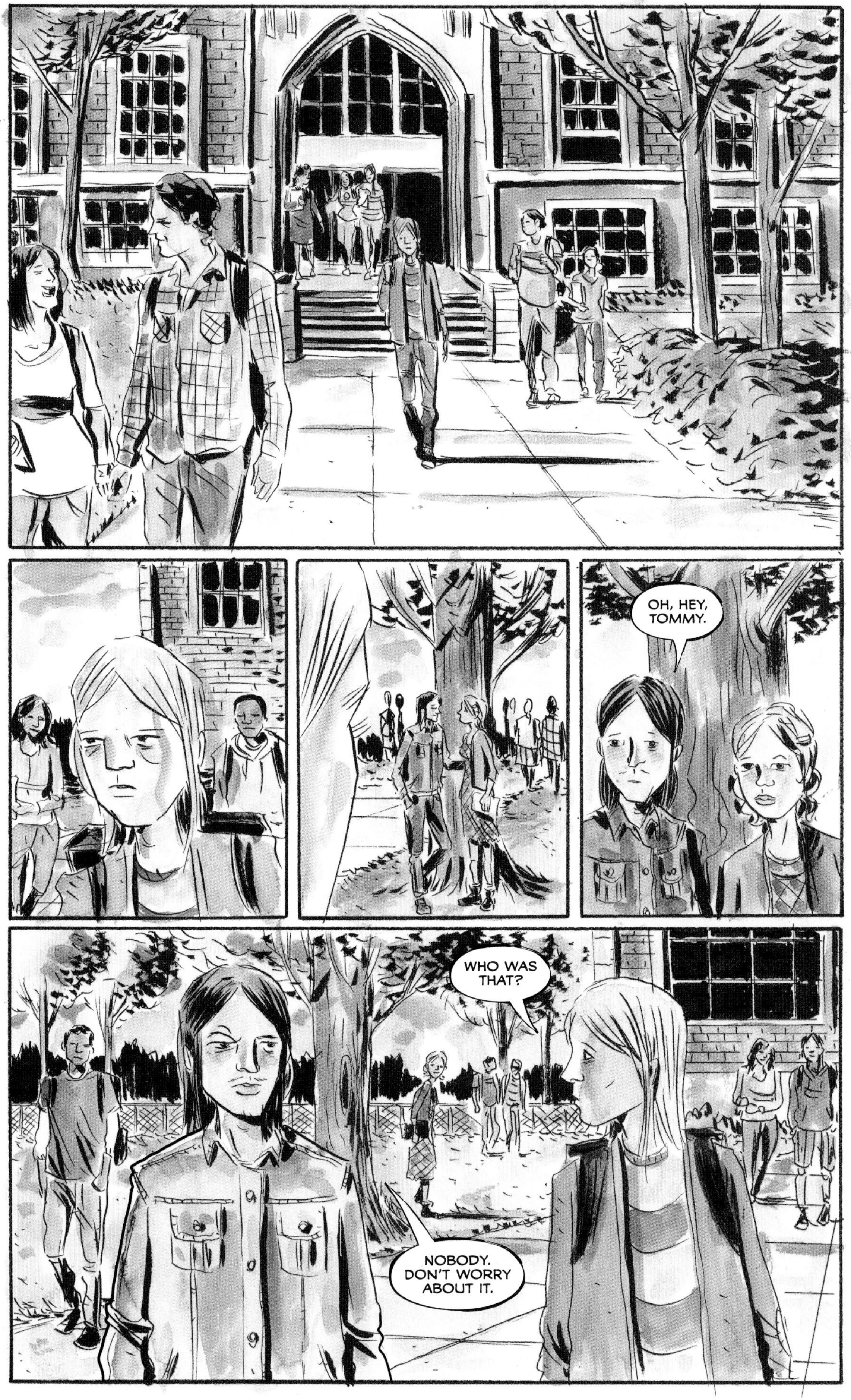
OH, HEY, TOMMY.
WHO WAS THAT?
NOBODY. DON'T WORRY ABOUT IT.

AND DON'T MENTION YOU SAW THAT WHEN YOU'RE AROUND CLARA. GOT IT?
I MEAN IT, TOMMY. IT'S NO BIG DEAL.
OKAY.
GOOD.
OKAY. FINE. I WON'T.
SO THERE IS A BIG PARTY TOMORROW NIGHT AT THE OLD FACTORY OUT ON ROUTE SIX. WANNA COME?
I DON'T KNOW. MAYBE.
COME ON. EVERYONE IS GOING. IT'LL BE FUN.
HEY. WHAT ARE YOU GUYS TALKING ABOUT?
NOTHING YOU WOULD CARE ABOUT.
FUCK OFF, RICHIE.
HE WAS JUST SAYING THAT THERE IS A PARTY AT THE OLD FACTORY TOMORROW. THAT ONE NEAR THE RIVER.

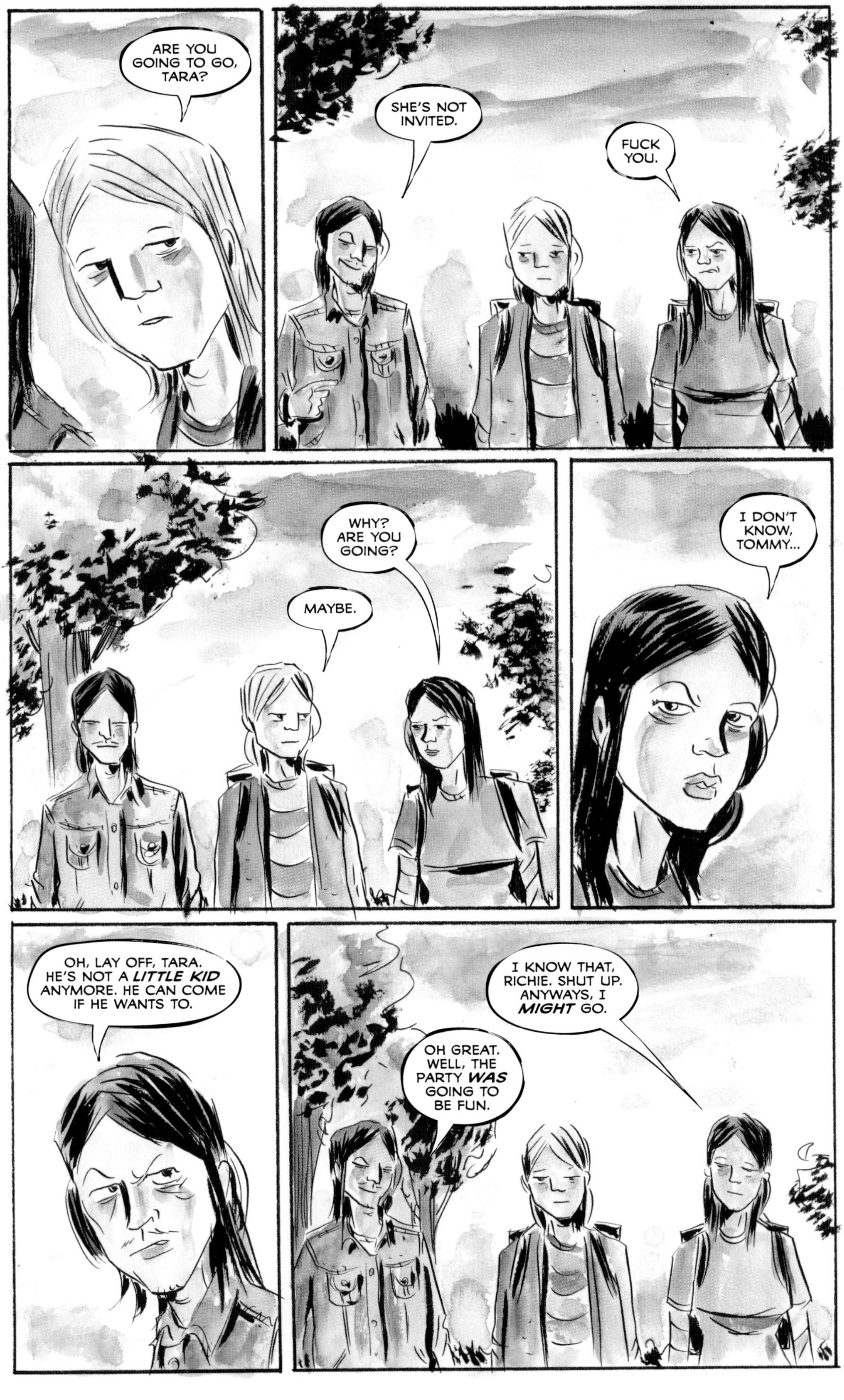
ARE YOU GOING TO GO, TARA?
SHE'S NOT INVITED.
FUCK YOU.
WHY? ARE YOU GOING?
MAYBE.
I DON'T KNOW, TOMMY...
OH, LAY OFF, TARA. HE'S NOT A LITTLE KID ANYMORE. HE CAN COME IF HE WANTS TO.
I KNOW THAT, RICHIE. SHUT UP. ANYWAYS, I MIGHT GO.
OH GREAT. WELL, THE PARTY WAS GOING TO BE FUN.

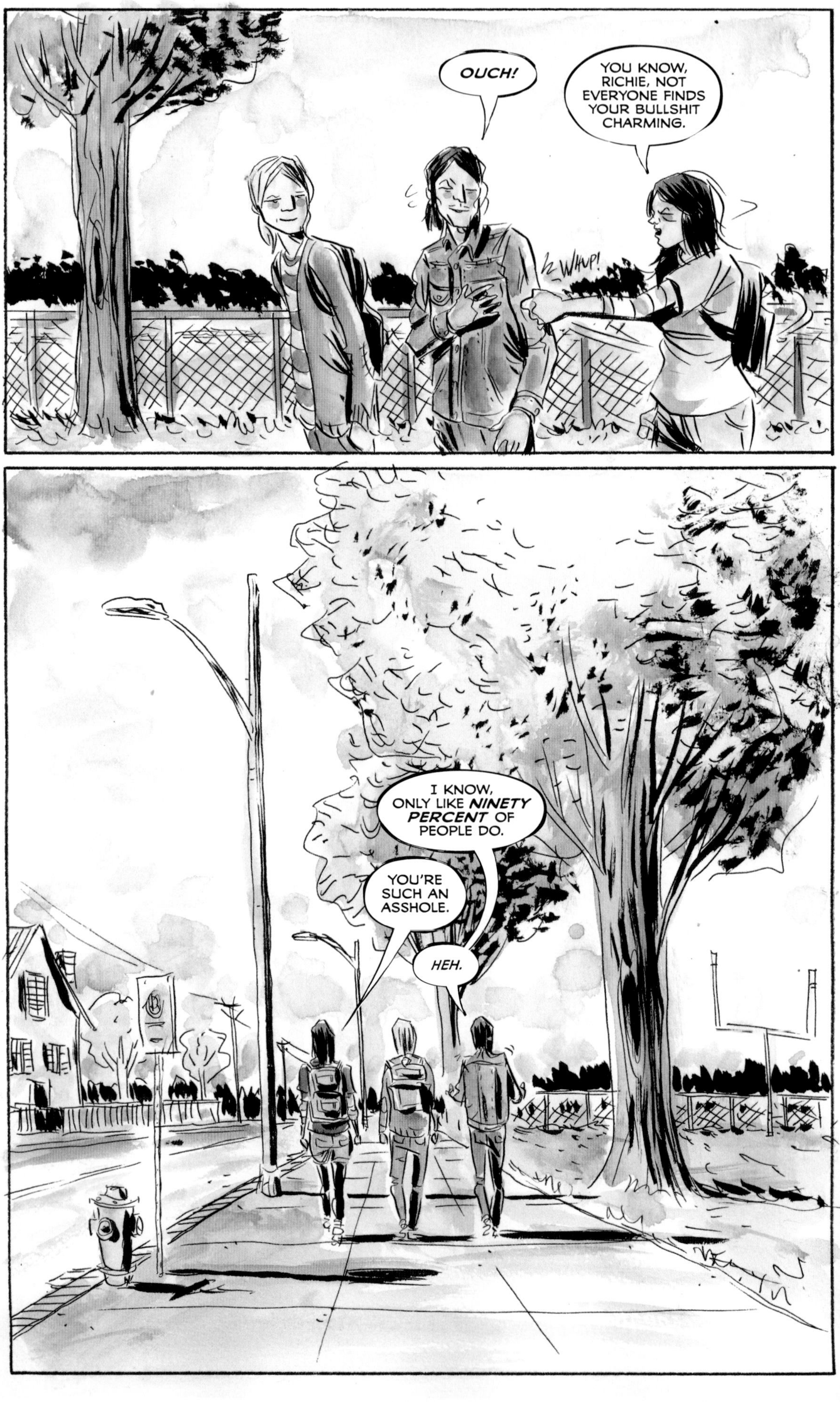
OUCH!
YOU KNOW, RICHIE, NOT EVERYONE FINDS YOUR BULLSHIT CHARMING.
WHUP!
I KNOW, ONLY LIKE NINETY PERCENT OF PEOPLE DO.
YOU'RE SUCH AN ASSHOLE.
HEH.

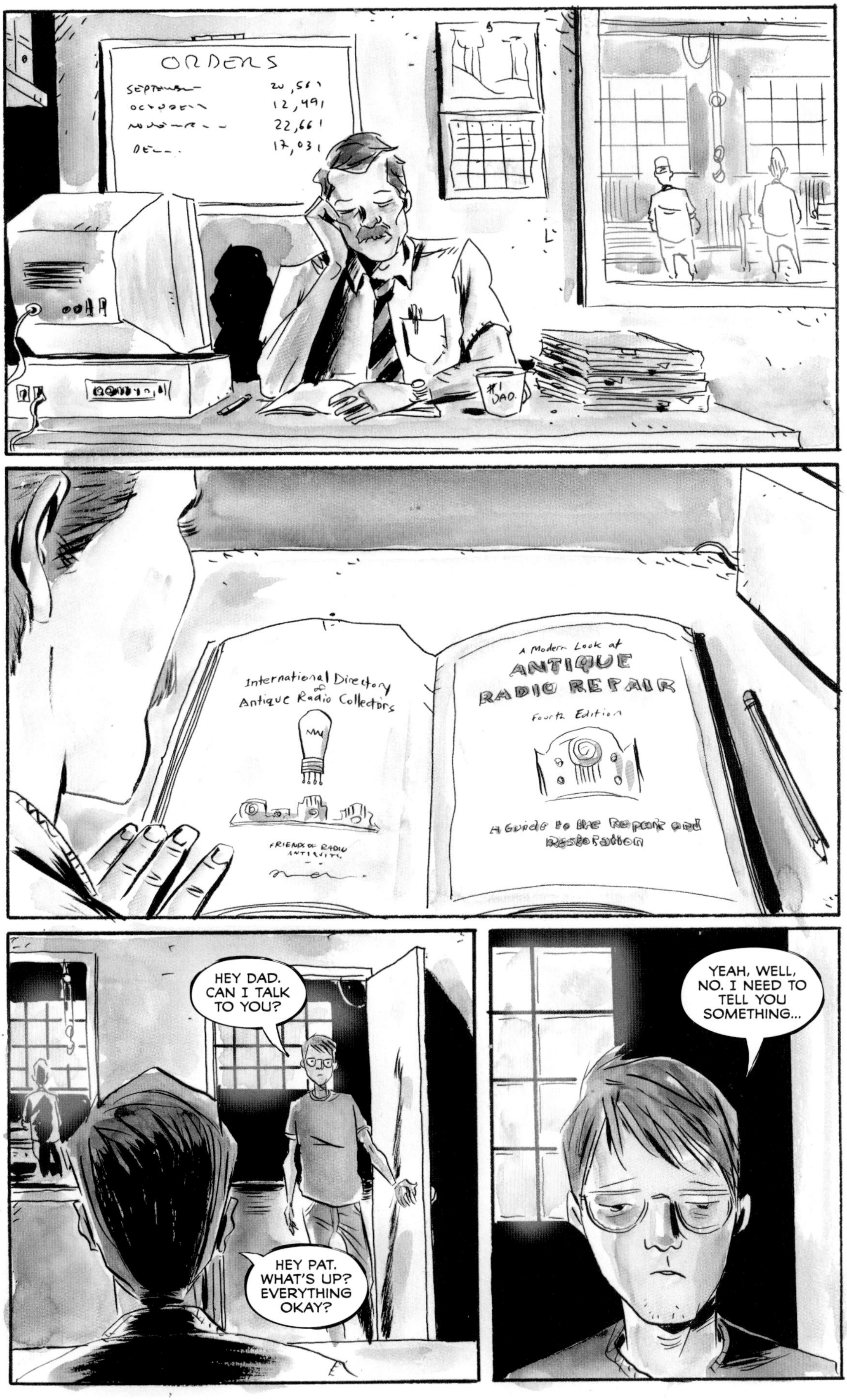
ORDERS
International Directory of Antique Radio Collectors
A Modern Look at
ANTIQUE RADIO REPAIR
Fourth Edition
HEY DAD. CAN I TALK TO YOU?
HEY PAT. WHAT'S UP? EVERYTHING OKAY?
YEAH, WELL, NO. I NEED TO TELL YOU SOMETHING...

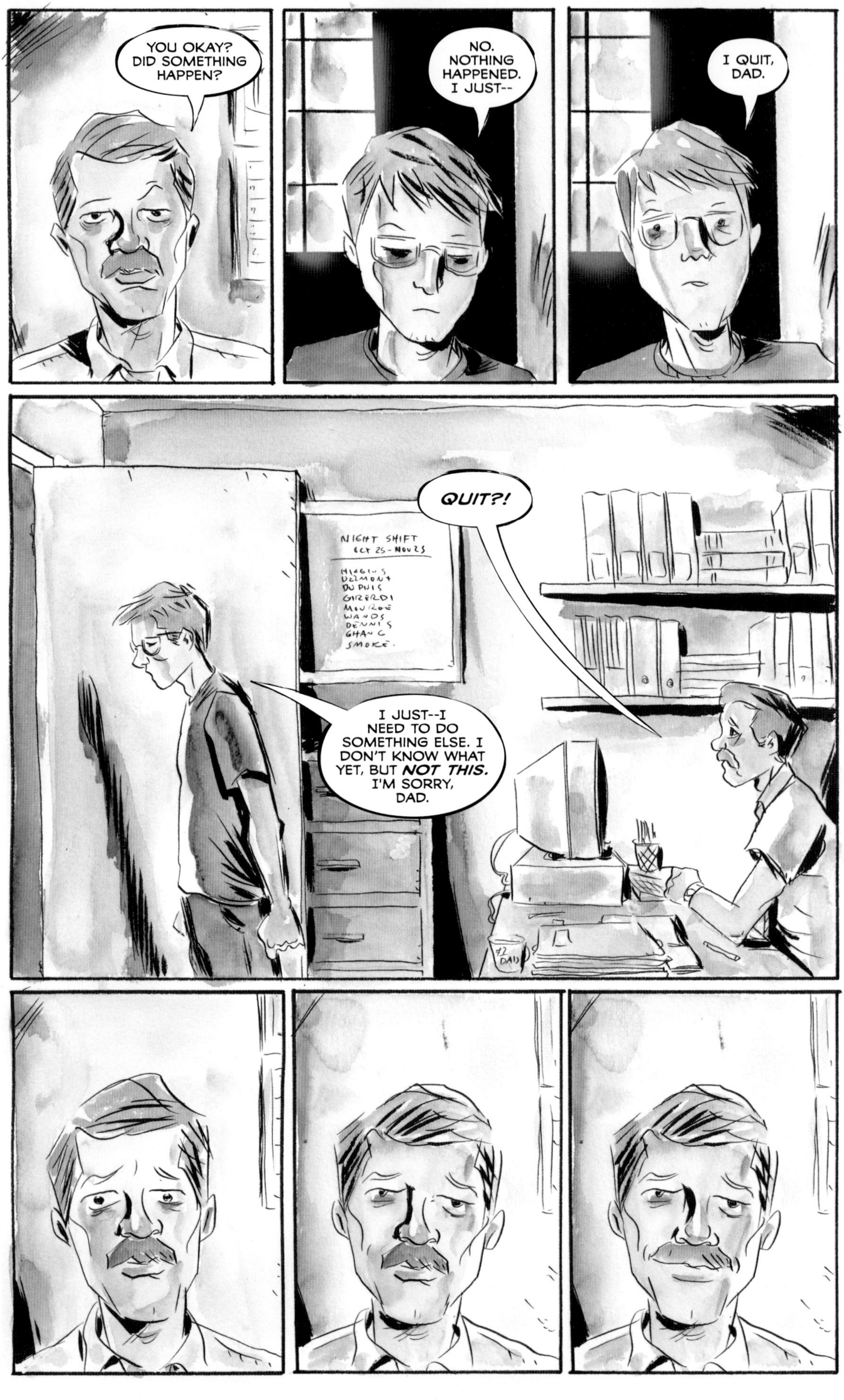

YOU OKAY? DID SOMETHING HAPPEN?
NO. NOTHING HAPPENED. I JUST--
I QUIT, DAD.
NIGHT SHIFT
QUIT?!
I JUST--I NEED TO DO SOMETHING ELSE. I DON'T KNOW WHAT YET, BUT ***NOT THIS.*** I'M SORRY, DAD.

CHAPTER TEN

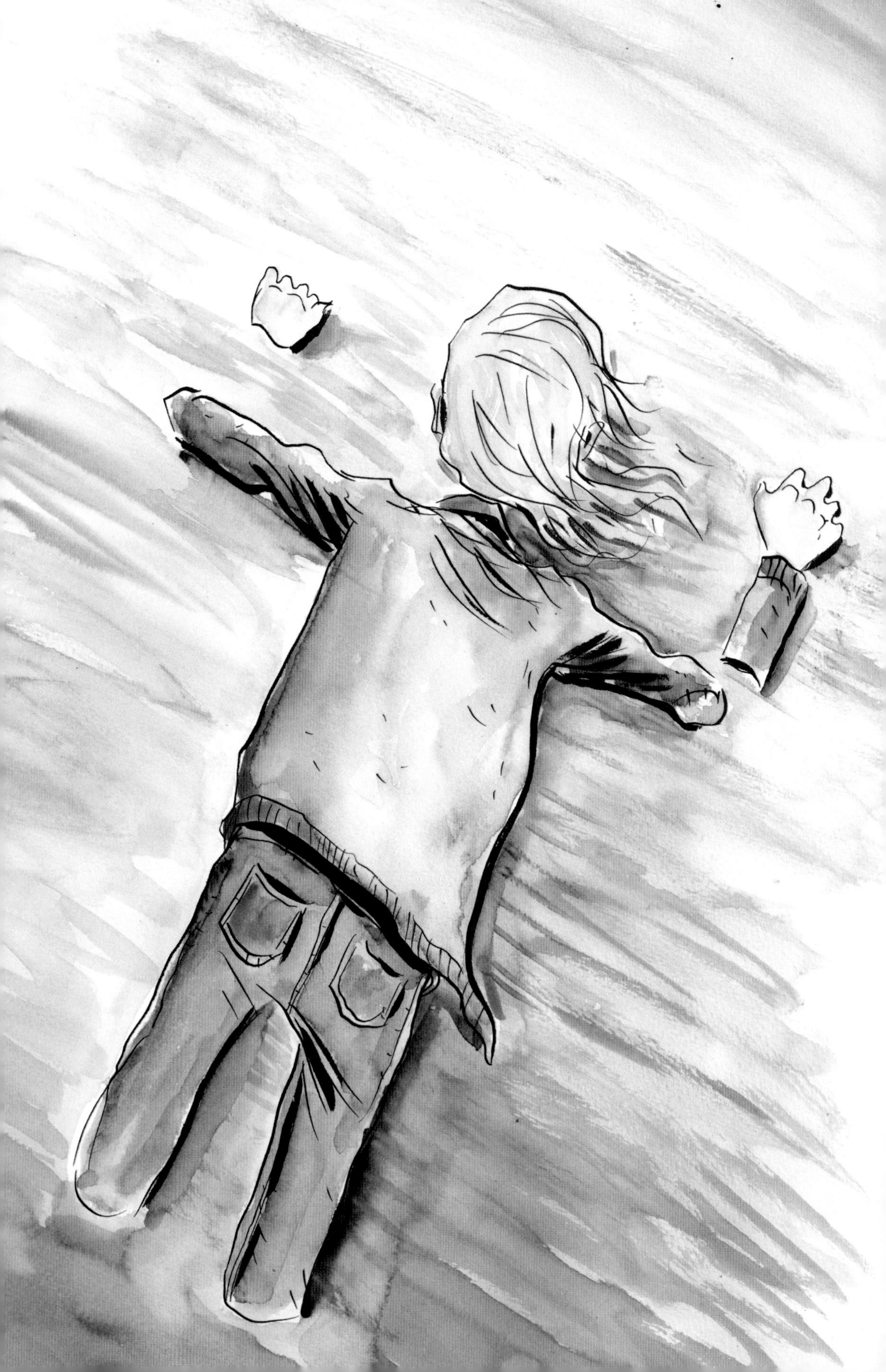

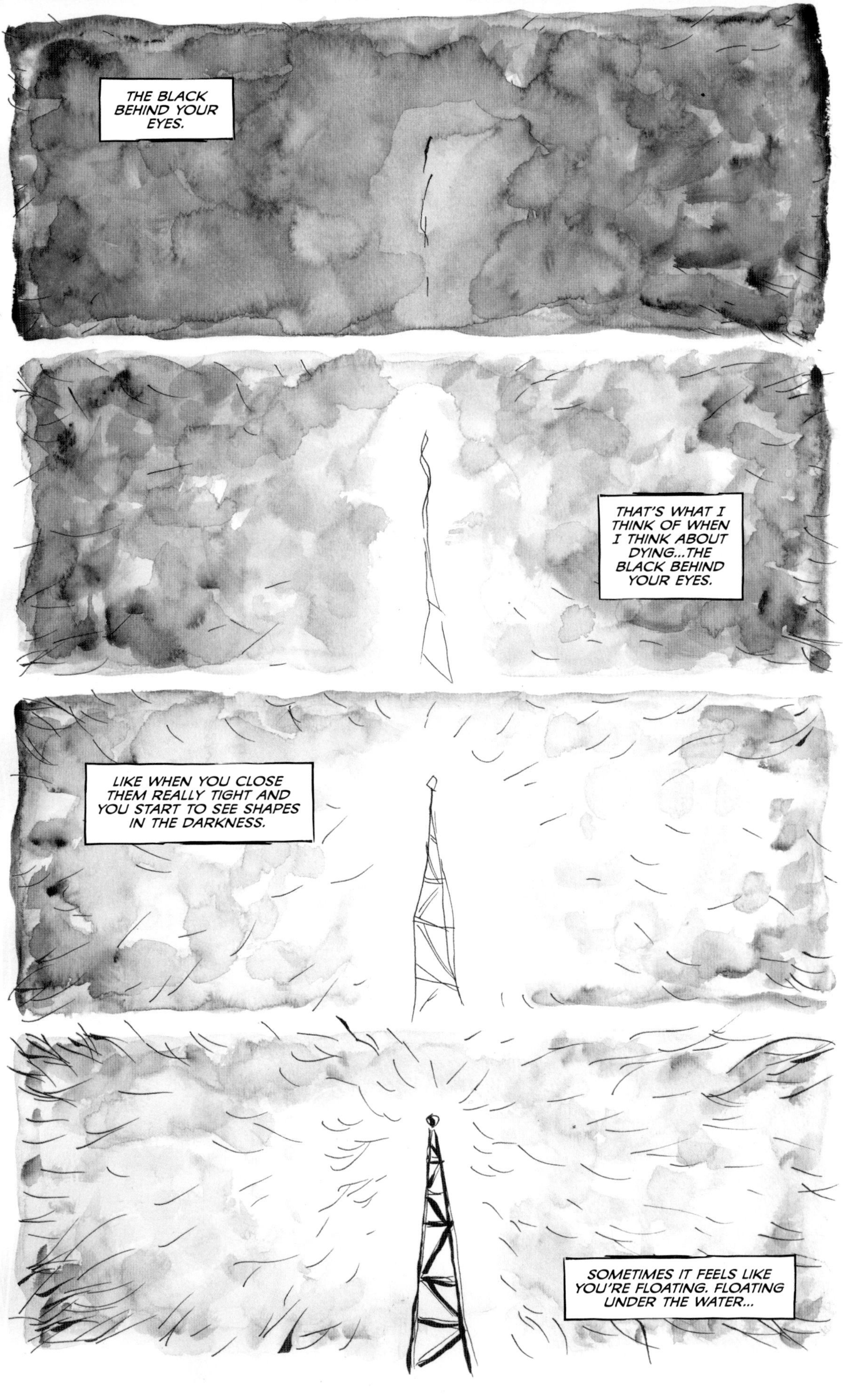
THE BLACK BEHIND YOUR EYES.
THAT'S WHAT I THINK OF WHEN I THINK ABOUT DYING...THE BLACK BEHIND YOUR EYES.
LIKE WHEN YOU CLOSE THEM REALLY TIGHT AND YOU START TO SEE SHAPES IN THE DARKNESS.
SOMETIMES IT FEELS LIKE YOU'RE FLOATING. FLOATING UNDER THE WATER...

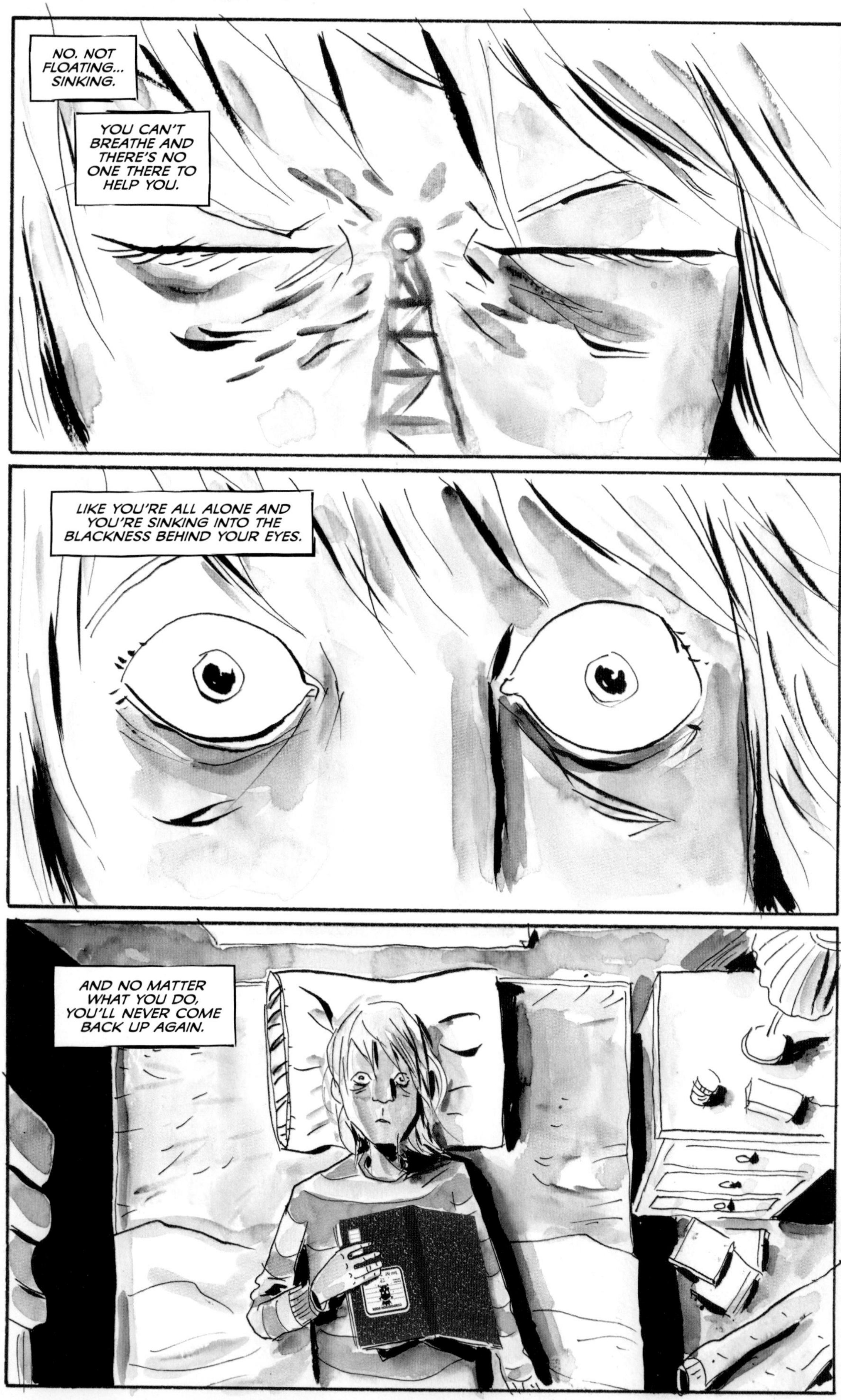
NO, NOT FLOATING... SINKING.
YOU CAN'T BREATHE AND THERE'S NO ONE THERE TO HELP YOU.
LIKE YOU'RE ALL ALONE AND YOU'RE SINKING INTO THE BLACKNESS BEHIND YOUR EYES.
AND NO MATTER WHAT YOU DO, YOU'LL NEVER COME BACK UP AGAIN.

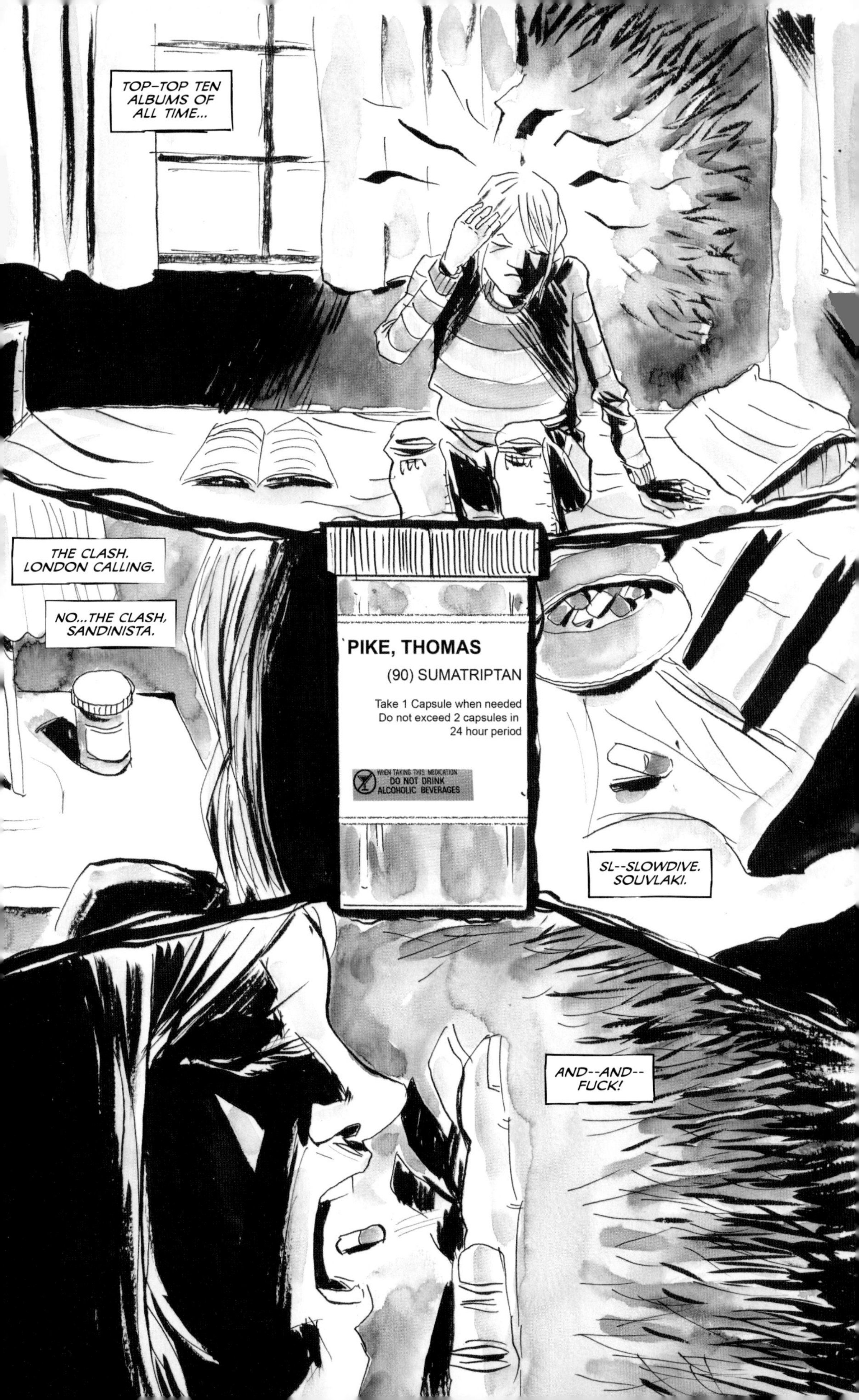
TOP-TOP TEN ALBUMS OF ALL TIME...
THE CLASH. LONDON CALLING.
NO...THE CLASH, SANDINISTA.
PIKE, THOMAS
(90) SUMATRIPTAN
Take 1 Capsule when needed
Do not exceed 2 capsules in 24 hour period
WHEN TAKING THIS MEDICATION DO NOT DRINK ALCOHOLIC BEVERAGES
SL--SLOWDIVE. SOUVLAKI.
AND--AND-- FUCK!

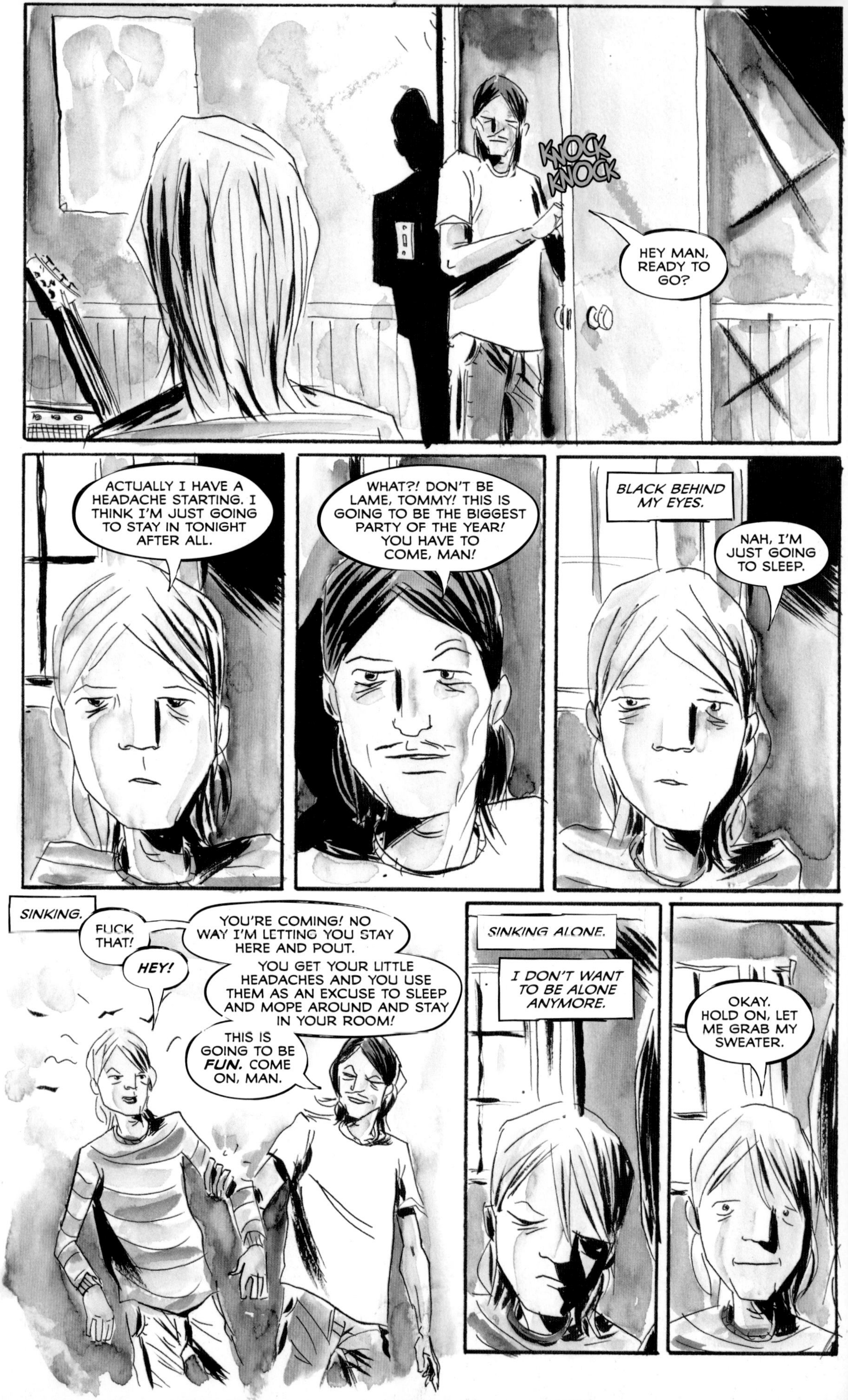
KNOCK KNOCK
HEY MAN, READY TO GO?
ACTUALLY I HAVE A HEADACHE STARTING. I THINK I'M JUST GOING TO STAY IN TONIGHT AFTER ALL.
WHAT?! DON'T BE LAME, TOMMY! THIS IS GOING TO BE THE BIGGEST PARTY OF THE YEAR! YOU HAVE TO COME, MAN!
BLACK BEHIND MY EYES.
NAH, I'M JUST GOING TO SLEEP.
SINKING.
FUCK THAT!
YOU'RE COMING! NO WAY I'M LETTING YOU STAY HERE AND POUT.
HEY!
YOU GET YOUR LITTLE HEADACHES AND YOU USE THEM AS AN EXCUSE TO SLEEP AND MOPE AROUND AND STAY IN YOUR ROOM!
THIS IS GOING TO BE FUN. COME ON, MAN.
SINKING ALONE.
I DON'T WANT TO BE ALONE ANYMORE.
OKAY. HOLD ON, LET ME GRAB MY SWEATER.

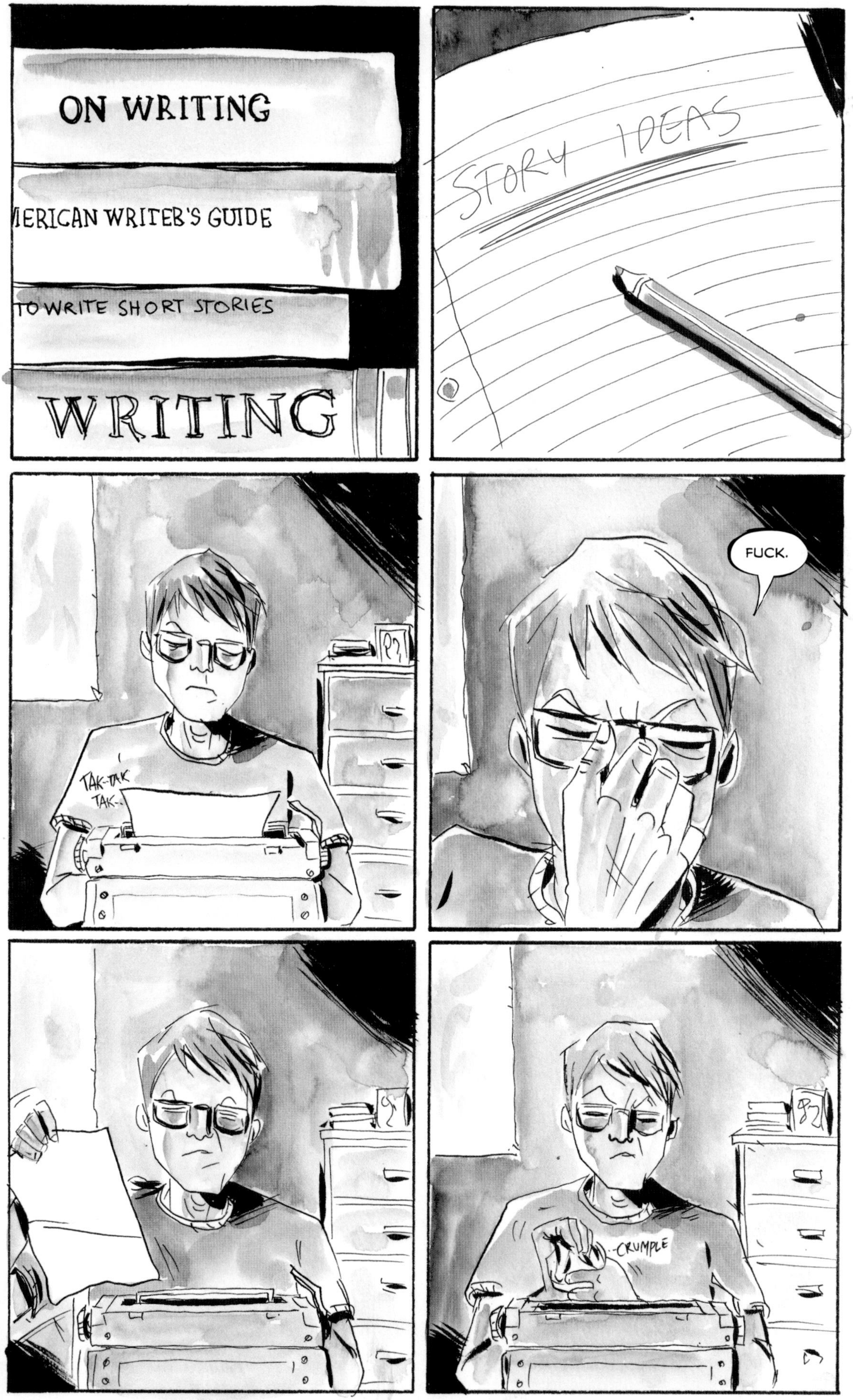
ON WRITING
IERICAN WRITER'S GUIDE
TO WRITE SHORT STORIES
WRITING
STORY IDEAS
TAK-TAK
TAK...
FUCK.
CRUMPLE

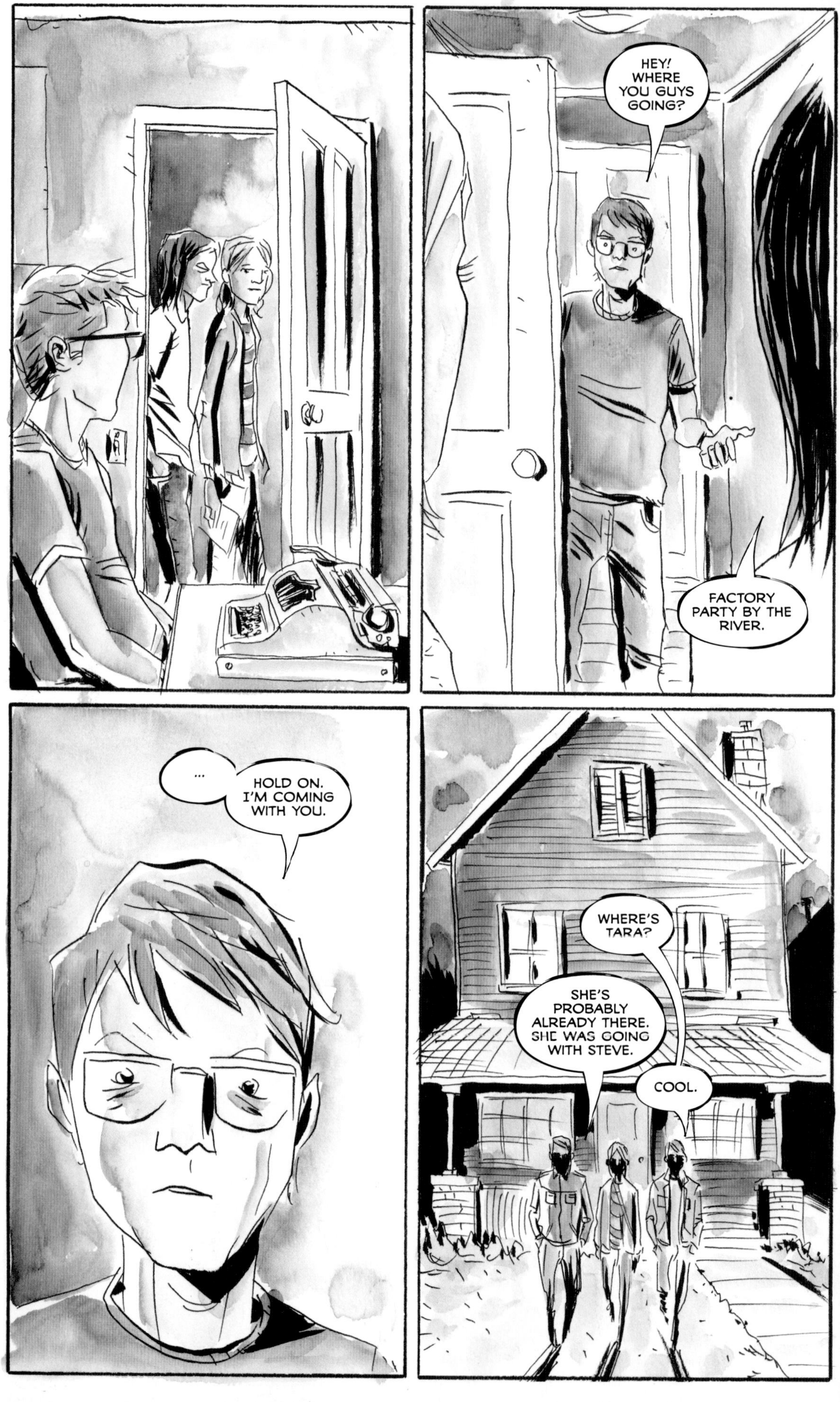
HEY! WHERE YOU GUYS GOING?
FACTORY PARTY BY THE RIVER.
...
HOLD ON. I'M COMING WITH YOU.
WHERE'S TARA?
SHE'S PROBABLY ALREADY THERE. SHE WAS GOING WITH STEVE.
COOL.

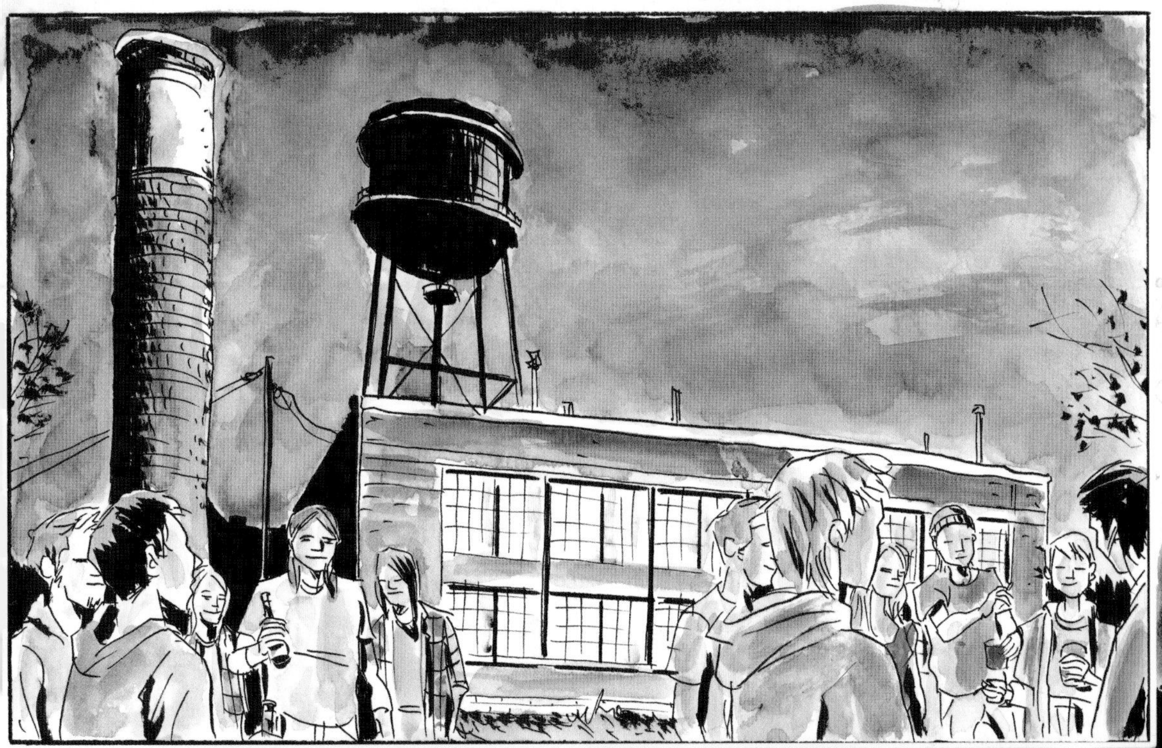

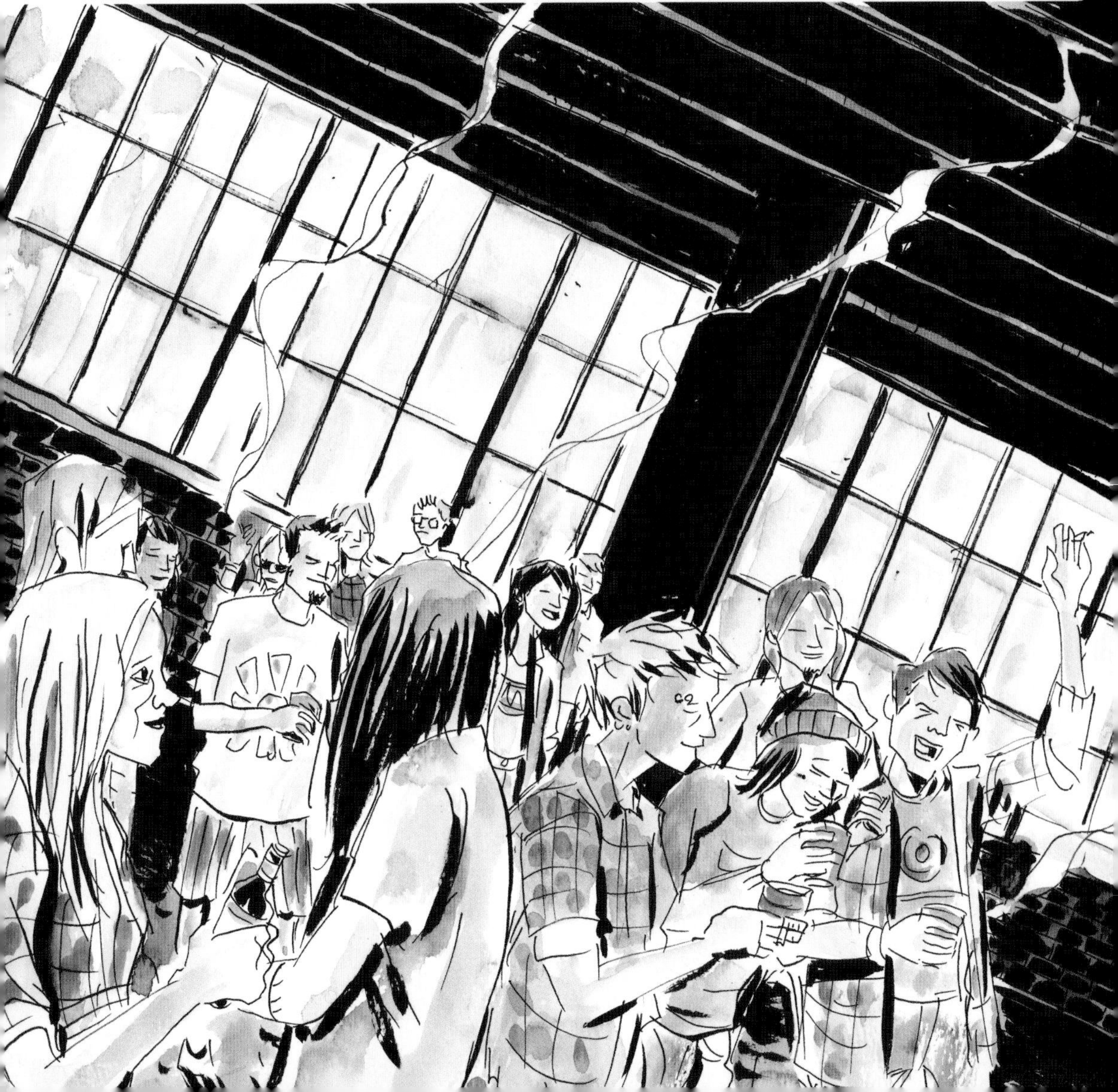

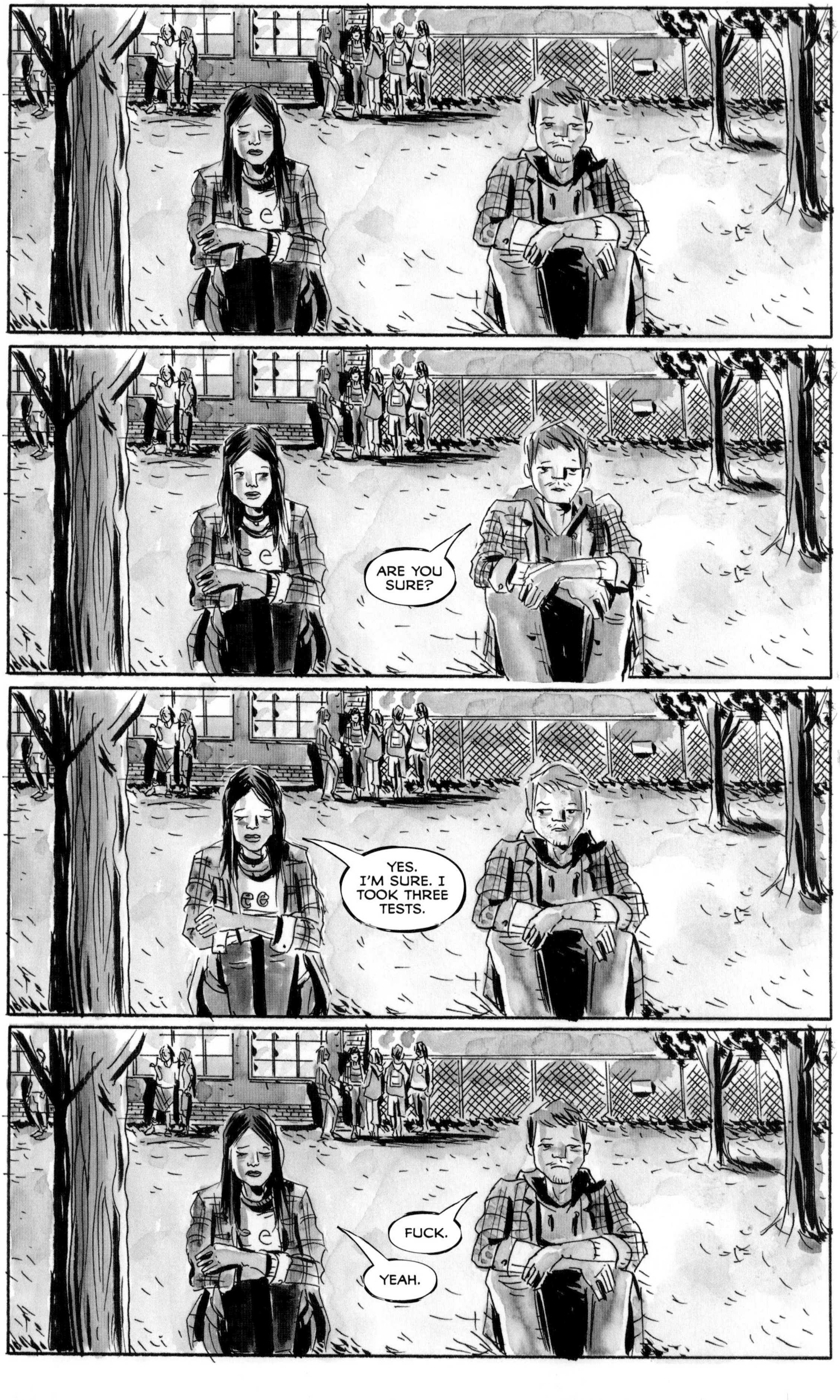
ARE YOU SURE?
YES. I'M SURE. I TOOK THREE TESTS.
FUCK.
YEAH.

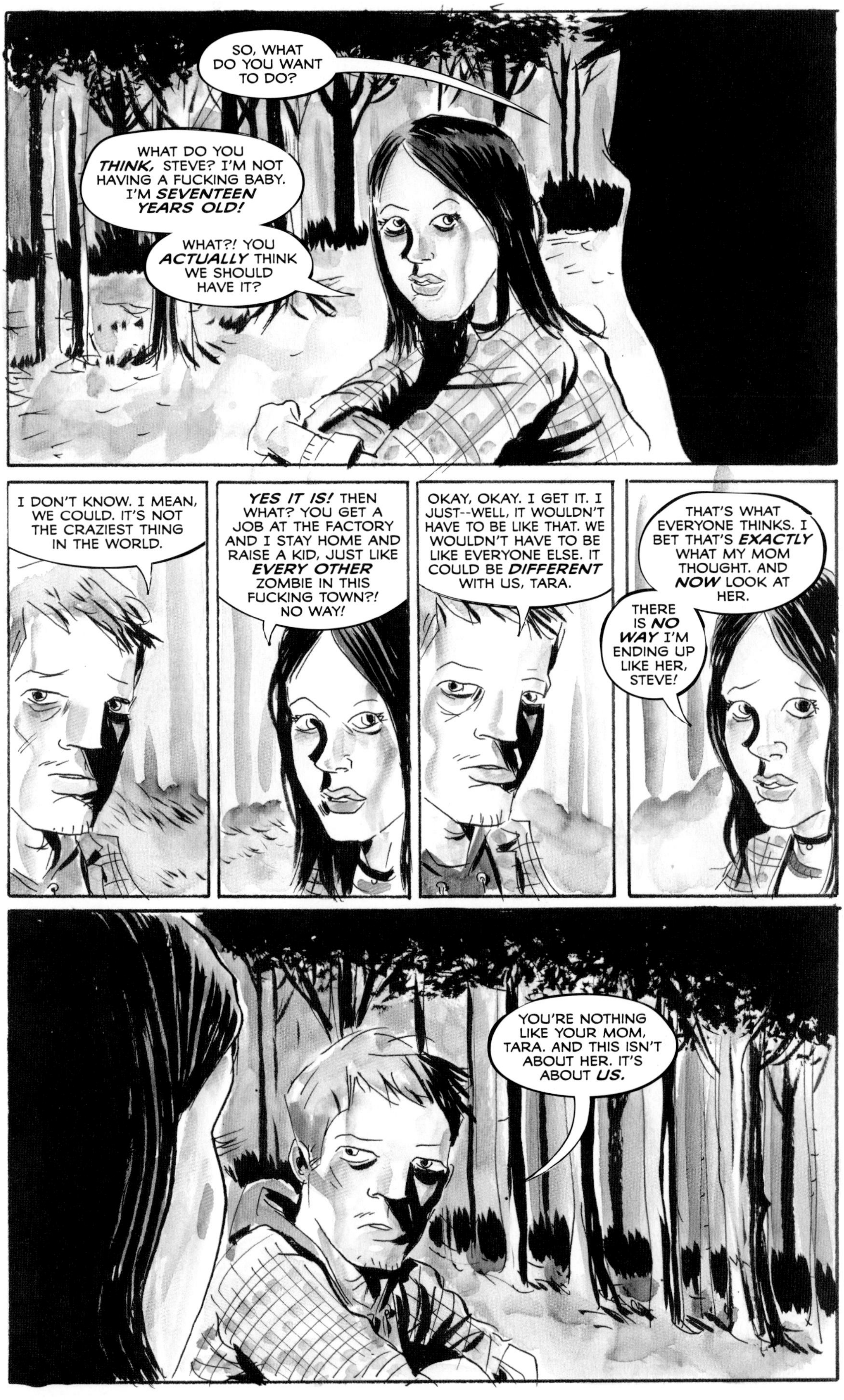
SO, WHAT DO YOU WANT TO DO?
WHAT DO YOU *THINK,* STEVE? I'M NOT HAVING A FUCKING BABY. I'M *SEVENTEEN YEARS OLD!*
WHAT?! YOU *ACTUALLY* THINK WE SHOULD HAVE IT?
I DON'T KNOW. I MEAN, WE COULD. IT'S NOT THE CRAZIEST THING IN THE WORLD.
YES IT IS! THEN WHAT? YOU GET A JOB AT THE FACTORY AND I STAY HOME AND RAISE A KID, JUST LIKE *EVERY OTHER* ZOMBIE IN THIS FUCKING TOWN?! NO WAY!
OKAY, OKAY. I GET IT. I JUST--WELL, IT WOULDN'T HAVE TO BE LIKE THAT. WE WOULDN'T HAVE TO BE LIKE EVERYONE ELSE. IT COULD BE *DIFFERENT* WITH US, TARA.
THAT'S WHAT EVERYONE THINKS. I BET THAT'S *EXACTLY* WHAT MY MOM THOUGHT. AND *NOW* LOOK AT HER.
THERE IS *NO WAY* I'M ENDING UP LIKE HER, STEVE!
YOU'RE NOTHING LIKE YOUR MOM, TARA. AND THIS ISN'T ABOUT HER. IT'S ABOUT *US.*

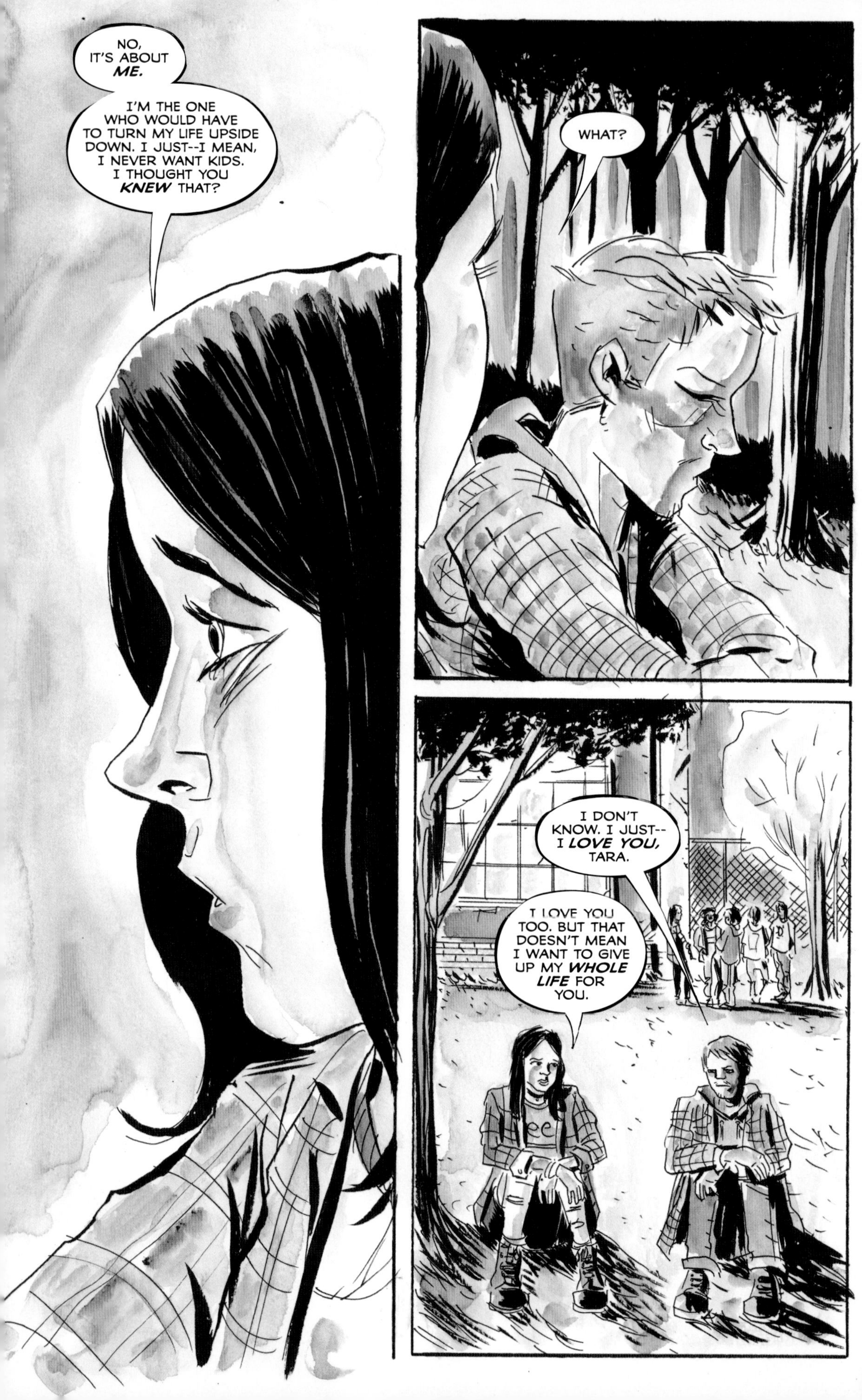
NO, IT'S ABOUT *ME.*
I'M THE ONE WHO WOULD HAVE TO TURN MY LIFE UPSIDE DOWN. I JUST--I MEAN, I NEVER WANT KIDS. I THOUGHT YOU *KNEW* THAT?
WHAT?
I DON'T KNOW. I JUST-- I *LOVE YOU,* TARA.
I LOVE YOU TOO. BUT THAT DOESN'T MEAN I WANT TO GIVE UP MY *WHOLE LIFE* FOR YOU.

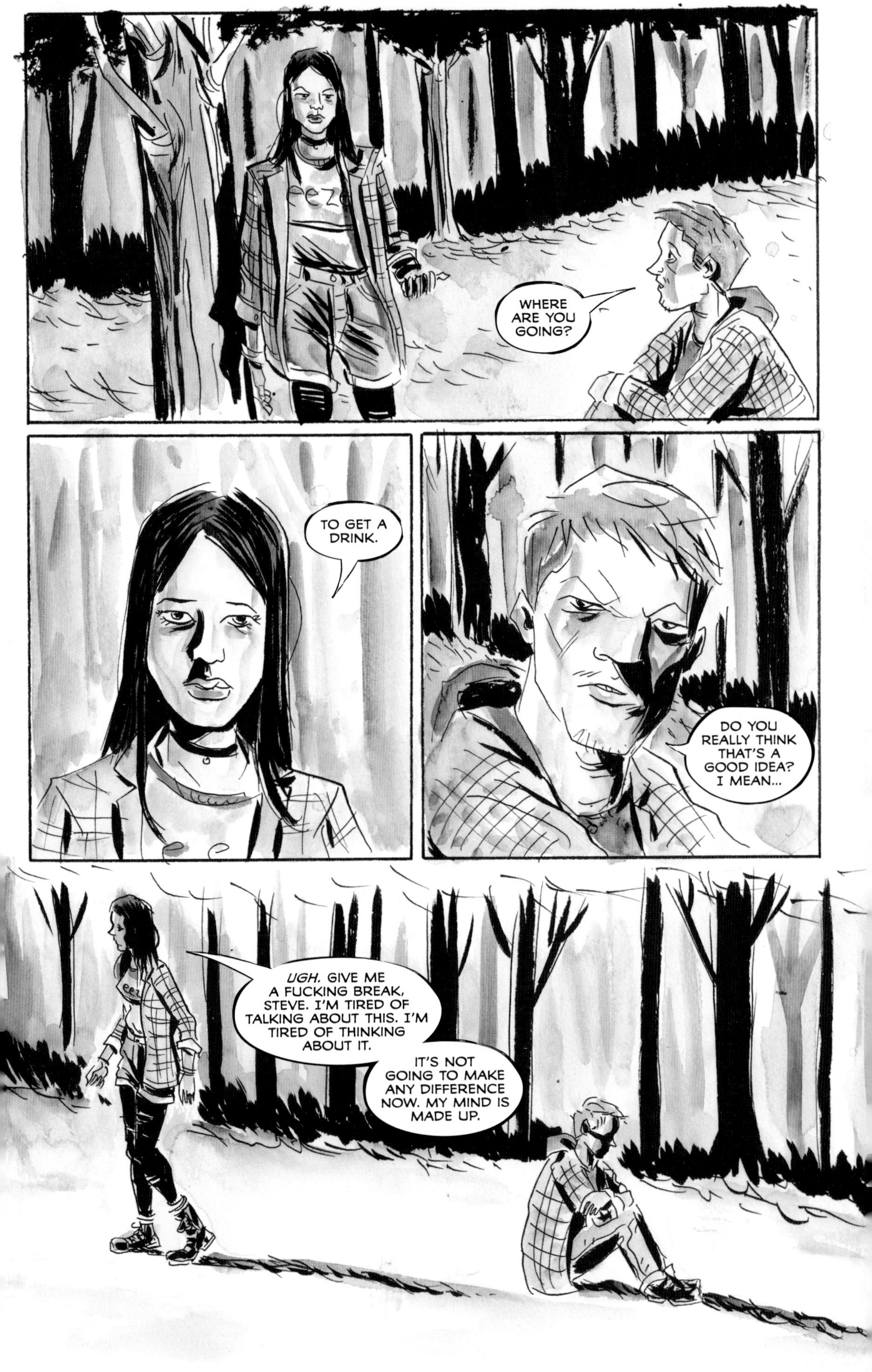
WHERE ARE YOU GOING?
TO GET A DRINK.
DO YOU REALLY THINK THAT'S A GOOD IDEA? I MEAN...
UGH. GIVE ME A FUCKING BREAK, STEVE. I'M TIRED OF TALKING ABOUT THIS. I'M TIRED OF THINKING ABOUT IT.
IT'S NOT GOING TO MAKE ANY DIFFERENCE NOW. MY MIND IS MADE UP.

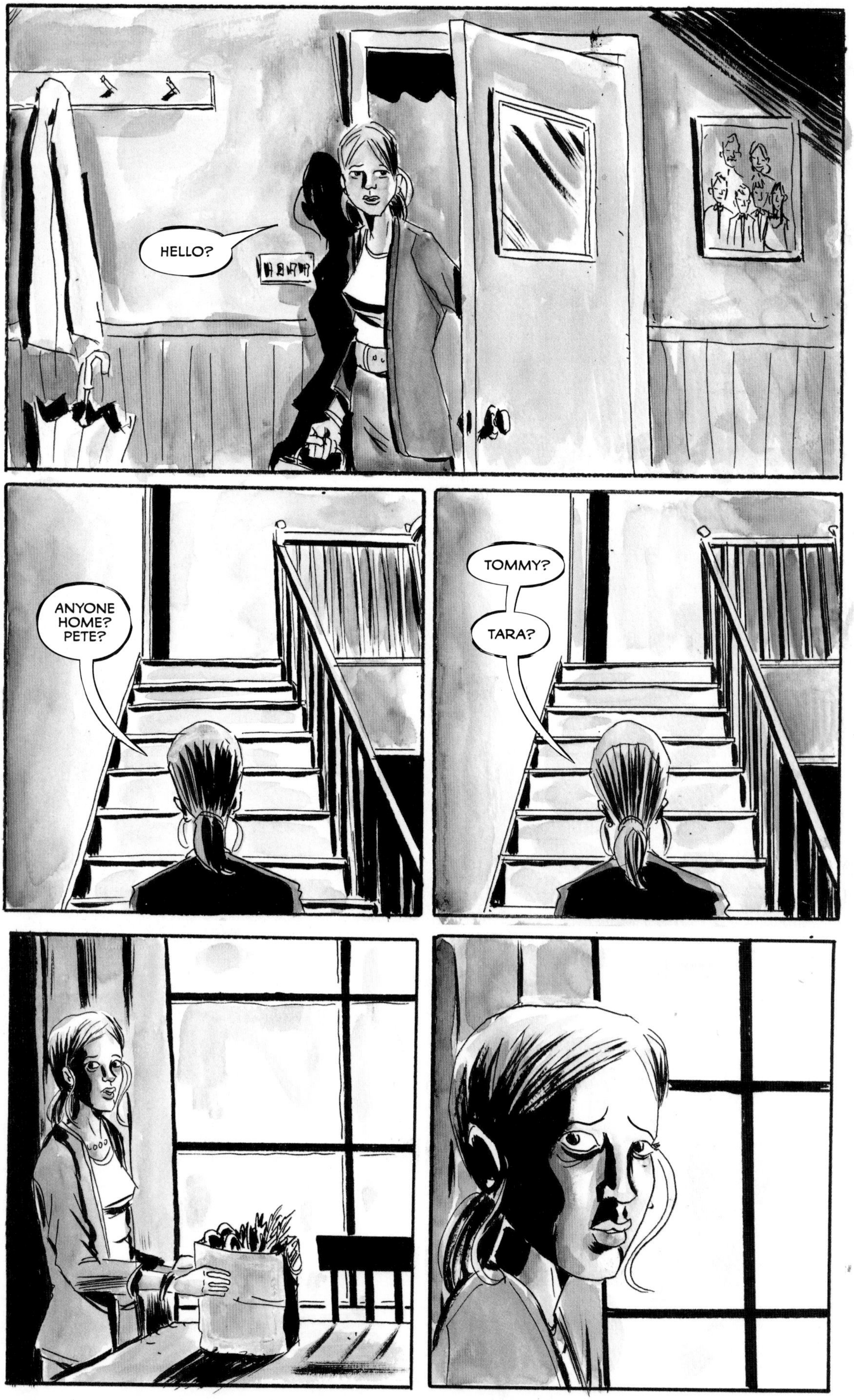
HELLO?
ANYONE HOME? PETE?
TOMMY?
TARA?

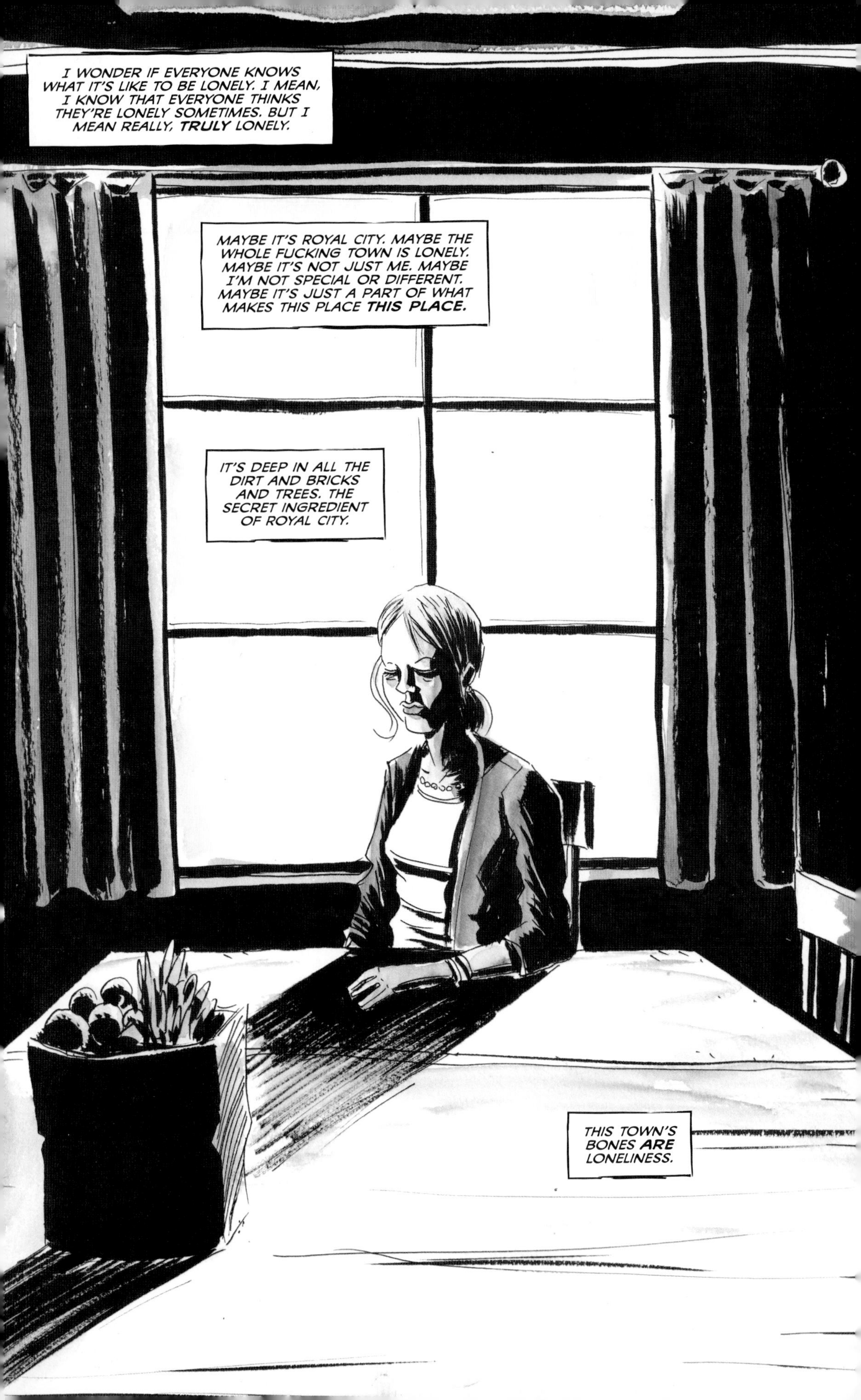
I WONDER IF EVERYONE KNOWS WHAT IT'S LIKE TO BE LONELY. I MEAN, I KNOW THAT EVERYONE THINKS THEY'RE LONELY SOMETIMES. BUT I MEAN REALLY, **TRULY** LONELY.
MAYBE IT'S ROYAL CITY. MAYBE THE WHOLE FUCKING TOWN IS LONELY. MAYBE IT'S NOT JUST ME. MAYBE I'M NOT SPECIAL OR DIFFERENT. MAYBE IT'S JUST A PART OF WHAT MAKES THIS PLACE **THIS PLACE.**
IT'S DEEP IN ALL THE DIRT AND BRICKS AND TREES. THE SECRET INGREDIENT OF ROYAL CITY.
THIS TOWN'S BONES **ARE** LONELINESS.

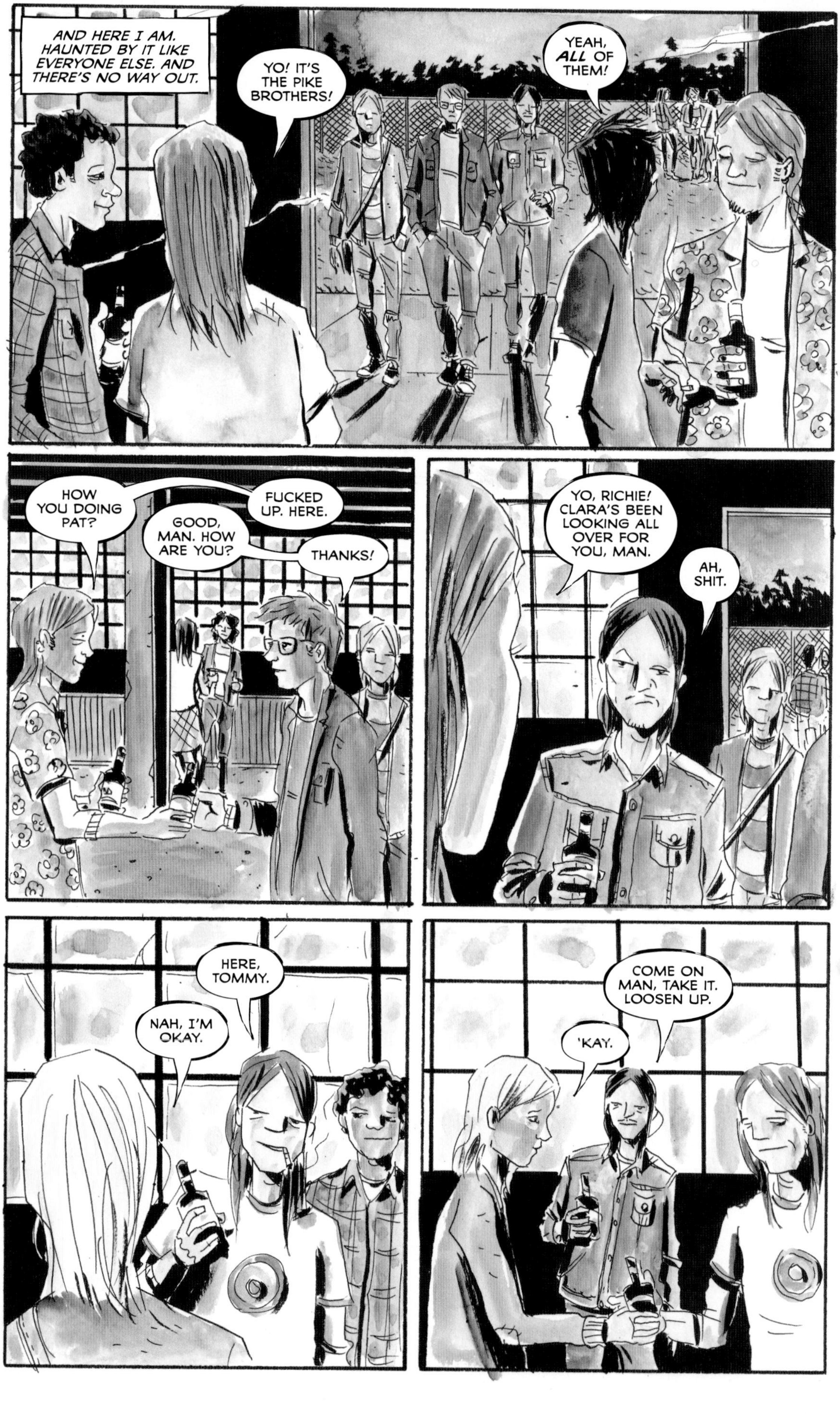
AND HERE I AM. HAUNTED BY IT LIKE EVERYONE ELSE. AND THERE'S NO WAY OUT.
YO! IT'S THE PIKE BROTHERS!
YEAH, ALL OF THEM!
HOW YOU DOING PAT?
FUCKED UP. HERE.
GOOD, MAN. HOW ARE YOU?
THANKS!
YO, RICHIE! CLARA'S BEEN LOOKING ALL OVER FOR YOU, MAN.
AH, SHIT.
HERE, TOMMY.
NAH, I'M OKAY.
COME ON MAN, TAKE IT. LOOSEN UP.
'KAY.

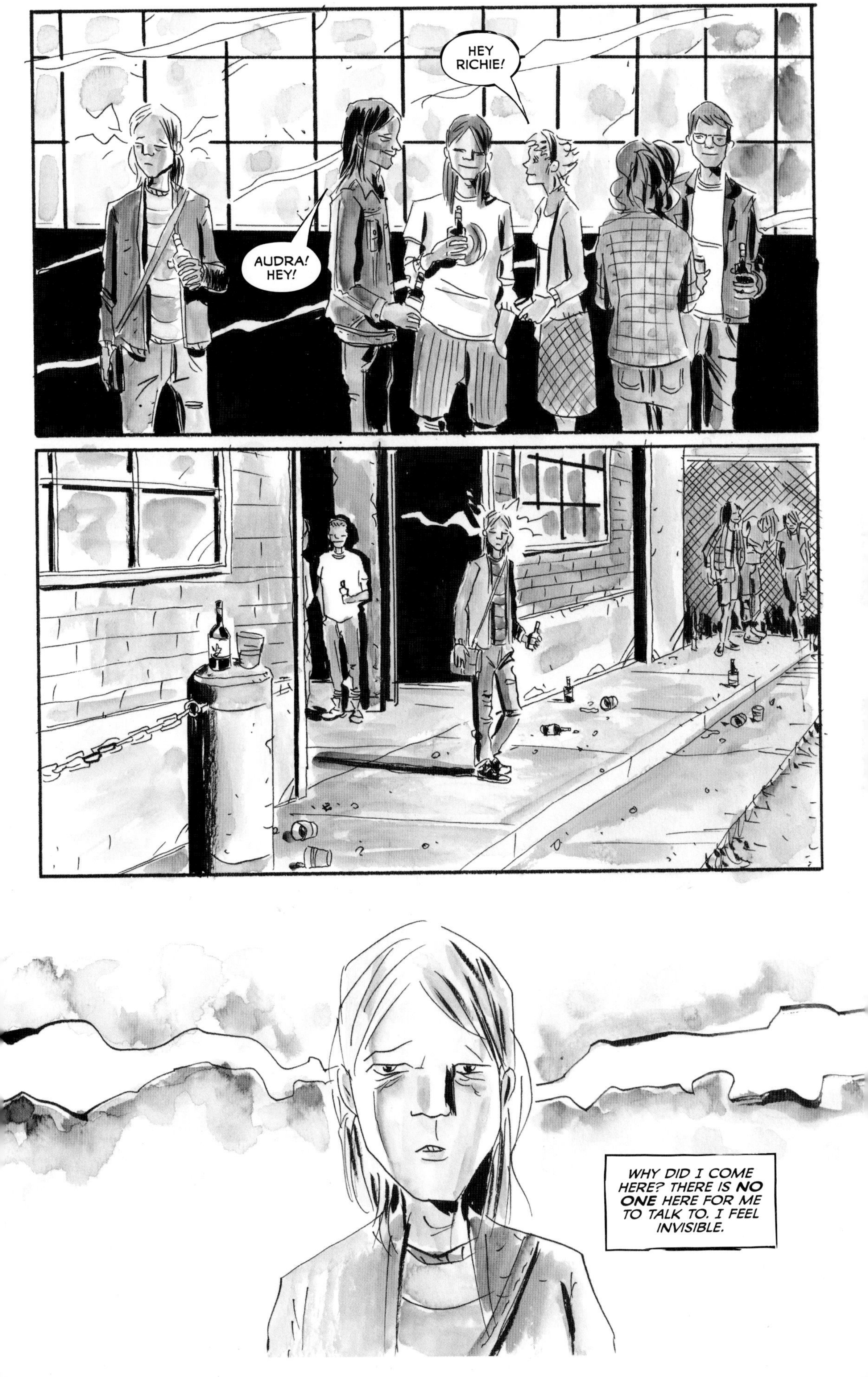
AUDRA! HEY!
HEY RICHIE!
WHY DID I COME HERE? THERE IS **NO ONE** HERE FOR ME TO TALK TO. I FEEL INVISIBLE.

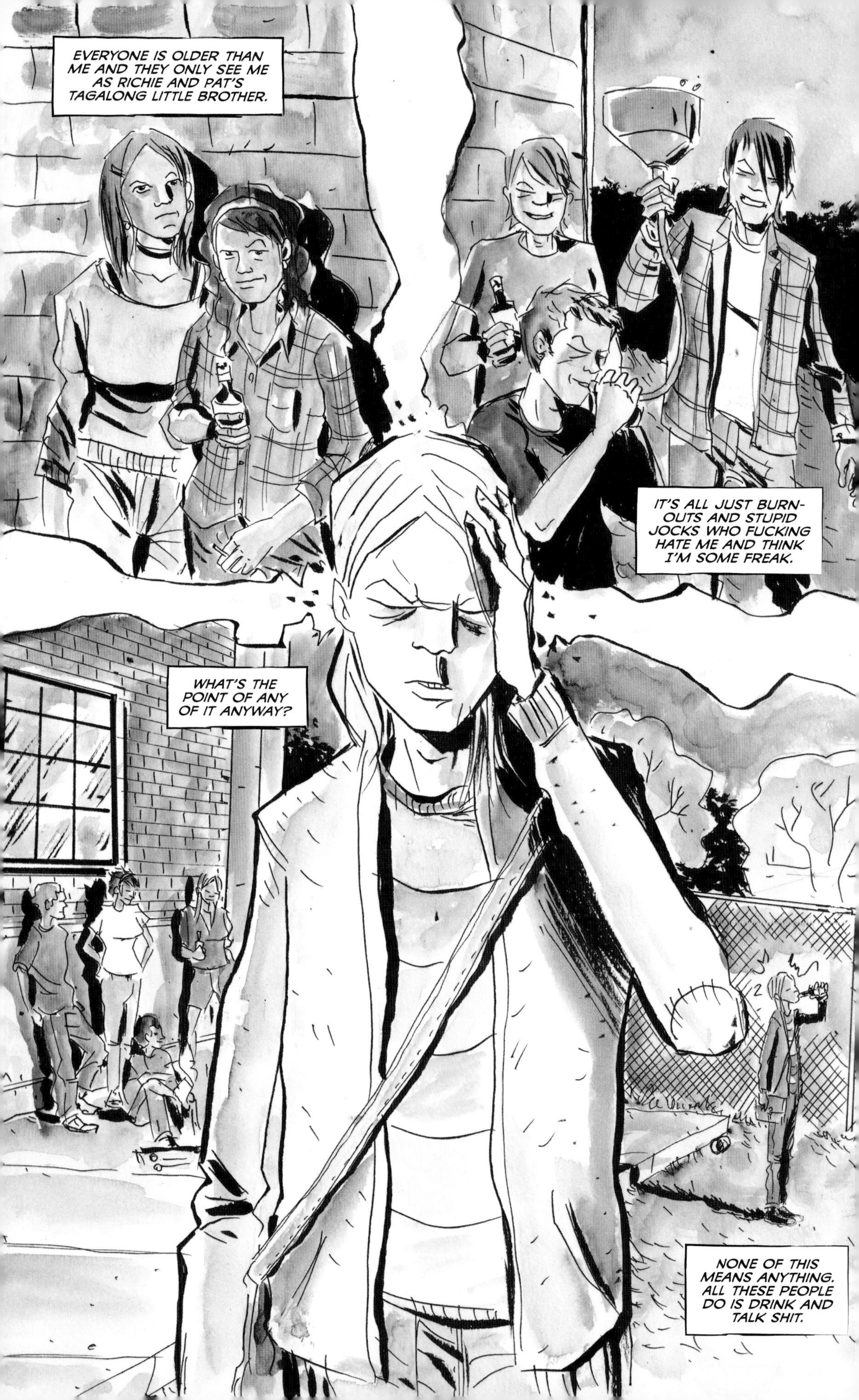
EVERYONE IS OLDER THAN ME AND THEY ONLY SEE ME AS RICHIE AND PAT'S TAGALONG LITTLE BROTHER.
IT'S ALL JUST BURN-OUTS AND STUPID JOCKS WHO FUCKING HATE ME AND THINK I'M SOME FREAK.
WHAT'S THE POINT OF ANY OF IT ANYWAY?
NONE OF THIS MEANS ANYTHING. ALL THESE PEOPLE DO IS DRINK AND TALK SHIT.

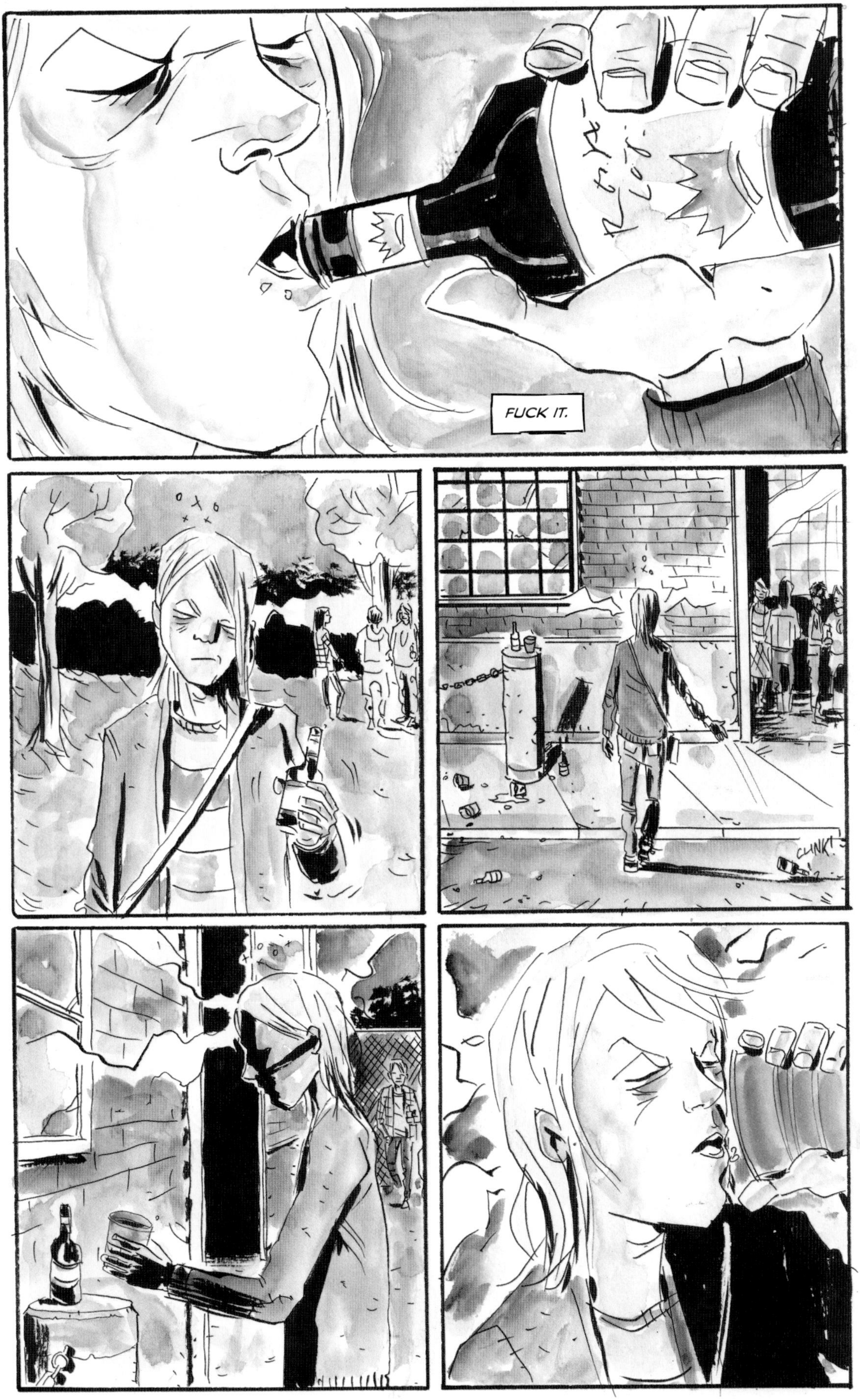
FUCK IT.
CLINK!

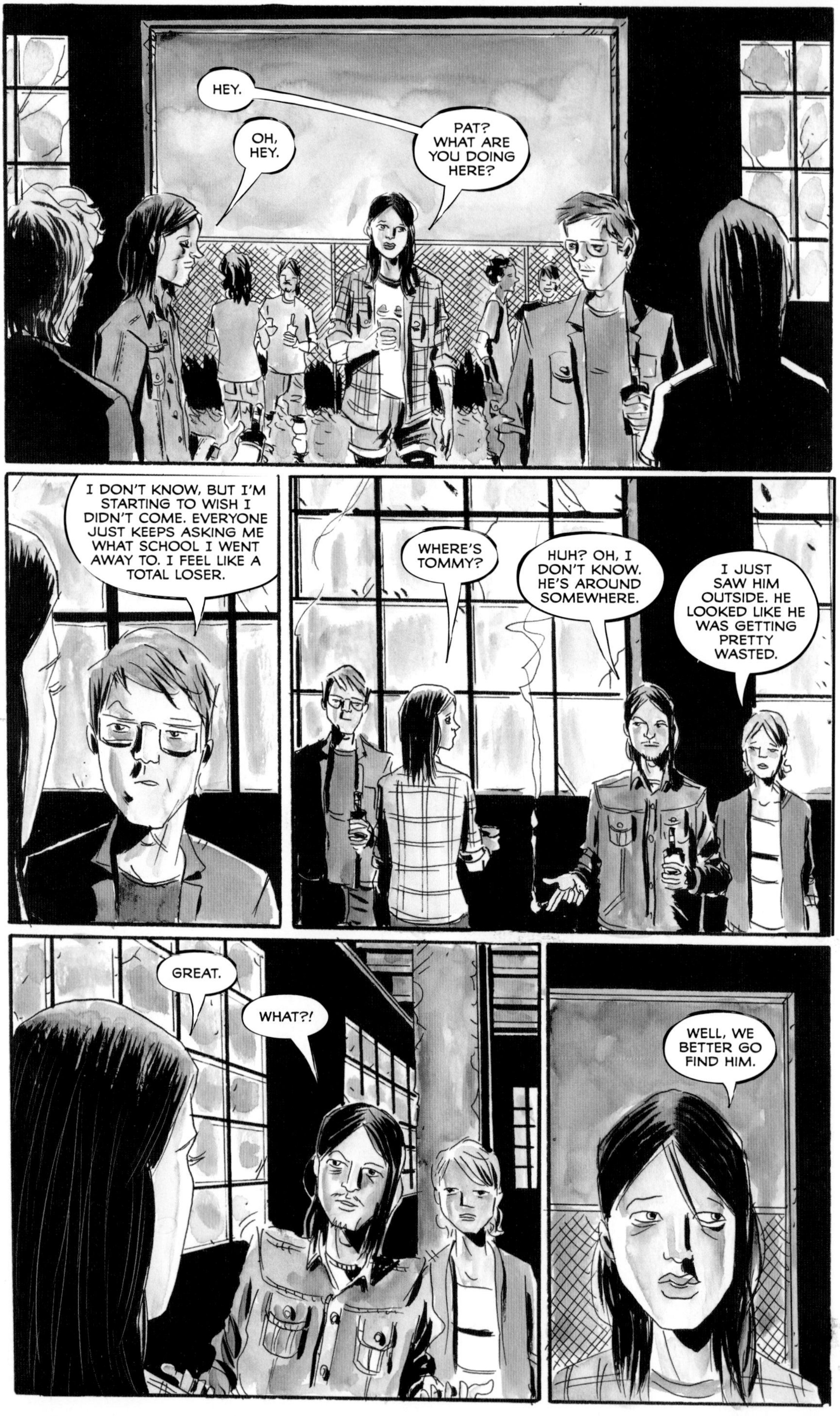
HEY.
OH, HEY.
PAT? WHAT ARE YOU DOING HERE?
I DON'T KNOW, BUT I'M STARTING TO WISH I DIDN'T COME. EVERYONE JUST KEEPS ASKING ME WHAT SCHOOL I WENT AWAY TO. I FEEL LIKE A TOTAL LOSER.
WHERE'S TOMMY?
HUH? OH, I DON'T KNOW. HE'S AROUND SOMEWHERE.
I JUST SAW HIM OUTSIDE. HE LOOKED LIKE HE WAS GETTING PRETTY WASTED.
GREAT.
WHAT?!
WELL, WE BETTER GO FIND HIM.

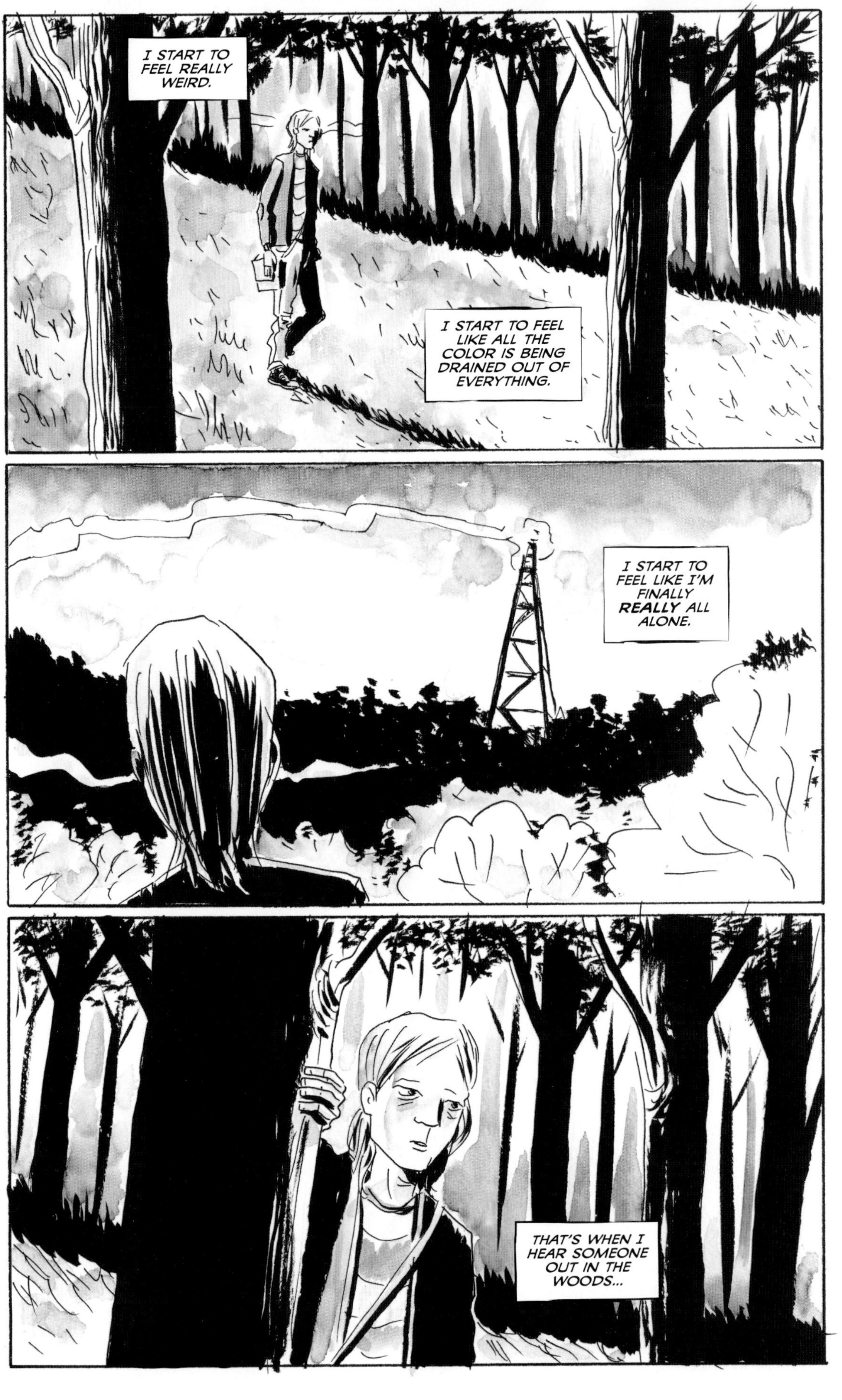
I START TO FEEL REALLY WEIRD.
I START TO FEEL LIKE ALL THE COLOR IS BEING DRAINED OUT OF EVERYTHING.
I START TO FEEL LIKE I'M FINALLY **REALLY** ALL ALONE.
THAT'S WHEN I HEAR SOMEONE OUT IN THE WOODS...

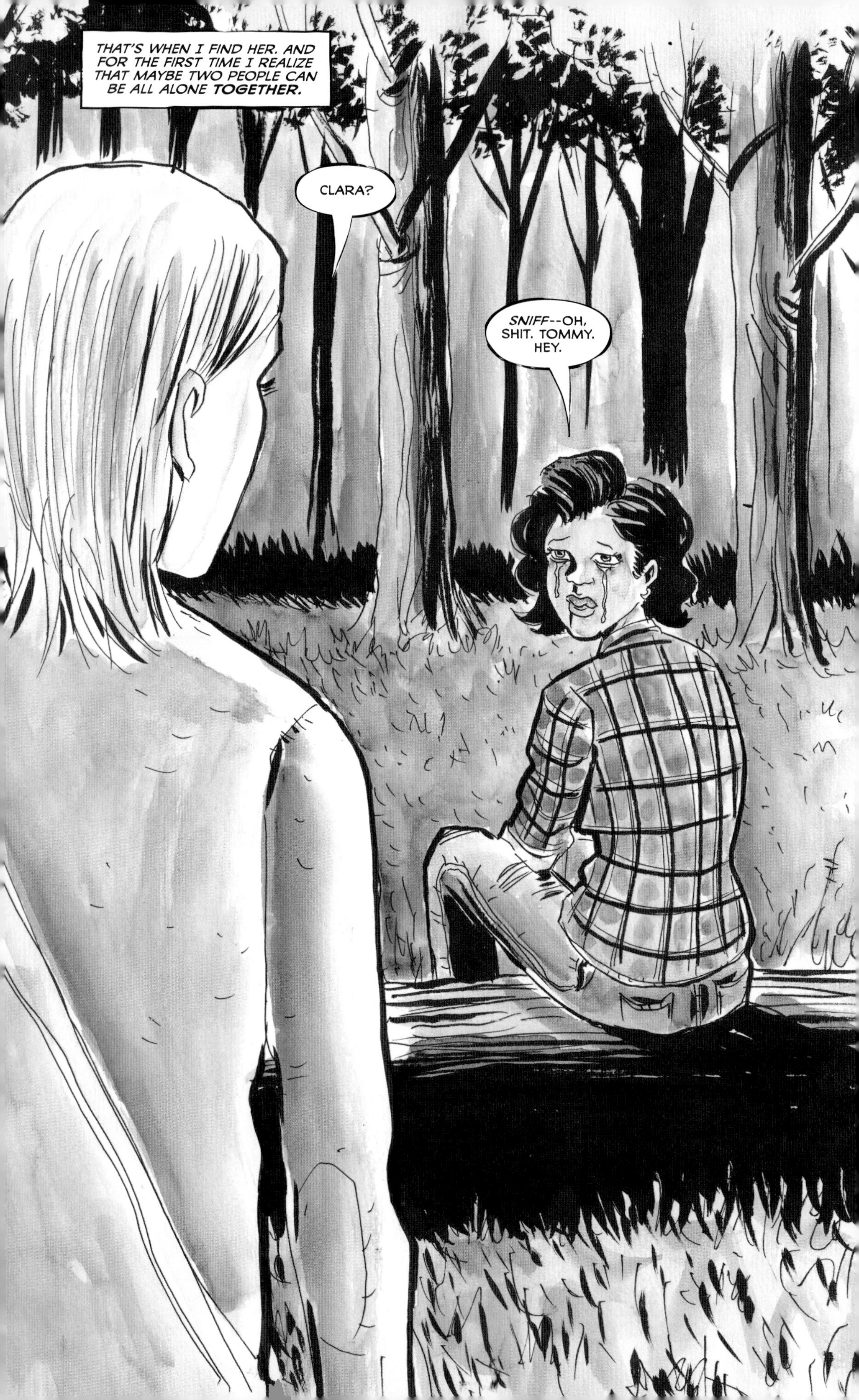
THAT'S WHEN I FIND HER. AND FOR THE FIRST TIME I REALIZE THAT MAYBE TWO PEOPLE CAN BE ALL ALONE **TOGETHER.**
CLARA?
SNIFF--OH, SHIT. TOMMY. HEY.

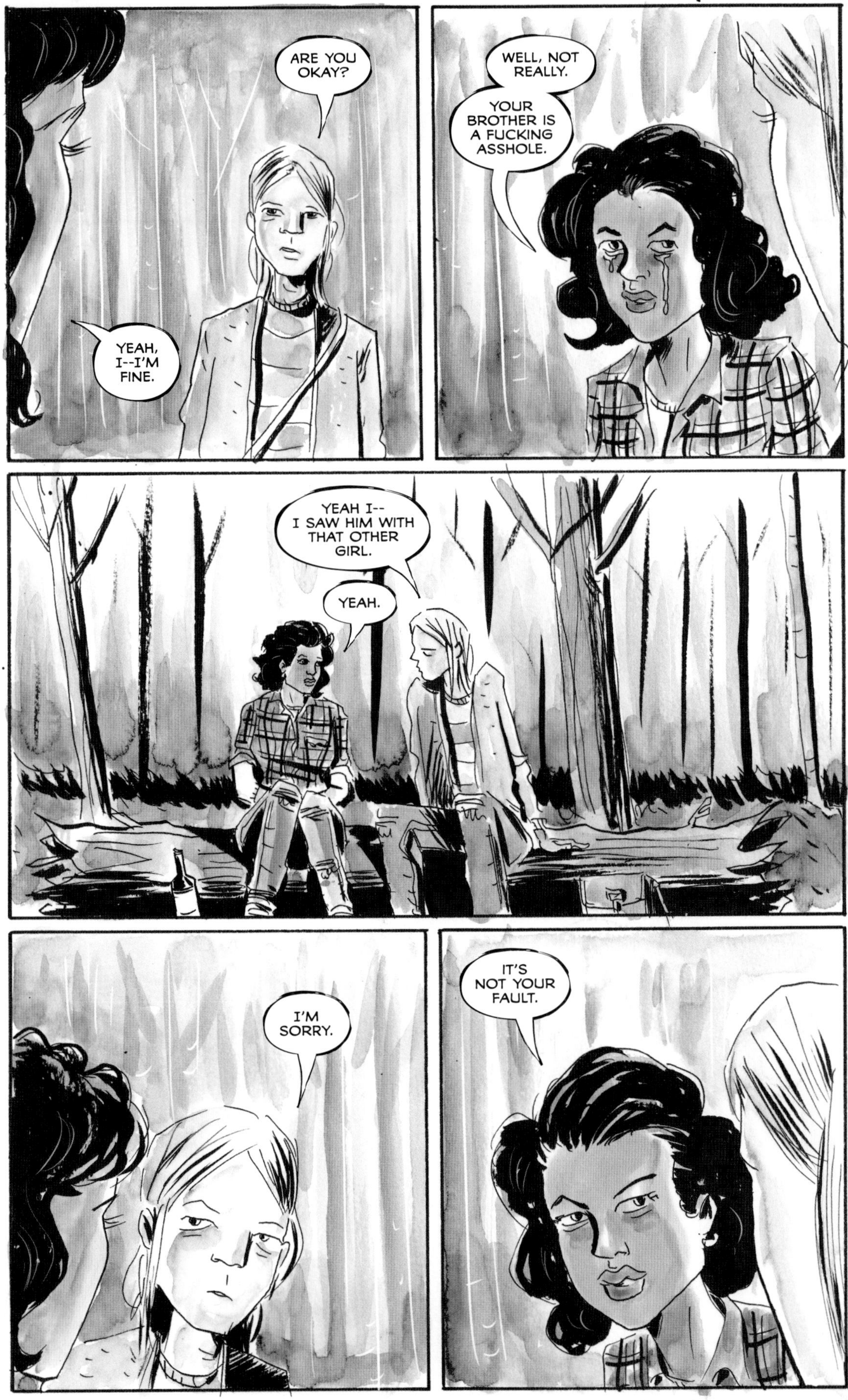
ARE YOU OKAY?
YEAH, I--I'M FINE.
WELL, NOT REALLY.
YOUR BROTHER IS A FUCKING ASSHOLE.
YEAH I-- I SAW HIM WITH THAT OTHER GIRL.
YEAH.
I'M SORRY.
IT'S NOT YOUR FAULT.

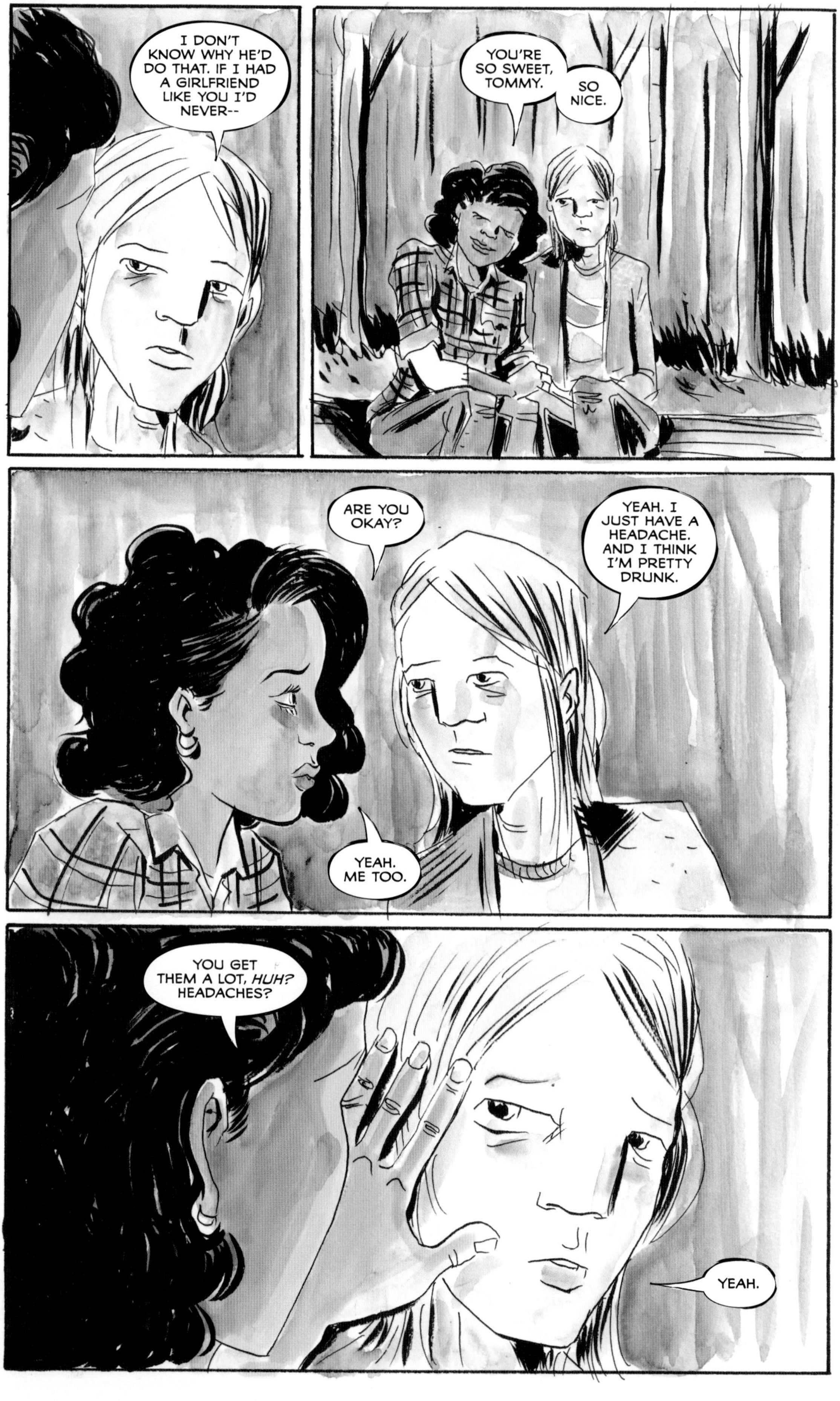
I DON'T KNOW WHY HE'D DO THAT. IF I HAD A GIRLFRIEND LIKE YOU I'D NEVER--
YOU'RE SO SWEET, TOMMY.
SO NICE.
ARE YOU OKAY?
YEAH. I JUST HAVE A HEADACHE. AND I THINK I'M PRETTY DRUNK.
YEAH. ME TOO.
YOU GET THEM A LOT, *HUH?* HEADACHES?
YEAH.

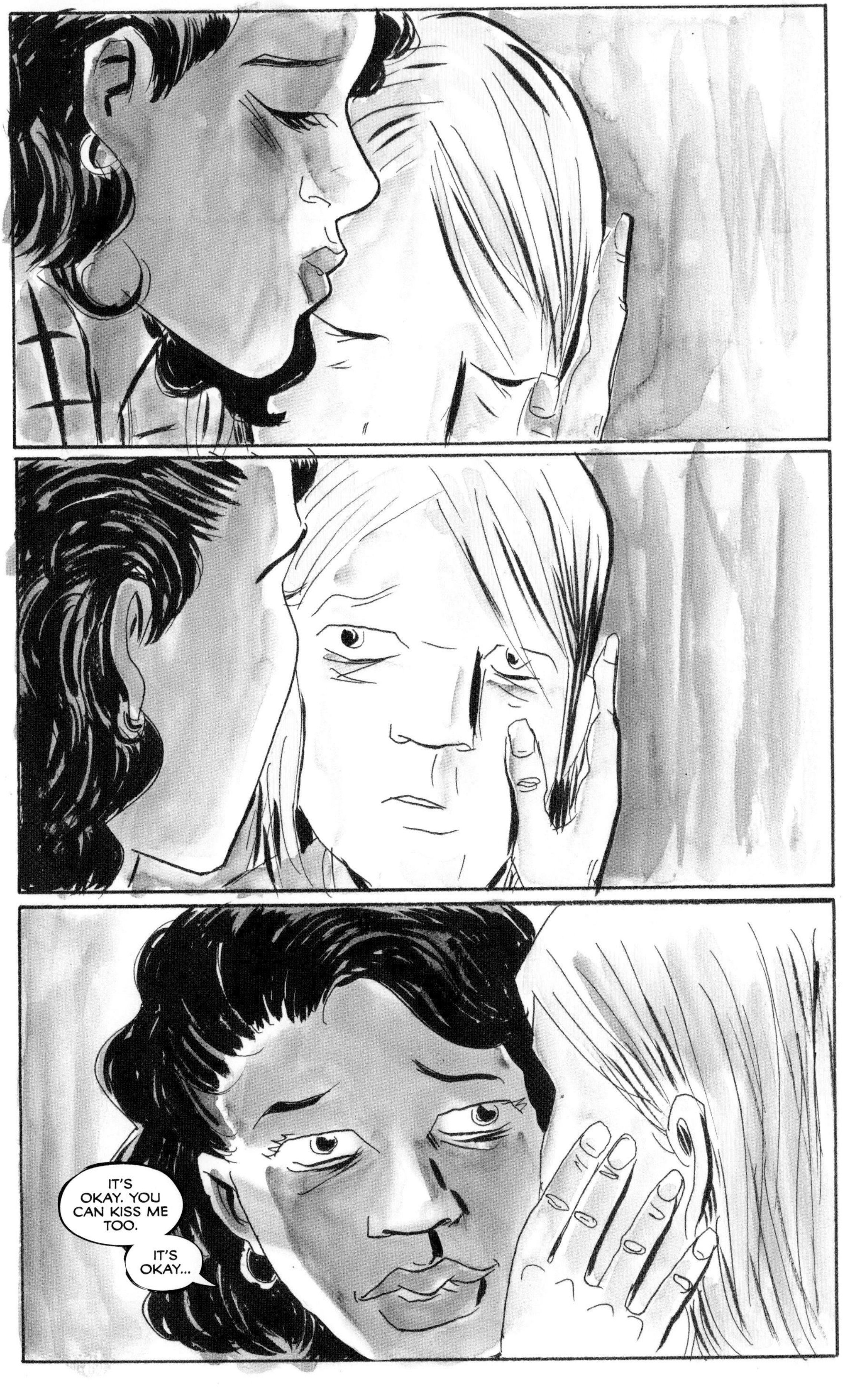
IT'S OKAY. YOU CAN KISS ME TOO.
IT'S OKAY...

And then it happens...

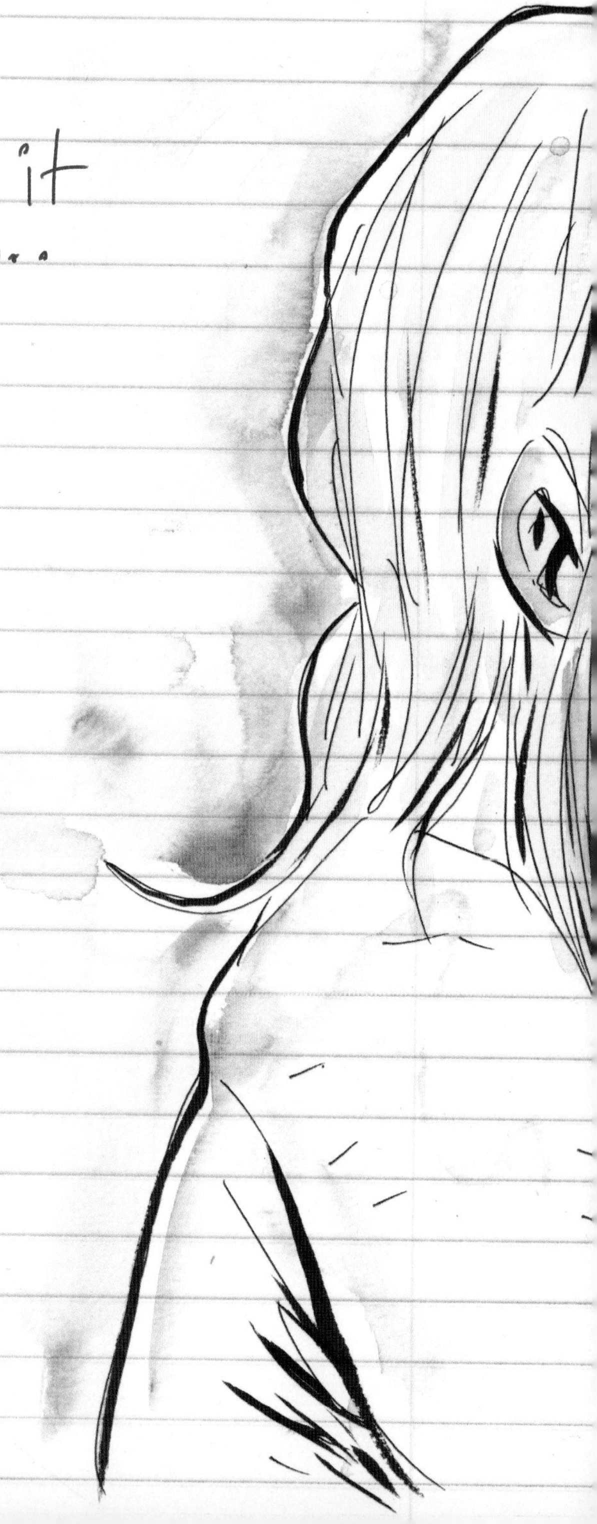

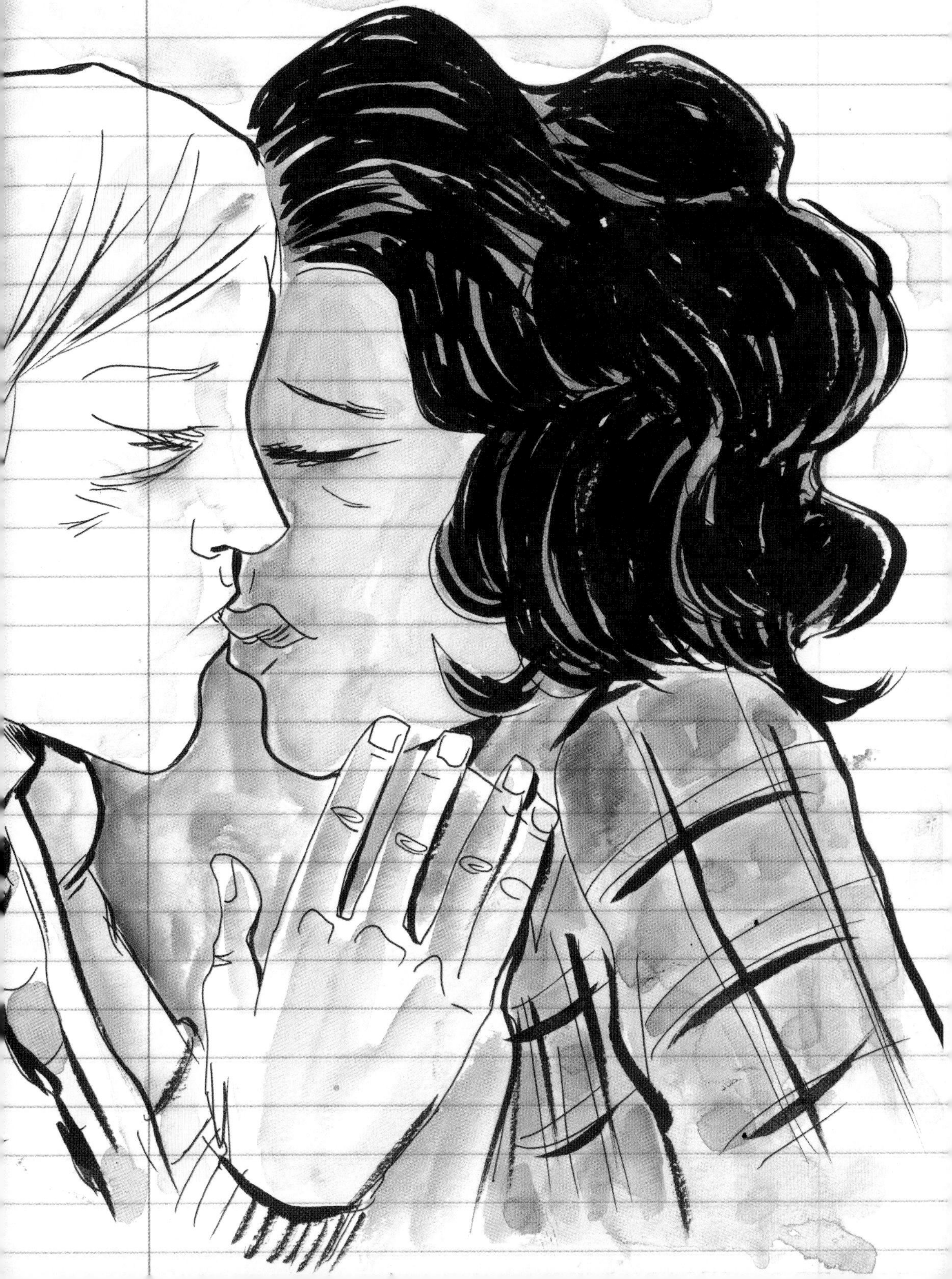

We stumble with our
clothes.

My head stops hurting, but
I stop noticing anyway.

It's my First time. I don't
Think it's hers but I don't ask.

it's awkward and embarassing
We're both drunk and it's
over pretty quickly.

Afterwards she gets really
quiet and I don't know
what to say to her.

Then my headache comes
back and it's even
worse than before.

And these words...

These are words I will
never actually write

This is the final journal
entry I will never
get a chance to make.

Because right after
this...

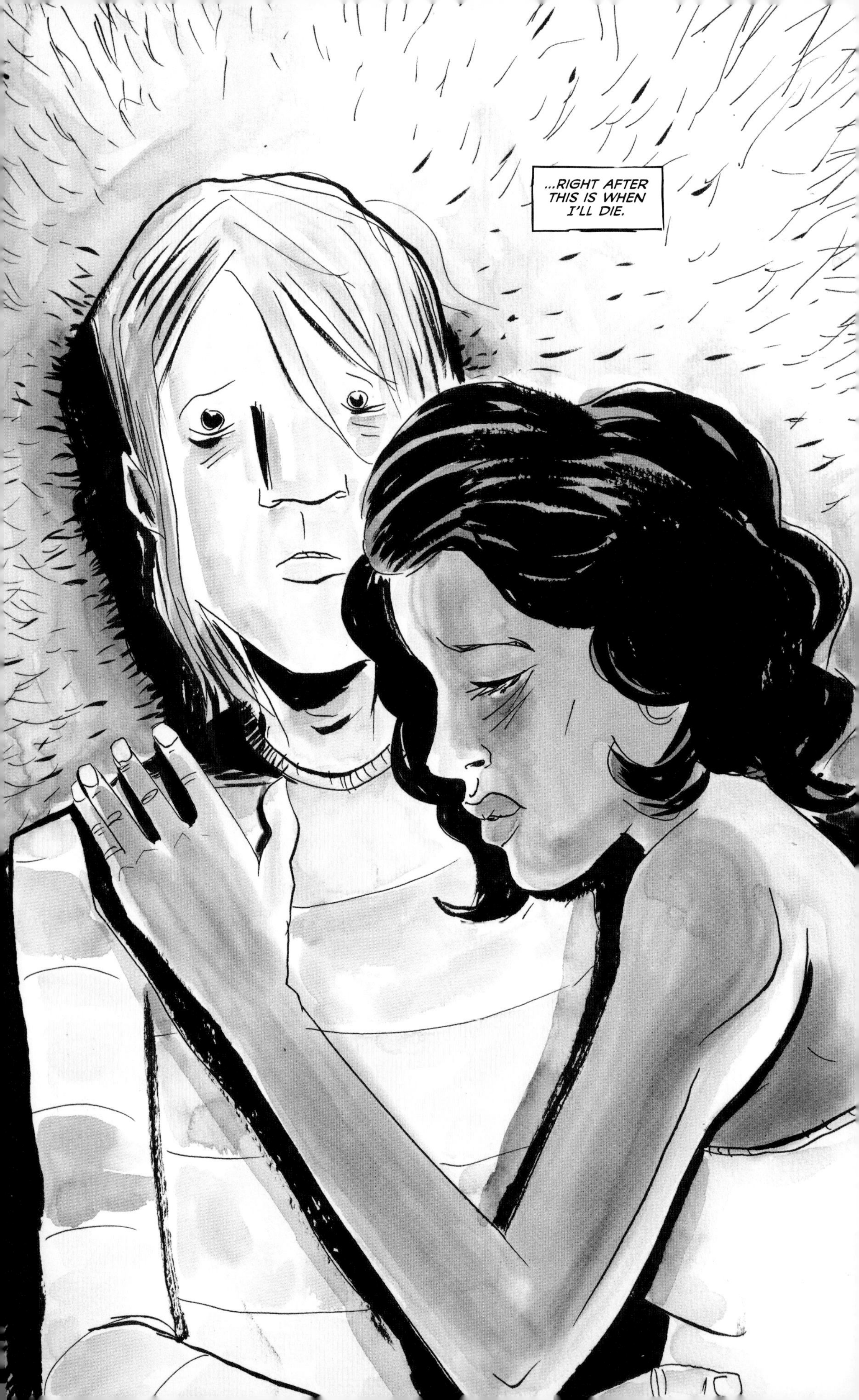
...RIGHT AFTER THIS IS WHEN I'LL DIE.

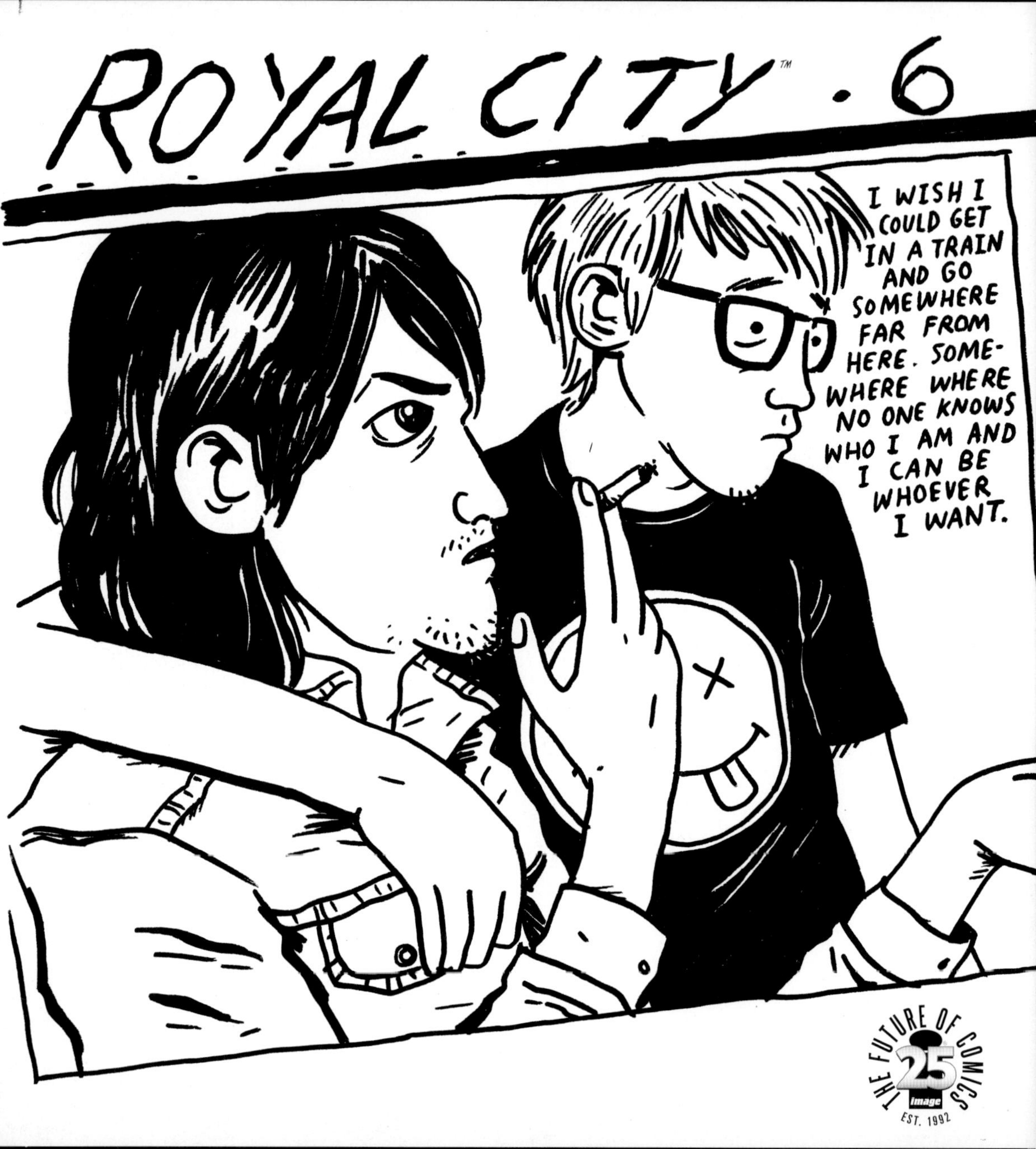

Jeffrey Brown

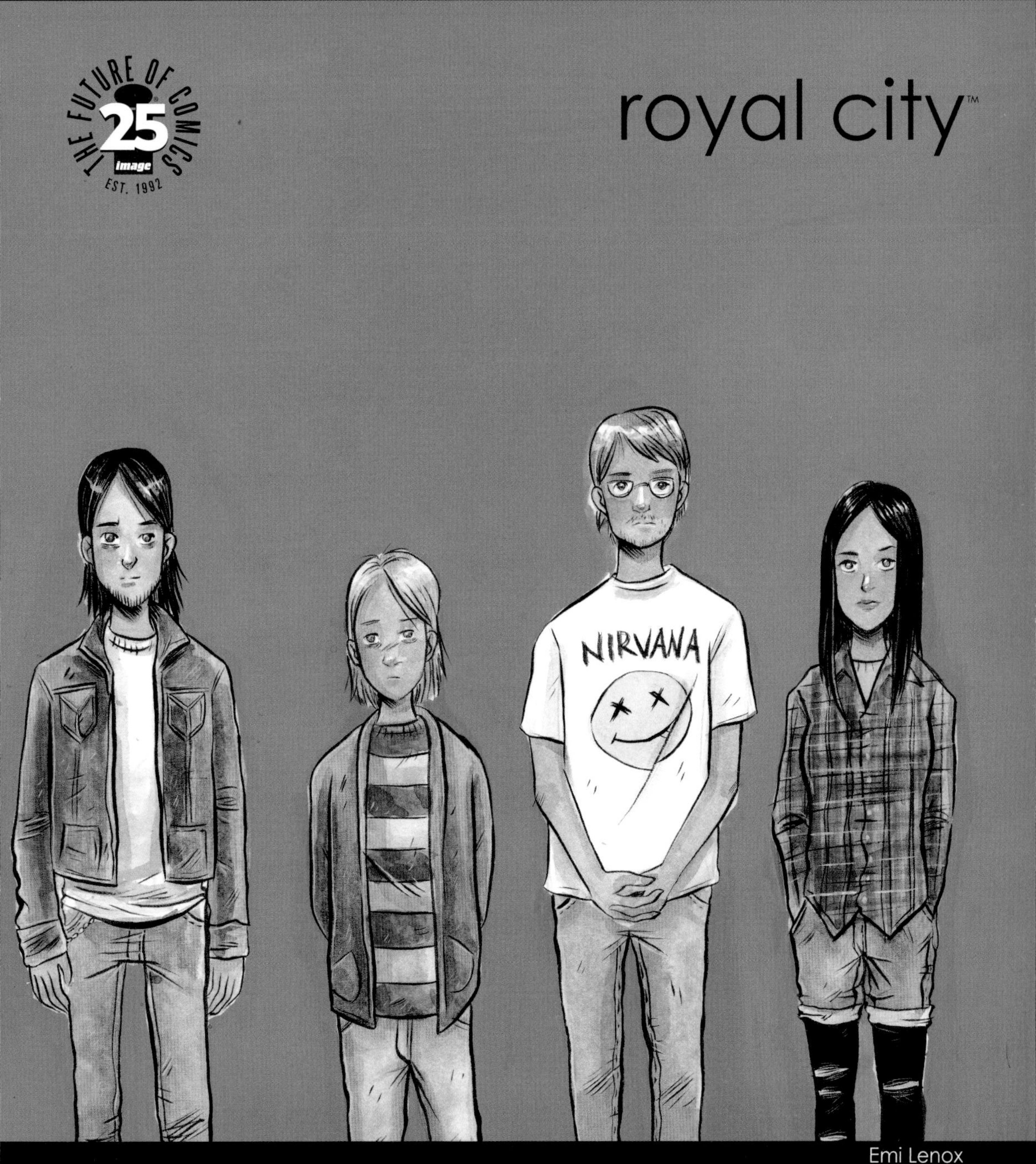
THE FUTURE OF COMICS
25
image
EST. 1992
royal city™
NIRVANA
Emi Lenox

ROYAL CITY #8
$3.99

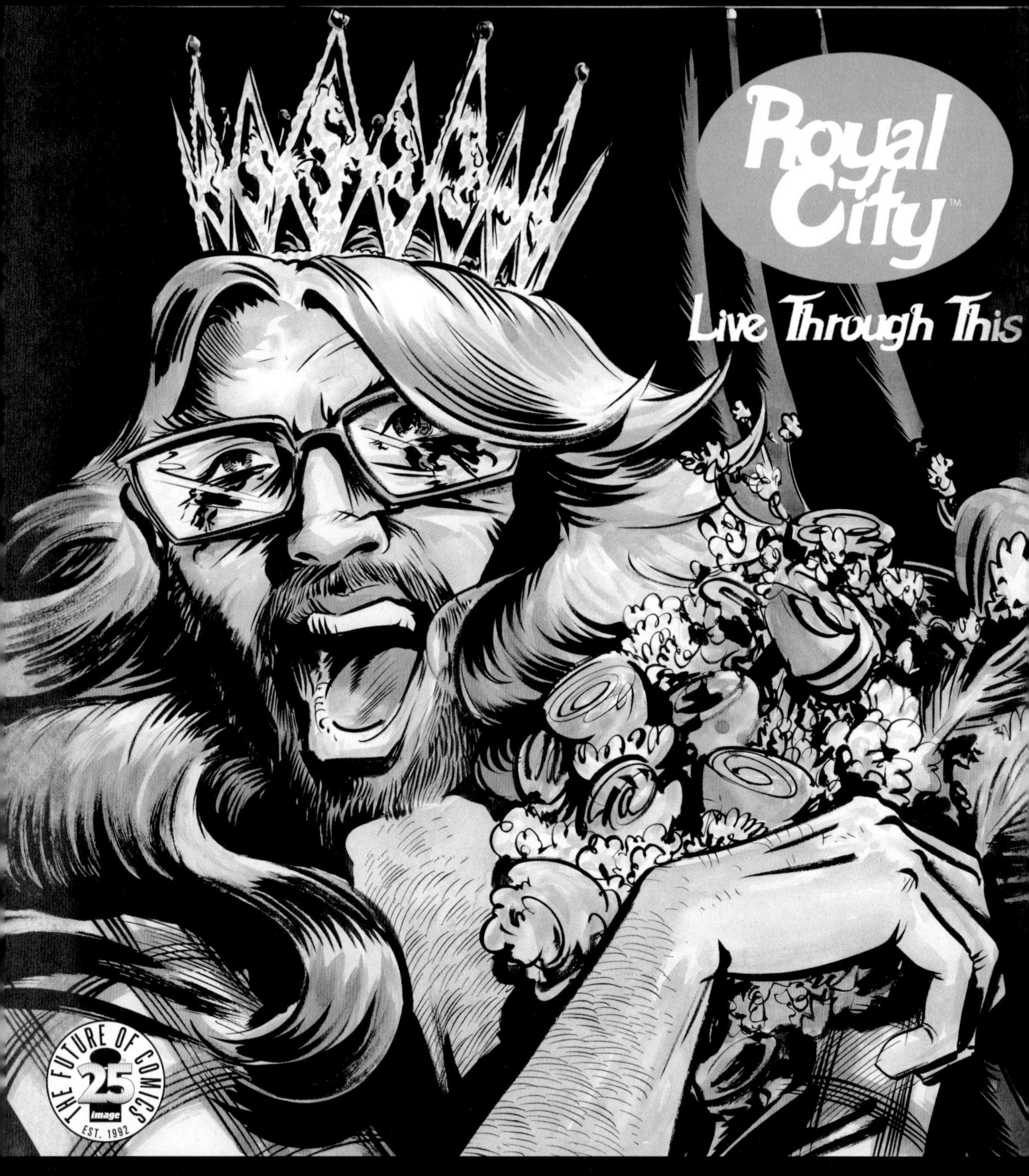
Royal City™
Live Through This
THE FUTURE OF COMICS
25
image
EST. 1992

Nate Powell

ROYAL CITY ™

ROYAL CITY #10
$3.99

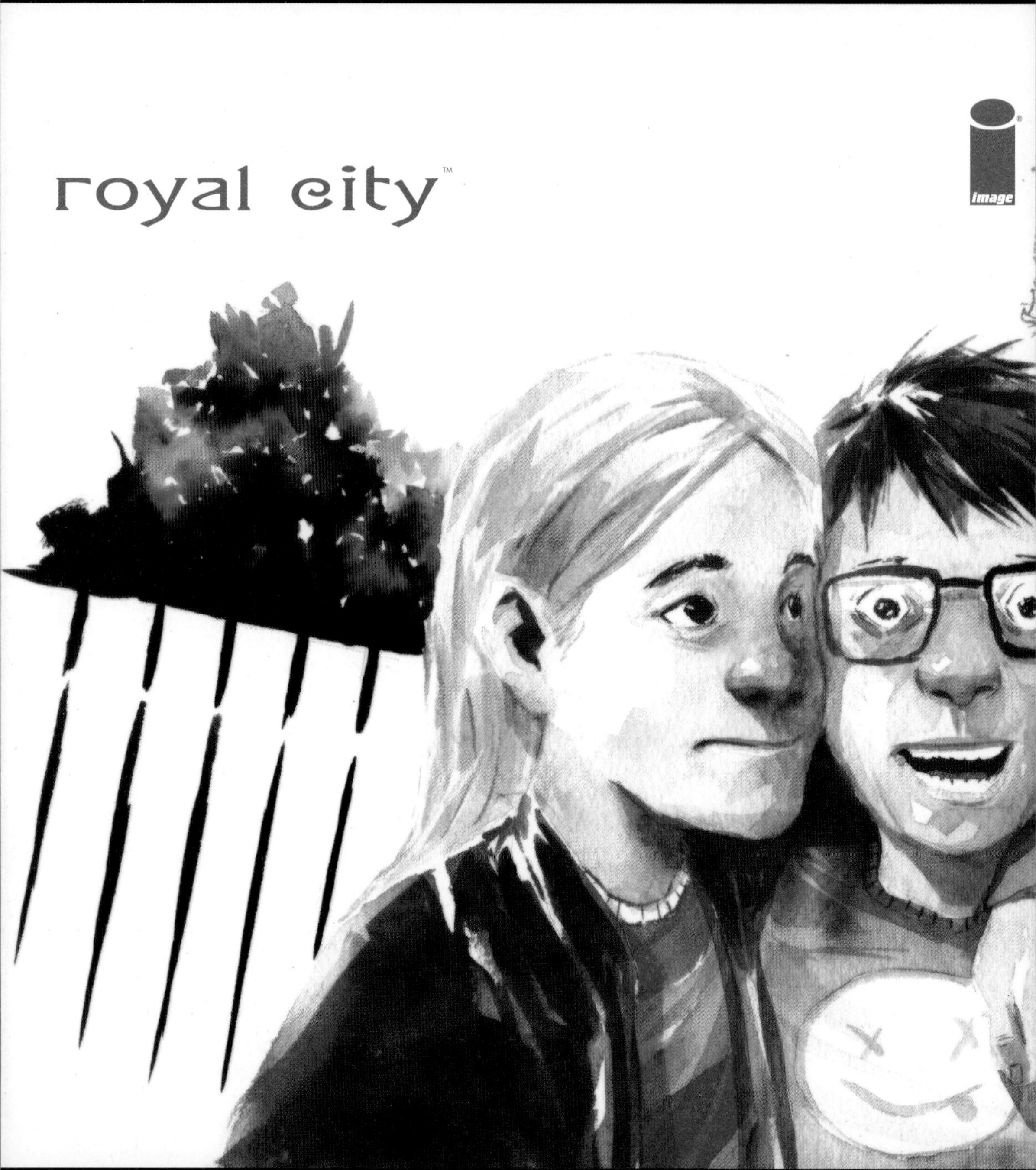
royal city™

Dustin Nguyen